AUSTRO-HUNGARIAN NAVAL POLICY
1904–14

To my wife Victoria

AUSTRO-HUNGARIAN NAVAL POLICY
1904–14

MILAN N. VEGO

Professor of Operations
US Naval War College
Newport, Rhode Island

FRANK CASS
LONDON • PORTLAND, OR

First Published 1996 in Great Britain by
FRANK CASS & Co. LTD.
Newbury House, 900 Eastern Avenue
London IG2 7HH

and in the United States of America by
FRANK CASS
c/o ISBS, 5804 N.E. Hassalo Street,
Portland, Oregon 97213-3644

© 1996 Milan N. Vego

British Library Cataloguing in Publication data
Vego, Milan N.
  Austro-Hungarian naval policy, 1904–14. – (Cass series.
  Naval history; 1)
  1. Sea-power – Austria – History –20th century 2. World
War, 1914–18 – Naval operations, Austrian 3. Austria –
History, Naval
I. Title
359'.009436

Library of Congress Cataloging-in-Publication data
Vego, Milan N.
  Austro-Hungarian naval policy, 1904–14 / Milan N. Vego.
    p. cm.
  Includes bibliographical references and index.
  ISBN 0-7146-4678-4 (hbk). – ISBN 0-7146-4209-6 (pbk)
  1. Austro-Hungarian Monarchy. Kriegsmarine – History.
  2. Sea-power – Austria – History – 20th century.
  3. Sea-power – Hungary – History – 20th century. 4. Austria –
History, Naval. 5. Hungary – History, Naval. I. Title.
VA473.V54   1966
359'.009436'09041 – dc20   95-53166
                                                              CIP

ISBN 0 7146 4678 4 (cloth)
ISBN 0 7146 4209 6 (paper)

Printed in Great Britain by
Bookcraft (Bath) Ltd, Midsomer Norton, Avon

Contents

List of illustrations

Maps and figures

Appendices

Glossary of geographic names

Italian/German	Croatian
Abbazzia	Opatija
Agram	Zagreb
Albona	Labin
Almissa	Omis
Antivari	Bar
Arbe	Rab
Arsa	Rasa
Barbana	
Benkovaz	Benkovac
Bocche di Cattaro	Boka Kotorska
Bossigliana	Bosiljina
Brazza	Brac
Bua	Ciovo
Budua	Budva
Calamotta	Kolocep
Capocesto	Primosten
Capodistria	Koper
Carlopago	Karlobag
Castelli	Kastela
Castelnuovo	Hercegnovi
Cattaro	Kotor
Cazza	Susac
Cetigne	Cetinje
Cherso	Cres
Cittavecchia	Starigrad
Clissa	Klis
Comisa	Komiza
Contado	Ravni Kotari
Crappano	Krapanj
Crivoscia	Krivosije
Curzola	Korcula

Dassa	Daksa
Divazza	Divaca
Dulcigno	Ulcinj
Eso	Iz
Fiume	Rijeka
Gelsa	Jelsa
Giuppana	Sipan
Gorizia	Gorica
Gravosa	Gruz
Grossa Isola	Dugi Otok
Incoronata	Kornati
Isto	Ist
Istria	Istra
Karlowitz	Karlovac
Lacroma	Lokrum
Lagosta	Lastovo
Laibach	Ljubljana
Lesina	Hvar
Lissa	Vis
Lussin Grande	Veliki Losinj
Lussin Piccolo	Mali Losinj
Makarsca	Makarska
Melada	Molat
Meleda	Mljet
Mezzo	Lopud
Monte Biloco	Biokovo
Morter	Murter
Narenta	Neretva
Neresine	Nerezine
Neusatz	Novi Sad
Nona	Nin
Novogradi	Novigrad

Olipa	Olip
Obbrovazzo	Obrovac
Ossero	Osor
Pago	Pag
Parenzo	Porec
Pasman	Pasman
Pelagosa	Palagruza
Perasto	Perast
Perkovich	Perkovic
Petrowardein	Petrovaradin
Pisino	Pazin
Pola	Pola
Ponte	Punat
Porto Rè	Kraljevica
Porto Tolero	Ploce
Provicchio	Prvic
Pucischie	Pucisca
Punta d'Ostro	Rt Ostro
Puntadura	Vir
Punta Planka	Rt Ploce
Punta Salvore	Rt Savudrija
Quarnero	Kvarner
Ragusa	Dubrovnik
Risano	Risan
Rogosnizza	Rogoznica
Rondoni	Mamula
Rovigno	Rovinj
Sabioncello	Peljesac
Sale	Sali
Salona	Solin
Sansego	Susak
San Stefano	Sv. Stefan
Scardona	Skradin
Scutari	Skadar
Sebenico	Sibenik
Segna	Senj
Selve	Silba

Sestrugno	Sestrunj
Sichelburg	Metljika
Signo	Sinj
Smoquizza	Smokvica
Solta	Solta
Spalato	Split
Spalmadori Isole	Pakleni Otoci
Spizza	Spic
Stagno	Ston
Stretto	Tijesno
Tenin	Knin
Teodo	Tivat
Tersatico	Trsat
Torcola	Scedro
Trau	Trogir
Trebocconi	Tribunj
Tuconio	Tkon
Ugliano	Uglijan
Ulbo	Olib
Vallegrande	Vela Luka
Veglia	Krk
Verbosca	Vrboska
Vergoraz	Vrgorac
Verlica	Vrlika
Vodizze	Vodice
Zapuntello	Zapuntel
Zara	Zadar
Zaravecchia	Biograd n.m.
Zengg	Senj
Zirona Grande	Veliki Drvenik
Zlarino	Zlarin
Zuri	Zirje

Preface

[handwritten: all depended on Italy's policy]

Austro-Hungarian naval policy after 1904 was influenced by a number of external and internal factors that differed greatly in significance. First and foremost, Italy's policies directly determined the Austro-Hungarian Navy's expansion and modernization. Italy was formally allied with Austria-Hungary in the Triple Alliance. However, there were deep-seated animosities and suspicions in the relations between these two European powers. 'Irredentists' wanted to unify about one million Italians living in Austria-Hungary with their kinsmen in the kingdom of Italy. Although irredentism enjoyed strong support among the Italian public, it did not exercise a visibly strong influence upon Rome's official relations with Vienna. However, the *irredenta* and the Austro-Hungarian reaction to it were powerful factors in the hands of those in both countries who urged a steady and rapid build-up of their countries' navies.

The implementation of Austro-Hungarian naval policy in respect to the size and composition of the fleet, the personnel strength to be maintained and trained, and the build-up of naval bases and coastal fortifications depended on several internal policy considerations: the willingness of the country's political leadership to support the steady expansion of the Navy and the strength of the opposition to such a policy course; the country's economic potential and strength, especially the state of its finances; public support for the Navy and maritime affairs in general. The Habsburg rulers in Austria, the court's advisors and the state bureaucracy traditionally had little interest in or understanding of the significance of sea power for the Empire. This was one of the major reasons for the slow and uneven development of the Austro-Hungarian Navy in the eighteenth and nineteenth centuries.

While foreign policy determined the political objectives of naval policy, the character of the probable war theatre and the identity of potential opponents at sea influenced the size and composition of the Austro-Hungarian fleet to be established and maintained. The small size of and short distances in the Adriatic favoured the creation of a fleet of battleships and cruisers with shorter steaming range and lower speed than those employed on the open oceans. For the same reasons, destroyers, torpedo craft and submarines could be used with a greater chance of success in narrow seas such as the Adriatic than in the

Mediterranean. Before 1904 the Austro-Hungarian fleet was a typical coastal defence force. However, the fleet's composition began to change after 1905 when larger battleships, cruisers and destroyers entered into service in large numbers.

The turning point in the development came in the spring of 1909 in the aftermath of the Austro-Hungarian annexation of Bosnia. Then the Navy announced plans to build its first dreadnought squadron; Italy had already decided to emulate other great powers in building dreadnoughts. These two developments signified a new phase in the Austro-Italian naval race. By 1909 Great Britain became increasingly concerned with the Austro-Hungarian and Italian naval build-up. Great Britain then confronted not only the steadily growing threat from the German High Seas fleet in the North Sea but also the prospect of losing control of the Mediterranean. Although Austria-Hungary and Italy continued to direct their naval build-up against each other, both countries were still partners in the Triple Alliance and as such were potential opponents of Britain.

The most important change in the naval situation in the Mediterranean came in 1912 due to the Turco-Italian war and the British failure to restrain Germany's naval build-up in the North Sea. Italy's acquisition of Libya and the Dodecanese Islands in the war with Turkey strengthened her strategic position in the central and eastern Mediterranean. However, by 1912, Italy's hitherto cordial relations with France rapidly deteriorated. As a result Italy decided to improve her relations with Austria-Hungary and Germany.

By 1912, because of Germany's threat in the North Sea, Great Britain announced a major redistribution of her fleet. Almost all the British battleships were concentrated against Germany's High Seas fleet in the North Sea, while only a few battle cruisers remained in the Mediterranean. France redeployed all her battle fleet from the Atlantic to the Mediterranean. Thus, for all practical purposes the protection of British interests in the Mediterranean was left to France. However, the French fleet faced a superior Austro-Italian combination. In effect Germany successfully weakened Triple Entente naval strength in the North Sea because British reinforcements in home waters were not adequate to cover the withdrawal of the French battleships to the Mediterranean.

After 1912 Austro-Italian naval policies entered a new phase. Although each country continued with its naval build-up, their main effort was directed to enhance Triple Alliance naval strength in the Mediterranean. To be sure, Italy and Austria-Hungary continued to be rivals for influence in Albania and in the Balkans, but this competition was overshadowed by the need to co-operate in the Mediterranean for the benefit of the Triple Alliance. The principal reason for this change of policy was that Germany, as the strongest partner in the Triple Alliance, wanted to employ the Italian and Austro-Hungarian fleets to improve her position against Great Britain in the North Sea. Italy, for her part, needed the Austro-Hungarian fleet to redress her unfavourable naval balance with France in the western Mediterranean.

Among all the partners of the Triple Alliance, only Austria-Hungary had no vital interests to protect in the Mediterranean. She was expected to sacrifice her fleet to protect both Germany's and Italy's interests. However, in the absence of any improvement in her relations with Russia, Austria-Hungary was obliged to co-operate with Italy because she needed Germany's support and friendship in a potential war against Russia and to maintain her status as a great power.

Many books and articles on the Austro-Hungarian Navy were published in the aftermath of the First World War. Perhaps, the single most important book was written in 1933 by a former naval officer, Hans Hugo Sokol, *Oesterreich-Ungarns Seekrieg 1914–1918* (Austro-Hungarian Naval War, 1914–1918). However, Sokol's work contains only a short description of the Austro-Hungarian Navy prior to outbreak of the First World War. The most significant work on the Austro-Hungarian Navy in the period before the First World War is Paul Halpern's *The Naval Situation in the Mediterranean, 1908–1914*. This work was based on excellent unpublished material from the Austro-Hungarian, Italian, British and French archives. Another important book, Gabriele Mariano's *Le Convenzioni Navale nella Triplece*, was written in 1969. It is a detailed account of the naval conversations and agreements among Germany, Italy and the Dual Monarchy during the period 1888–1913 that touches only briefly on other aspects of Austro-Hungarian naval policy and strategy in those years. One of the most recent works on the subject is *The Naval Policy of Austria-Hungary, 1867–1918: Navalism, Industrial Development, and the Politics of Dualism* by Lawrence Sondhaus. As the subtitle suggests, this book discusses naval policy in the context of industrial development and domestic policies. It is also largely based on secondary sources.

Most studies on the Austro-Hungarian Navy dealing with the period between 1900 and 1914 were unpublished manuscripts. The Vienna Kriegsarchiv has a collection of a dozen or so PhD dissertations dealing with the Austro-Hungarian Navy and written by the graduates of the University of Vienna. The most representative of these works are: Leo

Reiter, 'Die Entwicklung der K.u.K. Flotte und die Delegation des Reichsrates' (Development of the Imperial and Royal Fleet and Delegation of the Reichsrat); E. Krenslehner, 'Die K.u.K. Kriegsmarine als wirtschaftlicher Faktor in den Jahren 1875–1914' (The Imperial and Royal Navy As the Economic Factor in the Years of 1875–1914); A. Mayer, 'Die K.u.K. Kriegsmarine 1912–14 unter dem Kommando von Admiral Anton Haus' (The Imperial and Royal Navy 1912–14 Under the Command of Admiral Anton Haus); and Leo Gebhard, 'The Development of the Austro-Hungarian Navy 1897–1914: A Study in the Operation of Dualism'.

This study of Austro-Hungarian naval policy encompasses ten momentous years of European history between the spring of 1904 and the summer of 1914. For the Navy a new era began in the fall of 1904 when Admiral Count Rudolf Montecuccoli took the post of Navy Commander. He remained in this post until February 1913 and presided over the largest modernization and expansion programme in the Austro-Hungarian Navy's history. His successor was Admiral Anton Haus who essentially continued Montecuccoli's policies. Therefore, the entire ten-year period of the Austro-Hungarian Navy's development preceding the First World War can appropriately be considered the 'Montecuccoli era'. Another important event was the approval by the Delegations (Common Parliament) of the first multi-year special credit to be devoted to naval construction in 1904. This represented the first turning point in the Austro-Hungarian naval policy after 1867.

The year 1904 also saw the establishment of the Austrian Navy League which, like its counterparts in German and Italy, sought to increase public support for a considerable strengthening of the Austro-Hungarian Navy. Moreover, the influence of the heir to the throne, Archduke Francis Ferdinand, began to be felt more strongly upon both the internal and the foreign policies of Austria-Hungary from 1904 on. He was one of the staunchest and most consistent proponents of naval expansion. This, combined with his growing influence within the highest circles of the government, had the most positive effect upon the development of Austro-Hungarian sea power between 1904 and 1914. Coincidentally, in 1904 several external events shaped the course of Austro-Hungarian naval policy in the years to come. Italy came to consider Hungary and not France as the most likely opponent in a war. After 1904 Italy's foreign policy was aimed at expanding her influence in Albania and Montenegro as well as the other Balkan states, where Italy's interests clashed most directly with those of Austria-Hungary. Another significant event in 1904 was the Anglo-French rapprochement or 'entente cordiale'. It not only led to the redistribution of the British fleet but inaugurated steadily closer relations between Great Britain and France and later Russia.

The principal reason for the change in British policy was the growing strength of the German Navy that threatened Britain's hitherto-secure position as the world's leading sea power. The Anglo-German naval race was not only to exercise the most direct influence after 1900 on the foreign policy of the European powers, but also to have significant consequences upon the naval situation in the Mediterranean.

There are several reasons for this study of the Austro-Hungarian naval policy between 1904 and 1914. My 12 years of active service as an officer in the former Yugoslav Navy aroused my interest in Austrian and Austro-Hungarian naval history. The Versailles Peace Conference allocated many ex-Austro-Hungarian Navy ships to the then newly created kingdom of Serbs, Croats and Slovenes. Afterwards, many former officers of the Austro-Hungarian Navy served in the former Royal Yugoslav Navy. They introduced regulations and standards of education and training similar or identical to those in the Austro-Hungarian Navy.

I was deeply impressed with the durability of the old Austro-Hungarian forts around Pula, Sibenik and the Bay of Cattaro. They have survived the passage of time and human destruction. The piers and harbour installations along the eastern Adriatic coast built before 1918 are still in use, as are many old Austro-Hungarian signal stations along the coast and outlying islands.

Finally, it is important to bring into sharper focus the diplomatic and naval events in the Adriatic and the Mediterranean in the ten years preceding the outbreak of the First World War. This is especially pertinent today, because the conflict in the former Yugoslavia and the policies of major European powers eerily resemble the events that led to the outbreak of the First World War. The policies of Serbia, Montenegro and some other Balkan states as well as major European powers in 1908–9, 1912–13 and in 1914 bear many similarities with the situation today. Of course, in some ways the situation in Europe today is very different, but the similarities should be highlighted. Hence, the use of naval power by Austria-Hungary and other great powers of the day in the ten years preceding 1914 are well worth remembering. These events cannot tell us what to do in the future. However, they might provide us with some useful lessons on how to avoid errors of the past.

This study was originally a part of my doctoral dissertation, 'Anatomy of the Austrian Sea Power, 1904–1914', defended at the George

Washington University in 1981. However, the parts dealing with the Austro-Hungarian naval policy were extensively rewritten. The research for this study began in the autumn of 1974 during my service in the former West German merchant marine. During the next two years I spent my vacations in Vienna working in the Vienna Kriegsarchiv and the Haus- Hof- und Staatsarchiv. Thanks are due to Mr Franz Bilzer, Mr Josef Fleischer, Dr Kurt Peball, and the late Dr Walter Wagner for their great and invaluable help during my research at the Kriegsarchiv. My deep gratitude is due to Dr Kenneth McDonald, the former Professor of International Affairs at the George Washington University and currently the Chief Historian at CIA, the chairman of my doctoral committee and my principal adviser. He read my unedited draft, tackling illegible writing and often impenetrable prose with commendable patience and understanding. Without his frank criticism this study would be very different. Many thanks, too, to Professors Roderic Davison and Robert Kenny, two other members of my doctoral committee, for their forthright criticism and advice. I also want to thank Mrs Janet Martin-Surreil for her always highly efficient work in retyping my manuscript before it was submitted to the publisher. Finally, I wish to thank Mr Frank Cass and Dr Holger Herwig for making it possible for my manuscript to be published.

1

Framework

A naval policy can be defined as the sum of all the political, budgetary, social and purely military decisions by the country's highest leadership that affect a naval situation in general and the size and composition of naval forces in particular. Naval policy is heavily influenced by political conditions, both domestic and international. Foreign policy must define which countries or group of countries should be considered as friends, neutrals or potential opponents. It is the task of the country's foreign policy makers to ensure that their country will not be confronted by a group of powers superior in military strength. Naval policy and foreign policy are mutually dependent. Foreign policy should optimally prevent any change in the *status quo* that may lead to the weakening of the country's maritime position. However, foreign policy makers could conduct such a policy that would change the *status quo* to enhance or improve the country's maritime position. Likewise, naval policy aims must be taken into account by foreign policy makers.

A sound naval policy should be based on a clear definition of the goals to be accomplished and unwavering commitment to achieve these goals over time. The principal aim of a naval policy should be the establishment and maintenance of adequate naval strength in respect to potential opponents at sea. One's own naval strength is affected not only by the strength of potential opponents but also the country's geostrategic position and the characteristics of the probable maritime theatre. The size and composition of the fleet depends largely on the country's industrial capacity, financial strength, and the willingness of the country's political leadership to allocate sufficient resources for the expansion and modernization of the Navy. Hence, domestic policy considerations constitute a significant factor in the realization of naval policy objectives, while foreign policy comprises a *framework* for conduct of a naval policy.

Three foreign policy problems largely dictated the Dual Monarchy's naval policy between 1904 and 1914. First, the so-called 'Adriatic

1

Question' essentially involved the Dual Monarchy and Italy. However, Serbia, Montenegro, Greece and their patrons were also involved in that question at times. Secondly, the fate of the Turkish provinces in the Balkans that touched upon the interests not only of Austria-Hungary and all the small Balkan states, but also on those of Russia, Italy and, directly or indirectly, all the other great European powers. Thirdly, and not the least important, the problems in the Mediterranean. These three broad foreign policy issues provided both the framework and the background within which the Dual Monarchy's naval policy was conducted.

The Adriatic Question

This problem exercised by far the greatest influence upon the conduct of Austro-Hungarian and Italian naval policy. It in fact encompassed three related problems: Italy's *irredenta*; the fate of Albania; and Montenegro's efforts to annul an article of the Berlin Treaty of 1878 limiting her sovereignty in maritime matters.

By becoming allied with the Dual Monarchy and Germany in the Triple Alliance in 1882, Italy was rescued from her position of isolation and began to play a more prominent role in European affairs. By the 1890s, Italy, while outwardly loyal to the Triple Alliance partners, tried to remain on friendly terms with the other great European powers. Only Italy's relations with France until 1896 remained strained. In the wake of the Italian Army's humiliating defeat at Adowa that ended Italy's Abyssinian adventure, Rome initiated a new course in foreign policy aimed at reducing the country's excessive dependence on Germany. By 1901 Italy's foreign policy changed rather abruptly when the new government began to pursue a more assertive policy in the Balkans and North Africa. At the same time Italy continued to improve her relations with France.

For Austria-Hungary the greatly intensified irredentist agitation in Italy in 1903-4 was a source of much concern. The problem of Italian *irredenta*, or 'unredeemed' Italy, arose because over one million Italians were left within the Dual Monarchy's borders after Italian unification in 1859.

The irredentists claimed parts of the Dual Monarchy's littoral on historical, ethnic, and cultural grounds. They argued that as Istria and Dalmatia were territories formerly held by Venice, they rightfully belonged to her successor, the kingdom of Italy. While the province of Trentino (Welsch Tyrol) and the towns of Trieste, Zara, and Fiume could be claimed for reasons of nationality as parts of Italy, it was difficult to use this argument for other parts of the Austro-Hungarian littoral. In the Austrian province of Trentino, and the province of Goerz-Gradisca or Venezia Giulia, Italians made up about 30 per cent of the total population in 1910. In Trieste lived 119,000 Italians or 62 per cent of the total. In Istria, Italians made up 37 per cent of a total population of 404,000. However, only 18,000 Italians lived in Dalmatia, or three per cent of the population, according to the official Austrian statistics, as compared with 613,000 'Yugoslavs' mostly Croats. Italians in contrast claimed between 30,000 and 50,000 of their nationals in Dalmatia. In any case, Italians made up no more than ten per cent of Dalmatia's population. Italians comprised a majority only in the city of Zara. By 1910 roughly 243,000 Italians lived in Hungary, mostly in the coastal area. Only in Fiume did the Italians have a majority of 52 per cent.[1]

The most extreme Italian nationalists considered as 'unredeemed' lands the islands of Malta, Corsica, Corfú, and the entire eastern Adriatic shore as far south as Valona. However, even 'moderate nationalists' argued that Trentino and Trieste were parts of Italy.[2]

Although some Italian politicians flirted with the irredentists, this movement did not exercise any great influence on the conduct of Italian foreign policy before 1900. Nevertheless, irredentist agitation was a constant irritant that hindered all efforts to achieve better relations between Vienna and Rome. At the same time *irredenta* provided a powerful tool to those in both countries who advocated increased military and naval expenditures.

After 1878 another source of tension between Vienna and Rome was Albania. Both the Dual Monarchy and Italy aimed to obtain preponderant political, economic, and cultural influence in that Turkish province. Austria-Hungary initially had a more favourable position in Albania than Italy because of the many privileges given to her by Turkey. Austro-Italian rivalry in Albania became especially intense after 1900 as the Austro-Hungarian penetration of Albania was felt in the economic life of the province. But Italy, which in the 1890s had had a negligible share of Albanian trade, began to expand economically, thereby endangering the Dual Monarchy's hitherto secure position there. Both Italy and the Dual Monarchy also conducted vigorous political and propaganda activities among Albanians living in the province and abroad. By the turn of this century, about 150,000–200,000 Italo-Albanians lived in the Italian provinces of Calabria, Puglia, and Sicily.[3]

Besides Austria-Hungary and Italy, other countries with interests in Albania were Greece (which claimed the southern part of the province) and Montenegro (which had aspirations in the northern part). Serbia, because of her land-locked position, also wanted access to the sea through the Albanian territory. To this end, Belgrade advanced various railway schemes after 1904 aimed at obtaining direct access to the Adriatic and thereby reduce Serbia's economic dependence on the Dual Monarchy. Serbia then possessed only one normal-gauge railway, Belgrade–Nish. The Adriatic railway project (after 1910 known as the Timok Valley railway) in 1907 envisaged a line running from Nish to San Giovanni di Medua on the Albanian coast. Another branch of that railway was to run northwards from Nish to Prahovo on the Danube River where it was to be linked with the Rumanian system.

The principality of Montenegro was the only Balkan Slavic state bordering the Adriatic, a 22-mile-long coastal stretch. By the decision of the Berlin Congress of 1878, Montenegro acquired Podgorica, Gusinje, and Plava, as well as the port of Antivari that had previously belonged to Turkey's province of Albania. However, because of the Albanian protests, Gusinje and Plava were substituted for the port of Dulcigno in 1880. Article 29 of the Berlin Treaty of 1878 imposed serious restrictions on Montenegro. Any Montenegrin fortification on the Boyana River, except within four miles of Scutari, was prohibited. Montenegro was also barred from possessing any warships. The port of Antivari and all the Montenegrin waters were closed to naval vessels of all nations. The same article stipulated that sanitary policing of Antivari and the Montenegrin coast was to be entrusted to Austria-Hungary. Also, Montenegro had to adopt maritime legislation in return for which the Dual Monarchy extended consular protection to the Montenegrin merchant marine.[4] Not surprisingly, Montenegro chafed under these restrictions and tried repeatedly to enlist the support of the great powers to bring about the suppression of Article 29.

The Dual Monarchy and the Balkans

After the unifications of Germany and Italy, the attention of Austria-Hungary was directed away from central Europe and toward the extension of her political and economic influence in the Balkans. However, Austria-Hungary had to reckon with strong opposition by Tsarist Russia, which also had aspirations on the peninsula. Russia enjoyed traditionally close ties with the small Slavic states in the area. However, prior to 1905 Russia was unprepared to conduct an active policy in the Balkans because her involvement in the Far East made it imperative for her to avoid another possible major crisis elsewhere.

Relations between Vienna and Belgrade deteriorated rapidly after 1903 when in a palace coup in Belgrade the Austrophile King Alexander Obrenovic was overthrown and assassinated. His successor King Peter I from the House of Karadjordjevic almost immediately embarked on an active policy to create 'Greater Serbia'. Belgrade's primary goal was to

4

acquire Bosnia and Herzegovina where Serbs comprised about 40 per cent of the population. Serbia also coveted the Turkish province of Macedonia.

The Austro-Hungarian control of Bosnia and the Sanjak of Novibazar and her political and economic influence in Albania and Montenegro were perceived by Belgrade as an attempt to encircle and crush Serbia. Therefore, Serbia acutely felt the need for the support of a great power both to ensure her existence as a sovereign state and to realize her national aims. This was why the new regime in Belgrade began actively to seek Russia's backing for its policies in the Balkans.

The Dual Monarchy's policy toward Serbia was designed to prevent her from expanding into the nominally Turkish provinces of Bosnia and Herzegovina or Macedonia or Albania. While Vienna generally was not opposed to the creation of a 'greater' Bulgaria or Greece, it wanted an independent but weak Serbia, economically dependent on the Dual Monarchy.

In Montenegro the strongest political influence had traditionally been that of Russia. The latter in fact regarded the principality as a vanguard of Slavic interests against the Dual Monarchy in the Balkans. Montenegro needed Russia's support to preserve its independence against both Turkey and Austria-Hungary.

By the turn of this century the Dual Monarchy had succeeded in obtaining a dominant role in Montenegro's foreign trade. However, that position was challenged by Italy after 1896 when a daughter of Prince Nicholas I of Montenegro married the future Italian King Vittorio Emmanuele III. Italy tried to use this connection to expand her influence in Montenegro's economy and foreign policy. For example, an Italian company built the port (Pristan) in Antivari and in 1904 Italy negotiated the construction of the railway line Antivari–Virbazar. Nevertheless, Italy feared that because of Montenegro's dependence on Austria-Hungary, the principality could no longer be considered an effective roadblock between Dalmatia and Albania. Rome was also concerned that if Vienna chose to apply Article 25 of the Berlin Treaty and occupy the Sanjak of Novibazar (which formed a wedge between Montenegro and Serbia), Vienna's dominant position in Albania would become an accomplished fact.[5]

The Dual Monarchy on her part was concerned that Italy might become too closely associated with Montenegro. These apprehensions were not groundless because in 1896 Montenegro had proposed to Italy a division of Albania. Montenegro was to annex the northern part and Italy the southern part, except for the Vilayet of Janina which was to go to Greece.[6] While Austria-Hungary preferred the *status quo* in the Balkans, she was determined not to allow any expansion by Serbia or the establishment of a large south Slav state that would possibly intensify centrifugal forces within the Dual Monarchy and inhibit her expansion southward in the direction of Salonika.

The Dual Monarchy and the Mediterranean

The Dual Monarchy, by virtue of her position in the Adriatic, was a Mediterranean power. Besides Russia, she was the most directly involved of all the great European powers in the 'Eastern Question' that involved not only the fate of Turkish possessions in the Balkans and elsewhere in the Mediterranean, but also whether Turkey was to retain control of the Straits or whether Russia would succeed directly or indirectly in becoming mistress of that vital international waterway. Although the political and commercial interests of the Dual Monarchy in the Mediterranean were primarily secured through the active use of diplomacy, naval forces were also used at times.

The interests of the Dual Monarchy traditionally centred on the preservation of Turkey. Therefore, she was opposed to any action by Russia that might change the *status quo* in the Balkans or the Straits. Vienna always considered (with one notable exception in 1908) the opening of the Straits to Russian warships as an international issue concerning the interests of all the great European powers. Moreover, Austria-Hungary was strongly opposed to any Italian action against Turkish possessions in North Africa because this would reopen the perennial 'Eastern Question'.

The Dual Monarchy had an additional reason to be concerned about the preservation of the territorial integrity of the Turkish Empire – her highly developed and profitable trade in the Eastern Mediterranean (Levant). By 1904 the trade of the Dual Monarchy with the Mediterranean countries amounted to about 3.3 million metric tons or 31 per cent of her total seaborne trade, while seaborne trade with the Levant (Turkey, Greece, and Egypt) accounted for about 44 per cent of her trade with the Mediterranean countries.[7] In addition, Austria-Hungary was greatly concerned with the maintenance of an uninterrupted traffic through the Straits of Gibraltar, the Suez Canal, and the Turkish Straits.

In the aftermath of the Franco-Prussian War, European diplomacy was dominated by the German Chancellor Otto von Bismarck. He skilfully wove a complicated set of alliances and secret understandings between Germany and other great powers aimed at maintaining France's isolation and Germany's dominance on the continent. By 1873 Bismarck created an informal alliance among Germany, Austria-Hungary and Russia known as the Three Emperors' League (*Dreikaiserbund*). This alliance represented a revived form of the Holy Alliance. However, in practice, the Three Emperors' League was no more than a symbol of monarchical solidarity.

The 1875–78 crisis in the Balkans demonstrated the fragility of the Three Emperors' League. The Berlin Congress of 1878 forced the Russians to abandon their plans for a greater Bulgaria as stipulated by the San Stefano Treaty that they had imposed on the Turks. Among the foremost opponents of the San Stefano Treaty were the Dual Monarchy and Great Britain.

The Balkan crisis convinced Bismarck that Russia was an unreliable ally. This was the main reason that he reluctantly decided to have Germany conclude an alliance with Austria-Hungary. The treaty between Berlin and Vienna, known as the Dual Alliance, was signed in October 1879. The agreement was purely defensive in nature because both countries pledged mutual aid in case of an unprovoked Russian attack. At the same time the Dual Alliance was beneficial for Russia because it limited the Dual Monarchy's temptations to move closer to Great Britain. Bismarck succeeded in providing guarantees for Austria-Hungary's preservation as a great power, while at the same time he withheld full support of Vienna's foreign policy aims.

After 1879 Bismarck tried to renew friendship with Russia. He reached his goal in June 1881, when a new understanding, this time on paper, was concluded among Germany, the Dual Monarchy and Russia. The three courts recognized the European and mutually obligatory character of the principle of the closure of the Turkish Straits based on international law and confirmed by the Declaration of July 1878. While Europe was preoccupied with the Franco-Prussian War, Russia unilaterally denounced some provisions of the Peace of Paris that prohibited her from maintaining a fleet in the Black Sea. Russia's action led to the convening of the Black Sea Conference in London in January 1871. This conference, which ended in March, regulated the status of the Straits by amending the articles of the Treaty of Paris concerning the number and type of the vessels of the two contracting parties in the Black Sea. Russia was permitted to restore fortifications to Sevastopol. As compensation, the Sultan's powers in respect of the passage of warships through the Straits were increased. Although until then the Sultan was not empowered to allow the passage of warships in peacetime, the Treaty of London stipulated that the Sultan could open the Straits in time of peace to the warships of friendly or allied governments.[8] Germany and Austria-Hungary in effect guaranteed Russia's security in the Straits.

Russia also received an assurance from Germany and the Dual Monarchy that they were not opposed to the eventual union of Bulgaria and Eastern Rumelia. This represented a setback for Vienna's aims in the Balkans, but especially for Great Britain. The British government feared that Russia might use an enlarged Bulgaria to obtain eventual control over the Turkish Straits. The Dual Monarchy adhered to the renewed

Three Emperors' League unwillingly because of her deep mistrust of the Russian intentions regarding Turkey. Thus, Vienna became more interested in an anti-Russian alliance with Great Britain and Italy.

To satisfy the Dual Monarchy, Bismarck agreed to the adherence of Italy to the Dual Alliance in May 1882, thereby creating the Triple Alliance. In fact, Italy was thrown into the hands of the Dual Alliance by its deep resentment of the French action in Tunisia in 1881. The Triple Alliance promised to defend Italy against France, while Vienna was assured of Italy's neutrality in case of war with Russia. The Tunisia affair also showed Italy how important it would be to possess the active support of Great Britain to pursue successfully her colonial policies. Italy's highly favourable attitude toward Great Britain was also evident in the Triple Alliance Treaty of 1882 when at her insistence a clause was inserted stating the treaty could not be regarded as being directed against Great Britain.[9]

The Straits Question

The question of the viability of the Ottoman Empire was a recurrent issue in European diplomacy in the nineteenth century. The essence of the problem was the regulation of the passage of foreign warships through the 160 nautical mile-long Turkish Straits. The 'Straits Question' was principally an issue between Great Britain and Russia, though other great European powers were also involved.

British aims in the Mediterranean were limited because of her worldwide commitments. Traditionally, Great Britain sought to prevent any single power from dominating the Mediterranean and thereby threatening the security of her main sea route to India through the Suez Canal or the alternate route through Syria and Persia.

British aims were to ensure that her warships could enter the Black Sea at will. London also supported the continued independence of Turkey, thus blocking Russia's drive to Constantinople. Russia had more at stake in the Straits Question than any other great European power. A large share of Russia's trade overseas passed through the Straits. Control of the Straits would allow Russia to preserve her dominant position in the Black Sea. Moreover, the Russian Navy were to obtain unhindered access to the warm waters of the Mediterranean. Russia's minimum goal was to maintain the principle of closing of the Straits to non-riparian states.

After the mid-1870s British policy toward the Straits Question underwent changes. The purchase of shares of the Suez Canal Company made Great Britain wish to obtain direct political control over the still nominally Turkish dependency of Egypt. Hence, defence of the Suez Canal became more important for Great Britain than the Straits

Question. Yet Great Britain remained interested in seeing Russia's way to the Straits permanently blocked. The only powers whose interests in the Mediterranean were essentially identical with Great Britain's were the Dual Monarchy and Italy. The community of views between Austria-Hungary and Great Britain became especially evident during the 1885–87 crisis in the Balkans when both countries supported the anti-Russian party in Bulgaria. The British Foreign Secretary, Lord Salisbury, unlike Benjamin Disraeli in 1878, supported the establishment of a large anti-Russian Bulgaria. He hoped that in this way Russia's route to the Straits and the Aegean would be permanently closed. The Austro-Hungarian Foreign Minister, Count Gustav Kalnoky, regarded Great Britain as an important ally of the Dual Monarchy in the event of war with Russia.[10]

The Bulgarian crisis of 1885 effectively destroyed the Three Emperors' League. Bismarck's policy rested on the hope, which was not fulfilled, that Austria-Hungary and Russia would remain satisfied with a compromise on the Eastern Question.

The Mediterranean agreements

After 1886 Bismarck, unwilling to commit Germany to defend the Dual Monarchy's interests in the Balkans or the independence of Turkey, made great efforts to secure Vienna's interests against the other great powers. However, he was unsuccessful in his efforts to renew the Three Emperors' League, because Russia, on bad terms with the Dual Monarchy, refused. Nevertheless, Germany and Russia signed the so-called 'Reinsurance Treaty' in June 1887. By that treaty both powers only promised to stay neutral if one of them was attacked by a third party. However, Bismarck promised Russia diplomatic support with regard to the Straits Question and Bulgaria. This clause contradicted what Bismarck was trying to achieve in the Mediterranean.

During the Bulgarian crisis, Bismarck's policy was to urge both Italy and Austria-Hungary to form a league with Great Britain to maintain the *status quo* in the Mediterranean. Hence, any aggressive design by Russia with regard to Bulgaria and the Straits could be checked. Berlin would not join the league because Bismarck declined to involve Germany in the Straits Question. However, he did his best to help Vienna and Rome in their negotiations for the protection of their special interests.

Salisbury, for his part, declined to pledge his government to any concrete action in preventing Russia from seizing Constantinople. He placed great emphasis on the importance of protecting Italy from being crushed by France and generally was disposed to follow Bismarck's game because Germany was the strongest continental power. Salisbury opposed an alliance with Germany because in his view Great Britain's increased responsibilities would not be commensurate with the potential benefits she might gain.

In the end, Bismarck's efforts to bring about an understanding between the two Triple Alliance partners and Great Britain were successful. Italy and Great Britain signed an agreement concerning the Mediterranean on 12 February 1887 in London. The Italian note to the British government stated that both powers were to maintain as far as possible the status quo in the Adriatic, the Aegean and the Black Seas. However, if this proved to be impossible Italy and Great Britain were to prevent any modifications in the *status quo* that might be detrimental to their interests. Italy pledged to support British aims in Egypt, while Great Britain was to support Italy in North Africa, specifically in Tripolitania and Cyrenaica, against the encroachments of third powers. Also, Italy and Great Britain promised mutual support in case of any difference with a third power over their policies in the Mediterranean. Among other things, the British note to the Italian government said that both powers intended to prevent the extension of the domination of any great power in any part of the Adriatic, Aegean and North African coasts.[11]

By 24 March 1887, the Dual Monarchy acceded to the Italo-British agreement by an exchange of notes between the Austro-Hungarian ambassador in London, Count Karoly, and Salisbury. After expressing satisfaction with the understanding between Great Britain and Italy, the Austro-Hungarian note stated that

> although the question of the Mediterranean in general does not primarily affect the interests of Austria-Hungary, the Austro-Hungarian Government has the same interest so far as it concerns the Eastern question as a whole and therefore the same need of maintaining the status quo in the Orient so far as possible to prevent the aggrandizement of one power to the detriment of another and consequently of acting in concert in order to ensure these cardinal principles of their policy.[12]

By December 1887 at Vienna's initiative all three powers signed the second Mediterranean agreement that dealt primarily with the Straits Question. The Austro-Hungarian note delivered to London said that the policy of the three powers was aimed at the maintenance of the independence of Turkey as a guardian of the Straits. It stressed that in regard to the Straits, Turkey 'can neither cede any portion of her sovereign right nor delegate her authority to any other power in Asia Minor'. The Austro-Hungarian government concluded that all three powers should be associated with Turkey in the common defence of these principles.

The British note to the Austro-Hungarian government emphasized that if the Porte (Turkish imperial government) violated the principles guiding the use of the Straits, all three powers would feel justified in using force either jointly or unilaterally to occupy temporarily parts of Turkish territory and preserve the status quo.[13]

Both agreements were chiefly designed to preserve the status quo in the Mediterranean and the Black Sea against Russian and French action. Great Britain, although careful as always to avoid allying herself openly with the Triple Alliance, was eager to make these agreements to strengthen her position in the Straits.[14]

Search for the first naval convention

Although Austria-Hungary was uninterested in acquiring colonies in the Levant or North Africa, she had an active interest as a member of the Triple Alliance not to allow the change in the balance of power in the Mediterranean to the detriment of Italy and Germany. Italy, on her part, as the only Triple Alliance partner with extensive territorial and political pretensions in the Mediterranean, planned to conclude an agreement on naval co-operation with one or both of her allies. Such an agreement was aimed at protection against France and tying Germany and the Dual Monarchy to Italian policies in the Mediterranean. As early as 1888 Italian Prime Minister Giuseppe Crispi approached Austro-Hungarian Foreign Minister Count Gustav Kalnoky and broached the idea of concluding a naval convention between Italy and Austria-Hungary. This move resulted from the renewed French pressure to detach Italy from the Triple Alliance. However, Kalnoky rejected the Italian suggestion, and argued that the Austro-Hungarian Navy was a defensive force that could only be employed in the Adriatic. He advised Crispi that Italy should rely instead on the British Royal Navy for assistance in defending her Tyrrhenian coast and her outlying islands against any hostile action by the French fleet.[15]

Despite this discouraging response, Crispi raised the question of naval co-operation in the summer of 1889, both with Vienna and Berlin. The Italian ambassador in Berlin informed Crispi in July that the German government looked favourably upon the possibility of concluding a naval convention among the partners of the Triple Alliance. However, the German government suggested that Crispi should first discuss this idea with Vienna. The German Naval Office thought that Italy should rely on the entente with Great Britain because the addition of the Austro-Hungarian fleet alone would not be enough to achieve superiority over the French fleet.

By 6 August 1889 Crispi proposed to Kalnoky a naval agreement by which the Austro-Hungarian Navy was to protect Italy's Adriatic coast and thereby allow Italy to employ her entire fleet elsewhere in the

Mediterranean.[16] Moreover, Crispi proposed to Kalnoky that both a military and a naval convention be concluded between the two countries. Kalnoky, however, remained unmoved. The main reason for Vienna's cold attitude was apparently the feeling that any naval convention would work more to Italy's than to the Dual Monarchy's advantage.

After the renewal of the Triple Alliance in 1889 the new Italian Prime Minister, Antonio Di Rudini, instructed the Italian ambassadors in Berlin and Vienna in July 1891 to raise the question of a naval convention among the three partners. The Austro-Hungarian Navy's Commander, Admiral Sterneck, was favourably disposed to a naval agreement with Italy, but provided that he be appointed commander of the joint fleet in the event of war. However, the Italians were unwilling to yield on that point. Hence, no serious discussion of Italy's proposal took place.[17]

By 1887 France was diplomatically isolated and facing potential conflicts with Germany and Great Britain. Apparently aware of the existence of the Mediterranean agreements and perceiving Italy as the weakest link, France tried after 1888 to disrupt the Triple Alliance by driving Italy out of it. To accomplish that goal, France started a tariff war with Italy, intensified 'republican' intrigues and raised the question of the papacy.

By 1890, France's anti-Italian campaign was taking effect in Italy, as evidenced by rising anti-monarchical feeling, increased suspicion of the Triple Alliance, and a brief revival of the *irredenta* campaign. France's international position improved in 1890 when Bismarck fell from power. His less skilful successors failed to renew the Reinsurance Treaty and as a consequence Russia and Germany became estranged. Bismarck's fall also removed one great obstacle to France's eventual rapprochement with Russia. While France's threat to disrupt the Triple Alliance before 1890 was veiled and indirect, afterwards her policy was openly directed against Germany.

French–Russian agreement

By 1893 France concluded an alliance with Russia. This event also had a potentially profound influence on the situation in the Mediterranean. The French policy of seeking friendship with Russia was partly designed to prevent the conclusion of a new Mediterranean agreement between the Triple Alliance and Great Britain. For Russia the alliance with France offered among other advantages the presence of a strong French fleet in Toulon which would limit British ambitions in the Straits and the Levant and indirectly check British influence in Persia, Afghanistan and China.

By October 1893 the visit of the Russian naval squadron to Toulon caused the greatest apprehension as to future Franco-Russian intentions in the Mediterranean. There were rumours of a possible Franco-Russian naval convention, which, as events proved, were premature. In fact, French naval authorities showed little interest in a naval arrangement with Russia, because they believed that the French fleet in Toulon was able to check the Italian and Austro-Hungarian fleets alone. The Russian fleet was considered slightly weaker than the Austro-Hungarian fleet. The Russian fleet was not expected to become superior to the Austro-Hungarian fleet until 1897.[18] French interest in the Russian fleet was then limited to its utility as a symbol of Franco-Russian friendship and ability to defend the Russian Baltic coast in a possible war against Germany.

Vienna's attempt to create a Quadruple Alliance

New developments in the Mediterranean prompted Foreign Minister Kalnoky in 1893 to conceive a programme intended to: strengthen Italy's position, force Great Britain to take a definite stand in the Eastern Question and in the Mediterranean, and move Germany away from her policy of disinterestedness in the Eastern Question. Kalnoky in fact intended to create a Quadruple Alliance to protect the Turkish Straits. However, British Foreign Secretary Rosebery declined any such agreement and thought that the entire scheme was inspired by Germany.

After Gladstone became Foreign Secretary in February 1894, Kalnoky resumed his efforts to interest the British government in the plan. If London refused, he planned to threaten to conclude a pact with Russia in which the Dual Monarchy would obtain freedom of action in regard to Salonika and Russia in the Straits Question.[19] Subsequent talks between Vienna and London to conclude an agreement were fruitless. Rosebery told the Austro-Hungarian ambassador in London, Count Deym, that his government firmly adhered to the policy of closure of the Straits. Deym responded that his government could not expose itself to the danger of being unable to count with certainty on British protection of the Straits. Also, if Great Britain for any reason had to abandon her traditional policy, the Dual Monarchy would be compelled to confine her activities to the maintenance and safeguarding of her interests in the Balkans. Then, the Straits would be left to their fate: in other words, to be controlled by Russia. Rosebery responded by assuring Deym that even if Russia reached a favourable agreement with the Porte, she could not obtain free passage for her warships through the Straits without the concurrence of the other great powers and that Russia 'would never receive British consent'.

Rosebery had given Deym a rather gloomy prospect of Britain's ability to stand up to France and Russia in the Mediterranean. The Austro-Hungarian fleet was negligible and could not be of any help to

Great Britain. Rosebery had a similar view of the Italian fleet, despite the fact that it possessed a number of very good ships. Thus in case of conflict with the Dual Alliance, there was no other alternative for Great Britain but to withdraw her fleet from the Mediterranean. At a meeting in February 1894 Rosebery explained to Deym that Great Britain would defend the Straits alone against Russia. He also added that Great Britain would prefer not to have the Dual Monarchy as an ally because his government did not want to risk a European war over the Straits Question. However, Rosebery expressed the hope that in such a case the Triple Alliance would prevent France from taking an active part in the war on Russia's side.[20]

Growing colonial difficulties with France in the mid-1890s brought about a momentous change in British Mediterranean policy. As long as it had been possible for Great Britain to keep Russia in some sort of alliance with Germany, she had had a close identity of interests with the Triple Alliance powers. Great Britain then relied on her naval strength in the Mediterranean to sustain arrangements with Italy and the Dual Monarchy. However, after 1896 the alliance with Austria-Hungary for checking Russian pretensions to the Straits was no longer of any importance, for France, not Russia, had become Britain's principal opponent; and France, in the British view, could be handled without the assistance of the Triple Alliance.[21]

Moreover, British policy was to stick with Egypt as a key strategic position in the eastern Mediterranean and treat the Straits Question as negotiable. This change in British policy was not immediately apparent to Vienna, which approached London in February 1896 with the aim of concluding a new Mediterranean agreement. Ambassador Deym suggested to Salisbury that in case of a Russian attack against Turkey, Great Britain should defend Constantinople while the Dual Monarchy would come to Bulgaria's aid. However, Salisbury again avoided committing his government to anything that was likely to lead to a general European war. He stated that it was impossible to commit Great Britain to go to war in advance because so much would depend on the nature of prevailing public sentiment.[22]

At another meeting with Salisbury on 26 February, Deym revealed the apprehensions of Emperor Francis Joseph I regarding the uncertain course of British policy in the Mediterranean. He also told Salisbury that there was a fear in Vienna that the Dual Monarchy could no longer count on the British friendship and sympathy for the continued independence of Turkey. Salisbury then tried to assure Deym that regardless of the 'Armenian massacres' that had caused great revulsion in British public opinion, Great Britain would not be reconciled to eventual Russian control of the Straits. In fact, he was more concerned with the rapprochement between Russia and Bulgaria which was then taking place. As long as Bulgaria was hostile, any Russian expedition against Constantinople would depend on the security of sea communications in the Black Sea. These were in turn vulnerable to attack by any naval power stronger than Russia. Salisbury said that if Russia could command an uninterrupted road from the Prut River to the Bosphorus her communications would be secure and she would be comparatively indifferent to any danger that might menace her communications to Sevastopol.[23]

Ambassador Deym renewed his government's proposal to protect Turkey against Russia during a meeting with Salisbury in January 1897. He contended that in Vienna's view it was Great Britain who had the greatest stake in the maintenance of the status quo in the Straits and who therefore should take the lead in defending the Straits against Russian encroachments. Vienna proposed that if Great Britain sent her fleet to the Straits, the Dual Monarchy would then undertake the necessary measures on land to prevent Russia from obtaining a commanding position for an advance to the Straits. Salisbury responded by saying that although Great Britain was interested in the protection of the Straits, her interests were no greater than that of Italy and Austria-Hungary. He concluded that it was quite impossible for Great Britain to make such an agreement as Vienna wanted. Afterwards, there was no exchange of notes between Vienna and London on the renewal or confirmation of the previous Mediterranean agreements.[24]

Agreement with Russia

The British refusal to enter into a formal agreement with the Dual Monarchy regarding the Mediterranean was the principal reason that Foreign Minister Goluchowsky decided to reorient the country's policy to that of co-operation with Russia. In the agreement signed in Reval in 1897 Russia conceded that because 'the question of Constantinople and adjacent territory as well as that of the Straits have an eminently European character', they could not be made the subject of a separate understanding between the Dual Monarchy and Russia. Russian Foreign Minister Muravieff assured Goluchowsky that his government was not seeking any modification of the agreements concerning the use of the Straits then in force.[25] The long-standing policy of Vienna (which with one brief exception in 1908 remained unchanged until 1914) was that the Straits Question was a European problem that could be resolved only by co-operation among all the great powers.

The first naval convention

Italy made another attempt to conclude a naval agreement with her two partners in the Triple Alliance in the late 1890s. Although the Franco-Italian rapprochement was already underway, Italy's misgivings as to France's real intentions had not yet been dispelled. By early 1898 there were rumours in Italy that France and Russia had concluded a naval arrangement for joint operations in the Mediterranean and that Bizerte was to serve as a base for the Russian fleet. It was also believed that France intended actively to support Russian ambitions in regard to the Straits Question.

Although the rumours concerning the alleged Franco-Russian naval convention proved to be premature, they prompted Italy to seek some kind of arrangement to strengthen her position in the Mediterranean. By late 1898, the Chief of the Italian General Staff, General Tancredi Saletta, met with his German counterpart, General Alfred von Schlieffen, to discuss the tasks of the Triple Alliance fleets in the event of a war against the Franco-Russian combination (Dual Alliance). General Saletta also asked von Schlieffen to intercede in Vienna to persuade Austro-Hungarian military leaders to reach a naval agreement with Italy.[26]

Further talks concerning a naval convention among the Triple Alliance partners were held in late 1899, but no progress was recorded. The turning point came following the dispatch of a note from General Saletta to the Chief of the Austro-Hungarian General Staff, General Friedrich von Beck, on 6 June 1900. General Saletta proposed a conference to be held aimed at reaching an agreement on the employment of the Triple Alliance fleets in case of war that would respect the common interests of the Triple Alliance and remain within the political terms of the treaty. The Italian note did not surprise Vienna, because the need for such a conference had already been rumoured for some time. Saletta's initiative elicited a favourable reply from General Beck early in July. Although the Germans had no particular interests to protect in the Mediterranean at that time, they considered a combined action of their Triple Alliance partners against French troop reinforcements from North Africa to be of great potential value if Germany ever had to fight France on the continent.[27]

Talks among the Triple Alliance naval representatives began in Berlin on 5 November 1900 and were concluded exactly one month later with the signing of a naval convention. However, the naval convention merely provided a division of zones of operations among the three fleets. No joint naval command was envisaged in the event of war.[28] Only a few top officials in the Triple Alliance knew of the naval convention's existence or content. The naval convention of the Triple Alliance remained without practical effect after 1902 because of Italy's steadily improving relations with France and her increasingly ambiguous attitude toward the Triple Alliance.

The rapprochement between Italy and France continued after 1900 despite the fact that Italy signed a secret naval convention with the other two partners of the Triple Alliance that was aimed at France. By a new exchange of notes between Foreign Minister Prinetti and Ambassador Barrere in November 1902, both governments agreed to exercise full freedom of action in their respective zones of influence in North Africa. Moreover, Italy pledged to remain neutral in case France 'should be the object of direct or indirect aggression on the part of one or more powers'.[29] This clause clearly violated Italy's obligations under the terms of the Triple Alliance Treaty. The Franco-Italian understanding led in effect to a further weakening of the Triple Alliance's influence in the Mediterranean.

Franco-Russian naval convention

The much-rumoured Franco-Russian naval convention was signed on 21 December 1901. It provided a division of operational zones between the two fleets in case of war against Great Britain. In such a situation France was to concentrate a major part of her fleet in the Mediterranean, while deploying only second-class battleships and torpedo cruisers in the Atlantic, to tie the British fleet in its home waters. The convention stipulated that Russia's Baltic fleet was to remain on the defensive, while the Black Sea fleet was to transport one army corps and force its way through the Straits, then to proceed to Egypt and disembark the troops.

Rapprochement between France and Britain

The Franco-Russian naval convention was without much practical effect because of the rapprochement between Paris and London that started after 1900. By April 1904 the British and French governments signed two agreements aimed to resolve long-standing colonial disputes between the two countries.

The French government declared that it had no intention of changing the political status of Morocco, while Great Britain recognized France's right to provide Morocco with the assistance required to implement administrative, economic, financial and military reforms. France accorded identical rights to Great Britain in regard to Egypt. Finally, both countries agreed that to secure free passage through the Straits of Gibraltar no fortifications should be built on the Moroccan coast from Mellila to the heights commanding the right bank of the Sebou River.[30]

The Anglo-French understanding brought about a significant change in British foreign policy and strategy. One of the reasons why Great Britain sought reconciliation with France was a fear that if France intervened on Russia's side in the then ongoing war with Japan, Great Britain would be bound to aid her ally, Japan. In such an event,

Germany would exact a heavy price for staying neutral. But behind all British calculations was the growing strength of the German fleet. Great Britain simply could not allow a situation to arise in which the Royal Navy had to face simultaneously a German threat in the North Sea, an Italian threat in the Mediterranean, and an unfriendly France.

Naval balance in the Mediterranean

The Anglo-French understanding in 1904 immediately had a dramatic effect upon British naval strategy. The 'entente cordiale' almost completely removed the French fleet as the principal potential opponent of the British fleet in the Mediterranean. As a result, a new redistribution of the British Navy designed to concentrate in the North Sea was announced in December 1904. Under the new scheme, the British Mediterranean fleet based in Malta was to comprise eight instead of the hitherto 12 battleships. The former Channel fleet in Gibraltar was renamed the Atlantic fleet and allowed to retain its eight battleships. This fleet was to be employed either for the reinforcement of the Mediterranean fleet or the then newly created Channel fleet (formerly the 'Home fleet') based in Dover. Both the Mediterranean and Atlantic fleets had one extra battleship in reserve. In addition, each of these fleets had assigned to them one squadron of six armoured cruisers. The Mediterranean fleet comprised 15 destroyers plus seven in reserve, while the Atlantic fleet had ten and eight destroyers, respectively. Thus, if necessary, the Mediterranean fleet could have some 40 destroyers at its disposal.[31]

The French Navy after 1904, because of its disastrous administration, entered into an era of retrenchment and misguided reforms which crippled its strength. The French Mediterranean fleet in 1905 comprised six battleships in an active squadron plus two in reserve.[32]

The Russian Navy, following the catastrophic war with Japan, was reduced to the rank of a third-class power. By the spring of 1905 the Russian Black Sea fleet consisted of only two first-class and six second-class battleships.[33]

By the spring of 1905 the Triple Alliance enjoyed numerical superiority in almost every category of naval strength over its potential adversaries in the Dual Alliance. However, the total strength of the Triple Alliance fleets was not as great as it appeared on paper because the Austro-Hungarian Navy still remained essentially a coastal defence force that was incapable of sustained employment in the Mediterranean. The situation for the Triple Alliance was even more unfavourable if the British Mediterranean and Atlantic fleets were included on the side of the Dual Alliance.

By mid-1904 the combined Austro-Italian fleet had almost twice the number of battleships and destroyer-size vessels and three times as many cruisers as the Dual Alliance fleets (see Figure 1). However, if the British fleet in the Mediterranean was added then the Austro-Italian combination was approximately equal in strength to its potential adversaries. But it should be noted that while at that time the Austro-Hungarian fleet was not capable of sustained employment in the Mediterranean, all of its potential opponents were.

FIGURE 1
NAVAL BALANCE IN THE MEDITERRANEAN, MAY 1904

	Dual Alliance			Triple Alliance			
Type	France	Russia	Total	Britain	Italy	Austria-Hungary	Total
Battleships	8	10	18	12	18	11	29
Armoured cruisers	-	2	2	2	6	3	9
Protected cruisers	6	2	8	10	13	5	18
Destroyers	7	16	23	30	27	8	35
Torpedo boats	-	19	19	-	111	30	141
Submarines	NA	2	2	-	6	-	6
Total	21	51	72	54	181	57	238

Source: 'Uebersicht des schwimmenden Materials der groesseren Seemaechte', *Nauticus* (1904); 'Comparative strength' in *The Naval Annual 1905*, ed. Viscount Hythe Brassey and John Leyland (Portsmouth: J. Griffin Co., 1905), pp. 40–5.

NOTES

1. Theodore Veiter, *Die Italiener in der Oesterreichische-Ungarische Monarchie. Eine volkspolitische und nationalitaetenrechtliche Studie* (Vienna: Verlag fuer Geschichte und Politik, 1965) pp. 19, 46; and Gualtiero Castellini, *Trento e Trieste. L'irredentismo e il Problema Adriatico* (Milan: Fratelli Treves, 1918) p. 119.
2. William Ray Wallace, *Greater Italy* (New York: Charles Scribner's Sons, 1917) p. 23.
3. William C. Askew, 'Austro-Italian Antagonism, 1896-1914', in Lilian Parker Wallace and William C. Askew, *Power, Public Opinion and Diplomacy. Essays in Honor of Eber Malcolm Carroll by his Students* (Durham NC: Duke University Press, 1959) p. 199.
4. Bernadotte E. Schmitt, *The Annexation of Bosnia, 1908–09* (New York: Howard Fertig, 1970) p. 231.
5. *Italy's Foreign and Colonial Policy: A Selection From The Speeches Delivered in the Italian Parliament by Senator Tommaso Tittoni During His Six Years In Office 1903-1909* (London: Smith, Elder Co., 1914) p. 245.
6. W. Askew, 'Austro-Italian Antagonism', p. 20.
7. Statistical Department of Imperial Royal Trade Ministry, *Statistik des Auswaertigen Handels des Oesterreich-Ungarischen Zollgebietes im Jahre 1904*, Vol. 1: *Hauptergebnisse-Hafen verkehr* (Vienna: Hof- und Staatsdruckerei, 1905). pp. 485–507.
8. Coleman Phillipson and Noel Buxton, *The Question of the Bosphorus and Dardanelles* (London: Steven and Haynes, 1917) pp. 160–2.
9. Alfred F. Pribram, ed., *Secret Treaties of Austria-Hungary*, Vol. 1 (Cambridge, MA: Harvard University Press, 1920) pp. 69–73.
10. Bruno Malinverni, *Il Primo Accordo per il Mediterraneo, Febraio–Marzo 1887* (Milan: Marzorati Editore, 1967) p. 180.

11. Pribram, *Secret Treaties*, Vol. 3, p. 95.
12. Ibid., Vol. 1, p. 101.
13. Ibid., pp. 125–7.
14. Barbara Jelavich, *The Ottoman Empire, the Great Powers and the Straits Question 1870–1887* (Bloomington IN/London: Indiana University Press, 1973) p. 149.
15. G. Duca, 'Accordi e Convenzioni durante la Triplice Alleanza', *Rivista Marittima* (Rome, March 1935) p. 270.
16. Gabriele Mariano, *Le Convenzione Navali della Triplece* (Rome: Ufficio Storico della Marina, 1969) pp. 77–8.
17. Ibid., pp. 112–13.
18. Peter Jakobs, *Das Werden des Franzoesisch-Russischen Zweibundes 1890–1894* (Wiesbaden: Otto Harrassowitz, 1968) p. 170.
19. Helge Grenfelt, *Der Dreibund nach dem Sturze Bismarck*, Vol. 2, *Der Kampf um die Weltherrschaft 1895–1905* (Lund: CWK Gleery, 1964) p. 16.
20. Harold Temperley and Lillian M. Penson, *Foundations of British Foreign Policy from Pitt (1792) to Salisbury (1902)* (Cambridge: Cambridge University Press, 1938) p. 481.
21. Cedrio J. Lowe, *Salisbury and the Mediterranean 1886–1896* (London: Routledge & Kegan Paul, 1965) pp. 117–18.
22. Salisbury to E. Monson, 4 April 1896, no. 1, *British Documents on the Origins of the War 1898–1914*, ed. G. P. Gooch and Harold Temperley, 11 vols (London: HMSO, 1926–38) Vol. 8, p. 405.
23. Ibid., 26 Feb. 1896, no. 24, p. 5.
24. Temperley and Penson, *Foundations of British Foreign Policy*, pp. 496–7.
25. Jelavich, *The Ottoman Empire*, pp. 159–60.
26. Ibid., pp. 179–80.
27. Ibid., p. 205.
28. For details of the first Triple Alliance naval convention see Chapter 9.
29. Pribram, *Secret Treaties*, Vol. 1, pp. 249–55.
30. Thomas Barclay, *The Turco-Italian War and its Problems* (London: Constable and Co., 1912) pp. 181–3.
31. Arthur J. Marder, *The Anatomy of British Sea Power. A History of British Naval Policy in the pre-Dreadnought Era, 1880–1905* (New York: Alfred A. Knopf, 1940) pp. 441–2.
32. 'Comparative Strength', *Navy League Annual* (1905) p. 44.
33. Ibid.

2

Foundations

The term sea power has several definitions. This term is used to refer to where the preponderant strength of a nation lies. In a broader definition of the term, sea power encompasses the totality of the use of the sea by a nation. It includes political, economic, social, and military aspects. In a narrower understanding of the term, sea power is equated to the term naval power, that is, when referring to the pursuit of a country's or community's maritime interests primarily through their naval strength.

Admiral Alfred Thayer Mahan differentiated between a 'natural' and 'artificial' sea power. He claimed that the emergence of a 'natural' sea power has always been forced upon some peoples by the sheer necessity of geography, scarcity of natural resources and the national character. The want of natural resources often found an outlet in sea trading which then became the principal activity of the people or community. This, in turn, led to the growth of a large mercantile class. Thereby, a large number of the people and the nation's wealth and power depended upon the uninterrupted use of the sea. This natural and spontaneous growth of sea power in Mahan's view did not originate from a nation's rulers, though it could have been stimulated by them. Great Britain and Japan were among the 'natural' sea powers in modern times, because an uninterrupted use of the sea has been a matter of very survival for them. In similar but less critical positions were Holland, Portugal, Venice and various medieval Italian maritime city-states. There have also been such states as Spain and France, and perhaps the Austrian Empire and Austria-Hungary, whose sea power was 'natural' in that there was a great need for it. However, because the sources of their wealth were concentrated on land, these states were able to withstand extended interruption of their maritime trade in wartime.

'Artificial' sea power has been established primarily or exclusively for political purposes. Rome, the Ottoman Empire, the Russia of Peter the Great, and Wilhelmine Germany were prime examples of such sea powers. In fact, these powers were primarily naval powers, because the military aspects of the use of the sea overshadowed all other aspects.

Admiral Alfred Thayer Mahan enumerated six prerequisites for the development of 'natural' sea power: geographical position, physical conformation, extent of territory, population, national character and character of government. However, these prerequisites were more valid in the pre-industrial era; in the modern era, sea power depends heavily on the country's economic strength, especially her industrial capacity. Mahan's theories cannot be applied easily to Austria-Hungary, because of her multinational character and peculiar constitutional arrangement.

Position

Austria-Hungary, like France and Imperial Germany, occupied a favourable geostrategic position on land. The Habsburg rulers for most of their history devoted their attention to preserving or strengthening their power and influence on the Continent. Unlike France, Austria's seaboard faced a narrow sea (Adriatic) within a larger narrow sea (Mediterranean) rather than an open ocean. Both the Adriatic and the Mediterranean played a minor role in world trade between the discovery of the Americas in 1492 and the opening of the Suez Canal in 1869. Austria-Hungary's strategic position in the Mediterranean was unfavourable because the entrance to the Adriatic was controlled by potentially hostile powers and her seaborne trade was difficult to protect in wartime. However, her control of the highly indented eastern Adriatic shore, fronted with numerous offshore islands, gave her a commanding position over any potential opponent.

Coastline

Between 1878 and 1914 the Dual Monarchy's coastline stretched between Porto Buso and the Bay of Spizza – about 370 miles.[1] The main feature of the eastern Adriatic littoral is a large limestone belt that runs from the vicinity of Fiume southward for about 350 miles. The Dinaric chain ranges from 2,300 to 6,000 feet in height and varies in width between 40 and 60 miles. Toward the south-east the range broadens and rises, creating a significant obstacle for communication between the Pannonian plain and the Adriatic coast (see Map 1).

The eastern shore of the Adriatic is highly irregular and backed by steep and high mountains. Approximately 1,230 islands and islets front the shore. They are mostly elongated in the direction of the shore and flanked by channels elongated in the same direction. They are predominantly oblong in shape, rocky and hilly. The heavily indented coast offered numerous roomy natural harbours and anchorages.

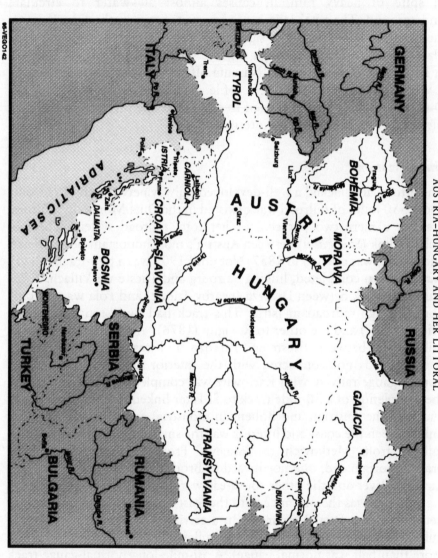

MAP 1

AUSTRIA-HUNGARY AND HER LITTORAL

Littoral area

One of the main features of the Austro-Hungarian littoral was a remarkable sparsity of drainage, because of the *Karst* landform which, in spite of heavy rainfall, causes almost all water to circulate underground. The total length of river waterways in the littoral was a mere 40 miles. The only significant river was the 142-mile-long Narenta, which breaks through the interior ranges and flows to the sea at Porto Tolero. But even the Narenta offered no easy route inland, for it was often restricted to a mere defile. The absence of rivers along the Dual Monarchy's littoral tended to emphasize the physical isolation of the coast from the country's interior.

Transportation

The littoral area lacked a well-developed railway network. By 1913 only about 550 miles of railroad track existed in the Dual Monarchy's littoral area, or a mere two per cent of her total railroad system. The first railroad link (*Suedbahn*) between Austria's most important port, Trieste, and Vienna was opened in 1857. Not until 1909 was a two-track railway (*Tauernbahn*) completed, linking Salzburg and Trieste via Villach. A 75-mile-long track between Divazza (nearby Trieste) and Pola was the only normal-gauge railroad in Istria. This track had two branches, one to Trieste (1887) and the other to Rovigno (1876).[2] Another narrow-gauge railroad was between Trieste and Parenzo, and was completed in 1902.

Fiume was not connected with the interior until 1873, when the normal-gauge railway with Karlowitz was completed. In the same year, the completion of a 30-mile track to St Peter linked Fiume with Laibach and with the Austrian and Bohemian industrial areas. Another railway link between the coast and interior was the small-capacity narrow-gauge railway from Metkovich to Sarajevo. From Sarajevo two railway branches originated, one northward to Brod (Slavonski Brod today) on the Sava River and the other south-eastward to Novibazar (Sandjak).

Dalmatia was the province with the least-developed communications network in the Dual Monarchy. In a territory of about 5,100 square miles, there were by 1914 only 180 miles of railroads (of which little more than half was normal-gauge). A 50-mile-long normal-gauge track connected Spalato and Tenin (via Perkovich), while another linked Tenin with Sebenico. However, these two railroads had only local importance and did not lessen Dalmatia's isolation from the country's interior. This problem might have been resolved by the construction of a railway through the Lika province. Although the Lika railway project was strongly supported by the Austrian government and the military, the Hungarians opposed it because they did not want the port of Spalato to flourish to the detriment of Fiume. Hungarian objections to construction of the Lika railway were not overcome until 1907, when both governments reached agreement to finance this project. The Hungarians agreed to the construction of the railway line Sichelburg–Karlowitz–Ogulin–Tenin in return for Austrian approval of a rival Hungarian railway through the Una River valley (Novi–Bihac–Tenin). After great difficulties, construction on the Lika railway project began in 1913 but was cut short by the outbreak of war.[3] In southern Dalmatia all existing railways were narrow-gauge. One railroad track linked Gravosa with Metkovich (via Uskopje), while another ran from Zelenika (Bay of Cattaro) to Uskopje.

Most of the roads in Istria were built on the western coast; in the eastern part of the peninsula the great lack of road communications was severely felt. Only two roads ran to Albona, one from Pisino and the other from Barbana. Toward the Bay of Quarnero the most important was the 'Kaiser Joseph II' road (via Poklon Saddle).

In Dalmatia the road network was only about 1,960 miles.[4] The principal road was the 330-mile-long Strada Maestra (or Strada Napoleon) that ran along the coast from Tersatico (Fiume) to Clambeto (near Obbrovazzo), and then to Tenin–Metkovich–Castelnuovo–Cattaro–Spizza. The Strada Littorale ran from Zara to Almissa, via Benkovaz. Another road ran from Zara to Obbrovazzo via Alpi Bebie, whence it linked northern Dalmatia with the interior of Croatia. After 1878, roads from Metkovich, Klek, and Ragusa were built to connect these ports with the newly acquired province of Bosnia and Herzegovina. Finally a road ran from Ragusa to Cattaro and thence via Mount Lovcen to the Montenegrin capital of Cetigne.

Population

The Dual Monarchy was a state with a dozen different nations and twice as many national groups. According to the last census before the war (1910), its total population was 51.4 million. The largest single national group were the Slavs with 47.5 per cent of the population; the politically dominant Germans and Magyars (Hungarians) made up 23.5 and 19.5 per cent respectively of the total. In the littoral area lived 1.3 million people, or only 2.5 per cent of the total population of the Dual Monarchy. Nevertheless the seafaring population of Istria and Dalmatia was sufficiently large to sustain the establishment and maintenance of a large merchant marine and Navy. Modern sea power also required a large pool of skilled mechanics to serve both onboard ships and ashore. However, the educational level of the Slavic population in the Austrian littoral was too low to satisfy these demands in 1910. About 65 per cent of the populace in Istria and Dalmatia was illiterate.[5] Yet, there was a large number of well-educated and skilled people in the industrially developed parts of the Dual Monarchy to satisfy the needs of the Navy and the merchant marine.

Seafaring traditions

Austria-Hungary was not a 'national' state in the accepted definition of the term and hence her 'national' character cannot be accurately defined. The population in the littoral, especially in the Italian-speaking part of Istria and the Croatian town of Ragusa, had a long and rich tradition in maritime trade and other commercial pursuits. However, they exercised little, if any, influence on the affairs of the Dual Monarchy. Moreover, the Germans, because of the relative self-sufficiency of their provinces in natural resources, were generally not uninterested in the development of foreign trade, especially commerce with overseas.

Perhaps the Austrian Empire might have developed into a great maritime nation in the eighteenth or nineteenth century if she had successfully embarked upon colonial expansion. Some attempts were made in that direction as early as 1774. William Bolts, an enterprising Englishman, founded the Trieste East India Trading Company (Triest Ostindische Handlungs Companie) and asked the government in Vienna to conduct trade in the east under the Austrian flag. In the same year the new company sent out two ships to establish a colonial settlement in Delagoa Bay on the east African coast. By 1778 the Trieste East India Trading Company seized control of the Nicobar Islands and successfully negotiated the lease of the Malabar Islands with the Sultan of Mysore. The company also established a consulate in Malaya at Pegu and in China at Canton. By 1782 it had extended its trade activities to China. However, the company eventually overextended itself and ran into financial difficulties. After the Austrian government refused to give it financial backing, the company went bankrupt in 1785 and shortly afterwards was dissolved.

The Dual Monarchy did not take part in the renewed scramble for colonies by the great European powers in the nineteenth century. The possibility of acquiring colonies was more than once alluded to in the

1870s at the highest level of government, but the Hungarians strongly opposed it. By the end of the nineteenth century, when spheres of interest were being carved out in China, Vienna reportedly thought of acquiring a strip of that country's coast. However, an enterprise of such magnitude would have required a substantial increase in the size of the Austro-Hungarian Navy, which the Magyars adamantly opposed.[6] In short, extra-European commercial enterprises were not an Austrian tradition.

The development of the Austrian sea power in the pre-industrial era was hindered by lack of interest in pursuing sea interests by the majority of her population. The interests of the Habsburgs were traditionally directed toward maintaining their rule in Germany, or elsewhere in Europe, and not in the Mediterranean and beyond. Most of the Habsburg rulers, with the exception of Empress Maria Theresa and Emperor Joseph II, did not show much interest in maritime affairs.

After 1867 the Dual Monarchy lagged behind in the development of sea power because of the consistent reluctance of the Hungarian government to strengthen the Navy. The Hungarians were in general unwilling to make a financial contribution to activities which they viewed as favouring Austrians.

Political arrangements

The Austrian Empire, following the *Ausgleich* (Compromise) reached between the Austrians and the Hungarians, was divided in November 1867 into two parts: Austria and Hungary. Both parts were *de facto* separate and equal states with their own legislative, judicial, administrative, and financial branches and locally-raised armed forces. The highest legislative bodies in Austria and Hungary were the Reichsrat and Parliament, respectively. Austria and Hungary were both united in the person of the Emperor. The political union between the two states was theoretically permanent. It depended upon two parallel arrangements between the Crown and the Magyar nation as represented by the Hungarian Parliament, and the unilateral constitutional statute promulgated by imperial authority in Austria and the Reichsrat. The Emperor was above the law and not accountable to any organ of the state for his imperial acts (see Figure 2).

Apart from the Austrian and Hungarian governments, there existed a common government in Vienna, consisting of three ministries: foreign affairs, finance, and war. Another common institution was the armed forces. There was also a kind of common parliament represented by the

FIGURE 2
THE AUSTRO–HUNGARIAN POLITICO-MILITARY SYSTEM

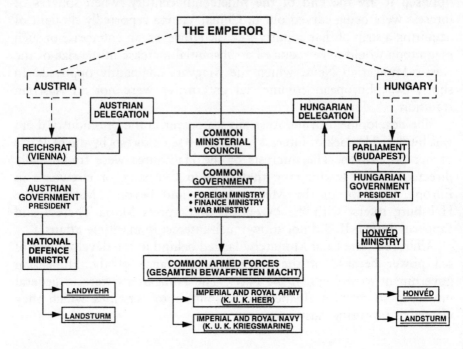

Delegations for Common Affairs (or Delegations in short). Austria and Hungary each sent 60 representatives to the Delegations, which met annually at Vienna or Budapest. Although they met simultaneously and in the same place, they deliberated separately and communicated decisions to each other in German and Hungarian, respectively. If mutual agreement was not reached, an equal number from each Delegation met and voted on the particular issue, but without any debate of the issues.

One of the most intractable problems between both parts of the Monarchy was their frequent inability to reach an agreement ('Quota') on sharing financial contributions for common expenditures. In 1867 it was mutually agreed that the 'Quota' between Austria and Hungary was to be 70 to 30 per cent respectively. Although Hungary's economic strength steadily grew, the Hungarians consistently opposed any change in the originally agreed ratio of contributions for common expenditures. The new 'Quota' agreement established the ratio of 65.4 to 34.6 per cent in November 1899, but did not come into force because of internal opposition in both Austria and Hungary. Instead, the Emperor, in accordance with his constitutional prerogatives, personally determined the 'Quota' ratio every year after 1900. Not until 1907 did Austria and Hungary negotiate a new 'Quota' agreement, which set the ratio at 63.6 to 36.4 and which remained in force until the outbreak of the First World War.

Natural resources

The Dual Monarchy possessed abundant sources of minerals such as coal and iron ore, which are the most important ingredients for the successful development of heavy industries. Total coal production in 1913 amounted to about 55 million tons, exceeded only by Germany and Great Britain. In the production of anthracite coal, Austria, with 27.6 million tons in 1913, ranked eighth in the world. While brown coal was exported (mostly to Germany), Austria in 1913 imported about 40 per cent of her anthracite.[7]

Iron ore was found in almost every part of the Dual Monarchy. By 1913, a total of about four million tons of iron ore was extracted, of which 80 per cent came from the Austrian part of the Empire. However, this production was insufficient to cover the ever-growing demand. Production of pig iron in 1913 amounted to about four million tons, almost evenly divided between the two parts of the Dual Monarchy.[8] Austria-Hungary was one of the world's largest producers of mercury, but lacked ores such as copper, lead and zinc.

The mineral resources of the Dual Monarchy were sufficiently large and varied to facilitate the rapid development of heavy industries after 1860. The need for railways, rolling stock and agricultural machinery provided the metallurgical industries with a home market. Although steel production rose from 1.1 million tons in 1900 to 2.7 million tons in 1913, it still amounted to only 6.3 per cent of total European steel production.[9]

Heavy industries

Machine-building industries in Austria-Hungary grew rapidly after 1868, but especially in the 1880s. Most of the factories were established to satisfy the demands of railway construction. Such plants were concentrated around Vienna, Wiener Neustadt, Graz, and Budapest. The largest heavy-industry concerns in Austria by 1913 were the Skoda Works (Pilsen) with 6,000 workers, the Machine Works (Simmering) with 3,700 workers, and the Ringhoffer Works (Prague) with 2,000 workers. In Hungary, the largest heavy-industry firms were the Diosgyör

Iron Works with 8,000 workers, and the MAVAG locomotive factory in Budapest.[10] However, because domestic production was unable to satisfy the ever-increasing demand, the Dual Monarchy remained highly dependent on imported machinery.

Naval shipbuilding and armament industries

The Dual Monarchy had well-developed shipbuilding and ship-repair and naval armament industries. By 1914 there were five large privately-owned and one state-owned shipyard employing between 10,000 and 12,000 workers.[11] The largest and best-known shipyard was the Stabilimento Tecnico Triestino in San Rocco (Trieste). This shipyard had five slipways from 350 to 500 feet, of which three served for the construction of battleships. The shipyard also operated a 350-foot dry dock and a 414-foot floating dock. The Austrian Lloyd Shipping Company (one of the co-owners of the Stabilimento Tecnico) had a 436-foot floating dock in Trieste. The Stabilimento Tecnico engine plant in San Andrea (Muggia Bay) manufactured boilers and reciprocating engines. A few years before the war this plant started production of the Parsons steam turbine under British licence. Between 1904 and 1913 the Stabilimento Tecnico workforce was expanded from 2,700 to about 3,200.[12]

The Cantiere Navale Triestino shipyard, established in 1907 (owned by the shipping company Fratelli Cosulich), had nine slipways for constructing ships up to 600 feet in length. This shipyard also operated one 13,000-ton and one 1,300-ton capacity floating dock. By 1914, the Cantiere Navale employed about 1,700 workers.

The only shipyard exclusively used for the construction of naval vessels was the Navy Yard (*Seearsenal*) in Pola. This yard was extensively modernized and expanded and by 1914 it employed about 2,000 full-time and 3,000 part-time workers.[13] The Navy Yard operated two dry docks (one of 470 feet for battleships and one of 400 feet for cruisers) and four floating docks (one with 22,000 tons capacity, one 15,000 tons, and two smaller docks for destroyer-size vessels).

In Hungary, the largest shipyard was Ganz & Co. in Fiume. After its merger with Danubius Co. of Budapest in 1905 it was known under the latter's name.[14] By 1912, this shipyard was expanded and modernized and was used for building battleships. However, Danubius's shipyard had too inexperienced a labour force for building dreadnoughts; and this problem was not resolved by 1914. By 1912 Danubius employed about 3,000 workers, in comparison to 1,200 workers four years earlier.

It operated two large slipways for the construction of battleships and three small slipways to handle up to destroyer-size ships. However Danubius operated only one 6,000-ton capacity floating dock. The same company also owned a small shipyard in Porto Rè (south of Fiume), which employed about 500 workers and after 1911 was engaged in the construction of destroyers.

After 1907, the Whitehead & Co. torpedo factory began to build submarines and torpedo craft. The company had one 1,300-ton floating dock used for submarine construction and repair. The naval armament industries were the best developed in the Austrian provinces of the Dual Monarchy. The Skoda Works was the largest manufacturer of naval guns in Austria, while the armour plates for warships built in the Austrian shipyards were produced mostly at the Vitkovice Armour and Steel Works (Ostrau). The Skoda Works plant at Poldhuette (near Prague) also manufactured armour plates for the Navy.

In Hungary the only gun factory was the state-owned Diosgyòr Steel Works built just before the outbreak of the First World War. Steel plates and armour plates were manufactured in Resicza while ammunition for naval guns was largely produced by the Manfred Weiss Co. in Budapest.

Besides the Skoda Works, the best-known and the most important armament factory in the Dual Monarchy was the Whitehead Co. in Fiume. It was established by the British engineer Robert Whitehead in 1872 and afterwards known by the Italian name Silurifico Whitehead. The Whitehead Co. was for some years the world's only manufacturer of torpedoes. It was also recognized as a world leader in torpedo design and production. By early 1914 it employed about 1,200 workers.

Agriculture

Despite great progress in industrial development, especially mining and heavy industries, the Dual Monarchy was predominantly an agricultural country. By 1910 about 53 per cent of the population in the Austrian provinces and about 70 per cent in Hungary were employed in agriculture.[15] Nevertheless, agriculture remained the least-developed sector of the Dual Monarchy's economy with productivity per hectare one of the lowest in Europe. Big landowners, especially those in Hungary who owned between 40 and 60 per cent of all available land, were more interested in the maintenance of high prices for agricultural products than in the intensive and rational exploitation of land. The inherent conservatism and high illiteracy of the peasantry, especially in Hungary, also retarded agricultural development. The only well-developed agricultural sectors in the Dual Monarchy were forestry and sugar-beet growing.

Foreign trade

Foreign trade did not play a significant role in Austro-Hungarian economic life. By the eve of the First World War, Austro-Hungarian foreign trade accounted for a mere 10 per cent of its gross national product as compared to 40 per cent for Great Britain and Germany. Although total foreign trade rose from 4.6 billion crowns in 1904 to 6.2 billion crowns in 1913, the trade deficit grew by 1913 to about 520 million crowns. This deficit was offset by remittances from the emigrants who left the Dual Monarchy in increasing numbers after 1900.[16]

Austria-Hungary's largest trading partner between 1880 and 1914 was Germany, from whom she received about 35–40 per cent of her imports and to whom she sent 40–50 per cent of her exports. Great Britain and France, on the other hand, made up only 8–9 and 3–6 per cent, respectively, of the Dual Monarchy's trade in the same period. Hungary's most important trading partners were the Austrian provinces, which received an average of 70–75 per cent of her exports, mostly agricultural products.[17]

The Dual Monarchy was highly dependent on seaborne trade for the export of her sugar, glassware, paper products, grain and wheat, and for the import of machinery and chemical products. Between 1904 and 1913 Austro-Hungary's total seaborne trade rose from about 770 million to 1.3 billion crowns, or 20 per cent of its foreign trade. Italy was the Dual Monarchy's leading trade partner in the Mediterranean.[18]

Although Austro-Hungary recorded impressive economic growth after 1867, but especially after 1900, it was at a rate below her potential and below that achieved by other European countries. A notable feature of the Dual Monarchy's economic development was that although industrial progress spread to every part of Austria-Hungary, wealth was concentrated in a few regions such as Lower Austria, Bohemia, and Budapest. More importantly, during the entire period between 1867 and 1914, Austria-Hungary continued to be dependent on foreign capital, particularly German and French.

To sum up, by 1904 the Dual Monarchy occupied a commanding geostrategical position in the Adriatic and the Balkans. She possessed a well-indented coast with numerous offshore islands offering many natural harbours and protected anchorages. Austria-Hungary's position in the Balkans offered her an opportunity to expand through Macedonia to the Aegean Sea or through Albania to the Ionian Sea. If either of these goals had been achieved, the Dual Monarchy would have become a true Mediterranean power. But there were also a few critical weaknesses that hindered Austria-Hungary from rapidly becoming a great sea power. Her seaboard faced the Adriatic Sea, which was too far from the main sea routes of the Mediterranean. Both shores of the entrance to the Adriatic were in the hands of other, potentially hostile powers.

Despite weaknesses in her economic development, by 1904 the Dual Monarchy possessed the solid industrial base needed for the maintenance of a strong Navy and merchant marine. By 1910, Austria-Hungary became largely self-sufficient in the construction of warships and naval weapons. Only a small part of her naval equipment had to be acquired from abroad. Austria-Hungary also had a relatively large, skilled and experienced seafaring population in the littoral. However, there was a marked lack of interest among almost all strata of the population in maritime affairs. Moreover, the proponents of an active policy to promote the sea interests of the Dual Monarchy were not influential until the aftermath of the Balkan Wars. A very awkward constitutional arrangement between the two parts of Austria-Hungary, combined with perennially weak finances, was another great obstacle to an active and sustained policy in the pursuit of sea interest. Nevertheless, this did not mean that Austria-Hungary was incapable of becoming a great sea power, for she still possessed great advantages by virtue of her size, population, civilization, and abundance of mineral and agricultural resources.

NOTES

1. Italian names of places and geographical points in the littoral were officially used in the Dual Monarchy. This practice changed in 1916 when the Croatian names were exclusively used. To make things simple, the Italian names will be used throughout the text.
2. Dates given are years of completion.
3. Work on the Lika railway resumed in 1921 and was completed four years later.
4. Foreign Office, Historical Section, *Dalmatia* (London: HMSO, 1920) p. 35.
5. Giotto Dainelli, *La Dalmazia. Cenni Geografici e Statistici* (Novara: Istituto Geografico de Agostini, 1918) p. 61.
6. Arthur J. May, *The Habsburg Monarchy 1867–1914* (Cambridge, MA: Harvard University Press, 1951) p. 405.
7. Alois Brusatti, ed., *Die Habsburger Monarchie 1848-1918*, Vol. 1, *Die Wirtschaftliche Entwicklung* (Vienna: Verlag der Oesterreichischen Akademie der Wissenschaften, 1973) pp. 153–4.
8. Ibid., p. 164.
9. Victor L. Tapié, *The Rise and Fall of the Habsburgs* (New York: Praeger Publishers, 1971) p. 326.
10. Ibid., pp. 184, 506.

11. Alfred Escher, *Triest und seine Aufgaben in Rahmen der oesterreichischen Volkswirtschaft* (Vienna, 1917) p. 34.
12. *Oesterreich am Vorabend des Ersten Weltkrieges* (Graz/Vienna: Stiasny Verlag, 1964) p. 69.
13. Hans Hugo Sokol and Theodor Braun, *La Guerra Marittima dell Austria-Ungheria 1914–1918*, 4 vols, trans. Raffaele De Courten (Rome: Istituto Poligrafico dell Stato Libreria, 1931–34) Vol. 1, p. 30.
14. Danubius Vereinigte Schiffbau und Maschinenfabrik.
15. *Oesterreich am Vorabend*, p. 71.
16. *Oesterreich am Vorabend*, p. 71; Statistical Department of Imperial-Royal Trade Ministry, *Statistik des Auswaertigen Handels des Oesterreich-Ungarischen Zollgebietes im Jahre 1904*, Vol. 1, *Hauptergebnisse–Hafenverkehr* (Vienna: Hof- und Staatsdruckerei, 1905) pp. 2–3; ibid., 1913, pp. 2–3; Hans Chmelar, *Hoehepunkte de Oesterreichischen Auswanderung. Die Auswanderung aus dem Reichsratvertretenen Koenigreiche und Laendern in den Jahren 1905–1914* (Vienna: Verlag der Oesterreichische Akademie der Wissenschaft, 1974) p. 71.
17. Brusatti, ed., *Die Habsburger Monarchie*, pp. 247, 486.
18. *Statistik des Auswaertigen Handels 1904*, pp. 321–3; ibid. 1913, pp. 322–9.

3

Launching the modern navy, 1904–7

By mid-1904 the Austro-Hungarian Navy consisted of 95 warships with about 131,000 tons. This included 10 battleships, three armoured cruisers, six protected cruisers, eight torpedo vessels and 68 torpedo craft. The Italian Navy in contrast consisted of 195 warships displacing 267,300 tons or twice the tonnage of the Austro-Hungarian Navy (see Figure 3). The Italians then had in service 13 battleships, 15 torpedo vessels, 145 torpedo craft, and two submarines. However, the Italian battleships, unlike their Austro-Hungarian counterparts, were designed for service in the Mediterranean. The Italian Navy also possessed numerical superiority over the Austro-Hungarian Navy in all other categories of warships.

Nevertheless, Italy was not as superior to the Dual Monarchy in naval strength as these numbers suggest, because of the considerably different maritime positions each country held. For example, the Austro-Hungarian fleet had to defend only about 370 miles along the coast, while the Italian Navy had to protect over 3,000 miles of the country's highly vulnerable coastline. Italy also had to protect her extended and exposed sea lines of communication and cope with several potential opponents at sea, a problem the Dual Monarchy was spared.

The Italian naval build-up until the turn of this century was primarily directed against France because conflicting interests in North Africa following the French annexation of Tunisia made Italy regard France as her most likely opponent in a war. However, after 1900 competition for influence in Albania and Montenegro and opposing aims in the Balkans led to growing rivalry between Vienna and Rome in the area, while Italy's relations with France markedly improved. As a result, Italy ceased to consider France as her potential opponent and began to prepare for a defensive war on land and an offensive war at sea against the Dual Monarchy. This change in attitude was the main reason for Italy's decision to increase her hitherto negligible naval strength in the Adriatic. By the spring of 1904 Italy announced the establishment of a naval Reserve Division based in Tarant consisting of four battleships, one cruiser, and 12 torpedo craft. This detachment was intended for deployment in the Ionian Sea and the Adriatic. A Torpedo Boat Inspectorate with seven torpedo craft stations was established in Civitavecchia. Two additional torpedo craft stations, at Ancona and Venice, were also planned to be established.

FIGURE 3
COMPARATIVE NAVAL STRENGTH OF ITALY AND AUSTRIA–HUNGARY, 1904

Type	Italy		Austria–Hungary		Italy/ Austria–Hungary Tonnage ratio
	No.	Tonnage	No.	Tonnage	
Battleships	13	166,724	10	85,560	1.9:1.0
Armoured cruisers	6	39,903	3	18,810	2.1:1.0
Protected cruisers	14	37,393	6	17,454	2.1:1.0
Torpedo vessels	15	12,848	8	5,070	2.5:1.0
First-class torpedo craft	9	1,135	1	134	8.4:1.0
Second-class torpedo craft	94	7,550	36	2,921	2.6:1.0
Third-class torpedo craft	42	1,792	31	1,297	1.4:1.0
Submarines	2	-	-	-	-
Total	195	267,345	95	131,246	2.3:1.0

Source: 'Uebersicht des schwimmenden Materials der groesseren Seemaechte', *Nauticus* (1904), pp. 479–89; 'Vergleich der beiderseitigen Streitkraefte, Kriegsfall I', 3 March 1906, Kriegsfaelle juengere Daten, *Kriegsarchiv Operations Kanzlei, Marinesektion-F8 1906.*

Navalists and their opponents

Italy's naval build-up in the Adriatic lent force to the arguments of those in Austria-Hungary who advocated a stronger navy. Industrial circles and financial institutions, such as those represented by the Austrian Industrial Council, consistently supported increases in naval expenditures. The profits of firms with the largest share in naval construction, such as the Stabilimento Tecnico shipyard, Skoda and Vitkovice, rose steadily as the design of naval vessels, especially those of battleships and cruisers, led to higher construction costs. Navy orders to domestic shipyards and armament plants also provided incentives to become self-sufficienct in naval construction so as to reduce dependence on orders from abroad.

The greatest single obstacle to the plans of Austrian navalists was the stubborn Hungarian opposition to any increase in naval outlays. Also, even when the Hungarian Delegation voted for such an increase, it avoided any commitment to a long-term construction programme.

Unlike Austria, Hungarian support for naval expansion was almost non-existent among high government officials and the public at large. Hungarians generally were not attracted to naval careers until after 1900. Hungary also had only two small shipyards in Fiume and Porto Rè, capable of building smaller torpedo vessels, and lacked well-developed armament industries before 1904. Therefore, it was understandable that the Hungarians were opposed to any large naval expenditures that brought in their view no tangible benefits to their country.

Another source of opposition to steady increases in the Navy's appropriations was the common Army. The views of the War Minister and the Chief of the General Staff were usually shared by Emperor Francis Joseph I, who regarded the Army as much more important than the Navy. Critics of the fleet's expansion were especially opposed to the construction of modern battleships, arguing that the Dual Monarchy's defences on the Adriatic should rest on coastal fortifications, harbour barricades, large numbers of torpedo craft, and large but inexpensive coastal defence ships. Advocates of a steady naval build-up countered that the fleet could obtain sea supremacy only by victory on the high seas, for which battleships were indispensable.[1]

Admiral Spaun's request

Italy's announced measures to improve her naval defences in the Adriatic roughly coincided with the request of the Navy's Commander, Admiral Hermann Freiherr Spaun, for a 120-million-crown special credit. Spaun's plan called for the continued construction of three *Erzherzog*-class battleships and the gradual replacement of the largely obsolete torpedo craft force. He believed that upon completion of this programme the Austro-Hungarian fleet would be adequate not only for the defence of the Adriatic but also for duty beyond that sea.[2]

Funds for the new fleet construction programme were included in the 500-million-crown special credit of the common armed forces presented in the spring of 1904 by War Minister General Heinrich von Pitreich. However, a dispute erupted between Admiral Spaun and General Pitreich over the way the special credit was to be financed. Although the Army's budget then averaged 500 million crowns per year while the Navy's expenditures were only 50 million, General Pitreich maintained that approval of the extraordinary credit depended upon a cut of 25 million crowns in the Navy's budget as opposed to a cut of only five million crowns in the Army's.[3] After his protest was rejected, Admiral Spaun resigned as the Navy Commander.

The new Navy Commander

A new era in the development of the Navy began in October 1904 when Vice-Admiral Montecuccoli assumed the post of Navy Commander. Born in Modena, Italy in 1843, the son of an army officer, he entered the Naval Academy in 1859 and saw action as a midshipman in the war against the French in the Adriatic. In 1866 he served on the frigate *Adria* during the Battle of Lissa and earned a medal for heroism. After many years of sea and staff duties ashore, Montecuccoli was promoted to the rank of Rear Admiral in 1897. Two years later, he took command of the *Active Eskadre* (operational fleet) and in July 1900 was appointed Commander of a newly organized fleet in east Asian waters, which he commanded during the Boxer Rebellion until September 1901. Upon his return from China, Montecuccoli headed the Navy's Technical Committee in Pola. By April 1903 he was appointed Deputy Chief of the Navy Section and a month later was promoted to the rank of Vice-Admiral.

The Austrian Navy League

Another factor that intensified agitation for the Navy's expansion and modernization was the establishment of the Austrian Navy League (*Oesterreichische Flottenverein*)[4] in September 1904. Founded in Vienna almost singlehandedly by a civil servant named Wladimir Kuk, the Austrian Navy League initially had only one local chapter (*Ortsgruppe*) with about 40 members.[5] Kuk's initial aim was to make the population at large understand that the merchant marine and overseas trade promoted the economic well-being of the Dual Monarchy. The League also supported maritime scientific research and promoted tourism on the Adriatic coast. In general, the Navy League awakened the enthusiasm of youth for a career at sea. However, soon after its founding, the League began to direct almost all its efforts into ensuring that the Dual Monarchy possessed a much larger Navy.

The Navy League was a *de facto* semi-official association. Under its auspices many books and pamphlets were published. Many of these biographies were written pseudonymously by retired naval officers or high officials on the subject of naval history, shipbuilding, and naval policy. The League's mouthpiece was the monthly journal, *Die Flagge* (*The Flag*).

Approval of special credit for ship construction

Vice-Admiral Montecuccoli continued the efforts begun by Admiral

Spaun to secure speedy approval of a special credit for ship construction. He requested 121 million crowns for the fleet's expansion in October 1904. With these funds he planned to complete within six years three *Erzherzog*-class battleships and to build 12 destroyers (*Divisionsboote*) and 36 high seas torpedo craft (*Hochseetorpedoboote*) of a new class. In the Russo-Japanese War of 1904–5 destroyers proved to be far superior to torpedo craft in speed, sailing range, armament, and seaworthiness. This was the main reason that after 1904 no major navy, except those of Austria-Hungary and Italy, initiated any new construction of torpedo craft. Torpedo craft were then classified as high seas (larger than 200 tons) or coastal types (less than 200 tons displacement).

By the autumn of 1904 the Navy ordered the construction of one 400-ton destroyer (*Huszar*) and one 200-ton high seas torpedo craft (*Kaiman*), both at Yarrow Ltd England. These ships were prototypes of their respective classes of destroyer and torpedo craft in domestic shipyards.[6]

By the spring of 1905 Montecuccoli (he was promoted to a full admiral in May 1905) planned a fleet consisting of 12 battleships, four armoured cruisers, eight scout-cruisers, 18 destroyers, 36 high seas torpedo craft, and six submarines.[7] However, this goal could be reached only through a long-term naval construction programme.

The Navy budget for 1905 provided 17 million crowns to start construction on the projected destroyers and 24 high seas torpedo craft.[8] By September 1905 both *Huszar* and *Kaiman* were completed in England, while three additional *Huszars* and five *Kaimans* were laid down at the Stabilimento Tecnico in Trieste. Hence, the long-overdue modernization of the torpedo force had begun. The Austro-Hungarian Navy also announced that all its second-class and old first-class torpedo craft would be gradually withdrawn from service.[9] These were to be replaced by 16 'flotilla' (*Flotillentorpedoboote*) or coastal torpedo craft of the new class.[10]

Because of the governmental crisis in Hungary the Delegations did not vote on Admiral Montecuccoli's proposed fleet construction programme until the end of 1905. Then they approved a 121-million-crown special credit for naval construction to be divided into three annual instalments, beginning retroactively in 1904.[11] This programme envisaged the completion of three *Erzherzog*-class battleships, one scout-cruiser, and six destroyers. Admiral Montecuccoli announced to the Delegations that he would seek funds in 1907 for the construction of three more battleships to replace older battleships. He also unveiled plans for the construction of the first domestically built submarine as soon as the funds from the special credit were available.

Hungarian approval of the 121-million-crown special credit was secured only after the Navy promised that some of the destroyers and high seas torpedo craft would be built by Hungarian industry. By 1905 the Navy decided to give orders for the five *Huszars* and 13 *Kaimans* to the Stabilimento Tecnico, while ordering six destroyers and ten high seas torpedo craft from the Danubius shipyard in Fiume. This decision was made despite the fact that Danubius did not yet have the capacity to build these warships.[12] The approval of the 121-million-crown special credit belatedly vindicated Admiral Spaun and represented the turning point in Austro-Hungarian naval policy after 1868.[13]

Despite the Delegations' approval of the 121-million-crown special credit, the continuing governmental crisis in Hungary prevented the promised funds for ship construction from becoming available to the Navy until the spring of 1906. However, by then only about 37 million of the 86 million crowns in the special credit for 1905 and 1906 were available. This caused a slowdown in construction of the *Huszars* and the *Kaimans*. Also, by April 1906 the Navy was forced to go into debt to shipbuilders to the tune of 36 million crowns. By the late spring when the governmental crisis in Hungary was resolved, there was steady funding for the three *Huszars* and five *Kaimans* under construction at the Stabilimento Tecnico.[14]

Also, by the spring of 1906 the Austrian and Hungarian governments reached an agreement that settled the shares of their industries in naval construction at 63.6 and 36.4 per cent respectively. This did not affect an earlier agreement signed in 1904 that stipulated that the armament industries in Austria and Hungary were to have an equal share in the production of ammunition and explosives for the Navy.

Proposed naval budget for 1907

Admiral Montecuccoli announced in the spring of 1906 that three old battleships (*Tegetthoff, Kronprinz Erzherzog Rudolf, Kronprinzessin Erzherzogin Stephanie*) and one cruiser (*Tiger*), all built between 1878 and 1887, would be put out of service.[15] In his first draft proposal for the naval budget of 1907 Admiral Montecuccoli requested funds to start construction on three new 14,500-ton battleships. He explained to the Delegations that plans for submarine construction were ready and could be implemented as soon as funds from the special credit became available. However, the common Ministerial Council did not approve

Montecuccoli's request for a large increase in the naval budget but directed him to formulate a new proposal.

Naval expenditures for the 1907 budget year approved by the Delegations totalled 65 million crowns. In addition to the funds for ships already under construction or approved, the funds were provided to start the construction of the three new 14,500-ton battleships (to replace those put out of service), one new 3,500-ton cruiser, two 230-ton *Lake*-class submarines, and the establishment of the first submarine base. Besides the 19 million crowns from the special credit of 1905, Admiral Montecuccoli requested 64.5 million crowns for naval construction in 1907. In addition, he asked that a total of 157 million crowns be allocated in 1908 and 1909. The 121-million-crown special credit in its final version was to be spread over four years (1904–7), and spent in four annual instalments (22.1, 52.9, 26.3 and 19.6 million crowns respectively).[16]

Role of Archduke Francis Ferdinand

The growing influence of the heir presumptive to the throne, Archduke Francis Ferdinand von Oesterreich-Este, greatly affected the conduct of the Dual Monarchy's naval policy between 1906 and 1914. Francis Ferdinand was the eldest son of Archduke Karl Ludwig, upon whose death in 1896 he became heir apparent to the throne. He was intelligent, energetic, impatient, and very temperamental. He had few confidants and many enemies.

Francis Ferdinand was a career officer who in 1892 reached the rank of Major General. Six years later he was officially put at the disposal of the Supreme Commander, in which capacity he took part in military conferences presided over by the Emperor. He was also well informed of all important military matters approved by the Emperor.

The heir to the throne repeatedly urged the Emperor to conduct a more active and assertive foreign policy. He felt a strong dislike and distrust of Italy, but favoured an understanding with Russia. He gradually became disenchanted with the Emperor because of his alleged weakness in the conduct of foreign policy and in dealing with Hungarian pretensions in domestic policy. This led to an increasingly bitter conflict between the Emperor's advisors and those around Francis Ferdinand.

The Archduke tried consistently to expand his prerogatives and influence in political and military matters. In the first serious test of will with the Emperor, in April 1906, he forced the resignation of the

41

Emperor's protégé, General Beck, as Chief of the General Staff and the appointment of General Franz Conrad von Hoetzendorf as his successor. However General Conrad proved to be a politician first and a soldier second. He regarded Italy, Serbia, and Montenegro with deep hostility. A great believer in the idea of preventive war, he repeatedly pressed these views to the highest government and military officials. He wanted to defeat the enemies of Austria-Hungary as they arose so as to avoid having to fight them all simultaneously. As a friend of Archduke Francis Ferdinand, Conrad exerted an inordinately great influence on the conduct of the Dual Monarchy's foreign policy.

Emperor Francis Joseph I and his closest advisors lacked both knowledge and interest in naval matters. Thus, it was Archduke Francis Ferdinand who was actively involved in almost every aspect of Austro-Hungarian naval policies. The Navy became his 'darling idea' (*Lieblingsidee*) and thanks to his growing influence, the Navy consistently obtained ever-larger funds for its expansion and modernization.

Francis Ferdinand acquired a permanent interest in the Navy and maritime affairs in general following his world cruise in 1892–93. In December 1892 he left Trieste on a voyage to Asia onboard the cruiser *Kaiserin Elisabeth*. After passing through the Suez Canal he visited Bombay, Ceylon, Singapore, Jakarta, Sydney, and Hong Kong and then arrived in Japan. From there the Archduke sailed aboard a steamer to Vancouver, travelled across Canada and the United States by train, took a passenger liner to Le Havre, and finally arrived in Vienna in October 1893. This trip convinced the Archduke that a country cannot achieve world-power status without a strong navy.[17]

Francis Ferdinand was also a close friend of the German Emperor William II whom he met on several occasions. Each of them was determined to make his country a strong sea power and this was undoubtedly the single most important factor in solidifying their friendship.[18] There is little doubt that Francis Ferdinand wanted to emulate the example of Emperor William II and become the principal proponent of the development of Austrian sea power. He often attended the annual manoeuvres of the German fleet and was invariably impressed.

As early as 1898 Francis Ferdinand urged the Emperor to approve the building of large 8,000–10,000-ton battleships in order to strengthen 'our fine navy'. This began the Archduke's efforts to modernize the fleet, which he afterwards pursued with great energy and firmness.

Archduke Francis Ferdinand's motives in supporting the expansion of the Austro-Hungarian fleet were based on his sincere belief that the value of sea power for the Empire was bound to increase in the future and on his strong animosity toward Italy. Therefore, Austria-Hungary must obtain a commanding position in the Adriatic. He wanted the Austro-Hungarian Navy to close the gap which separated her from the other great sea powers as quickly as possible; his ultimate aim was to make the Austro-Hungarian fleet a power factor in the Mediterranean. He wanted the fleet to have good ships and excellent crews in order to offset its numerical inferiority.[19] The Archduke was promoted to the honorary rank of Admiral in 1902. However he apparently did not interfere in the Navy's everyday activities, although he was keenly interested in the Navy's development and paid close attention to the naval budget, organization, and appointments of flag officers.[20]

Transformation of the fleet

By the end of the summer manoeuvres of the Austro-Hungarian Navy in August 1906, Admiral Montecuccoli issued an order of the day in the Archduke's name praising the combat readiness of the fleet despite inadequate naval budgets. The Archduke said that despite some progress made, expenditures were still insufficient for the Navy's needs. He declared that the Austro-Hungarian fleet should be strong enough to accomplish its tasks in the Adriatic fully, that is, to be able *to seek and beat the enemy on the high seas* instead of being restricted to the defence of the coast.[21]

Not surprisingly, the Archduke's remarks were unwelcome in Italy, because his statement implied that the Austro-Hungarian naval build-up was directed against Italy. Many editorials in the Italian press criticized the Dual Monarchy's attitude toward Italy. For example, in an article published in *Il Mattino* in October 1906, the Italian deputy Frederico de Palma argued that Italy must continue with its naval build-up to achieve supremacy in the Adriatic and to blockade the Dual Monarchy's naval bases in the event of war.[22]

Italy's plan to build her first dreadnought led to a strong reaction among Austrian navalists. Admiral Montecuccoli stated in the spring of 1907 that the Austro-Hungarian 14,500-ton battleships were inferior to Italy's newest 19,000-ton battleships. He announced that the Navy planned to increase the armament of the battleships to be built in the future. He also explained that the Austro-Hungarian Navy did not intend to build dreadnoughts because its tasks were limited in scope and the coal supplies were restricted. Montecuccoli argued that the country's naval policy was influenced 'by the role which the fleet plays in national defence and by the importance of Austro-Hungarian maritime interests'. Therefore, the fleet's construction programme had to be drawn up with regard to probable rather than possible opponents at sea.[23] Hence, it was obvious from Montecuccoli's statement that Austria-Hungary did not plan at that time to respond to Italy's dreadnoughts by constructing her own.

Naval progress

By 1907 the construction of the new Austro-Hungarian battleships and the modernization of the torpedo force were in full swing. In that year the two last 10,600-ton *Erzherzogs* were commissioned. These ships were the first Austro-Hungarian battleships that incorporated the lessons of the Russo-Japanese War. Moreover, the two new 14,500-ton *Schlachtschiff*-I/-II (later known as the *Radetzky*-class) semi-dread-noughts and the first 3,500-ton *Admiral Spaun* scout-cruiser were laid down at the Stabilimento Tecnico and the Navy Yard. In addition three *Huszars* and three more *Kaimans*, all built at the Stabilimento Tecnico, entered service. Also, the two *Lake*-class and two *Germania*-class submarines were laid down at Pola.

Naval budget for 1908

Admiral Montecuccoli presented the naval budget for 1908 to the Delegations on 20 December 1907. Among other things, he requested about five million crowns for the construction of a dozen 110-ton new coastal torpedo craft. The 34-million-crown special credit (1904–7) allocated for the modernization of the torpedo craft force was considered as completely inadequate to build all 48 projected destroyers and torpedo craft. Montecuccoli explained that the Russo-Japanese War showed that only the 200-ton or larger torpedo craft could be employed on the high seas, while the 100-ton torpedo craft were the most suitable for defence of the coast.[24]

The naval budget of 1908 envisaged 17 million crowns allocated for ship construction and modernization. This included the funds for the start of work on the first of a dozen new 110-ton coastal torpedo craft. This order was evenly divided between the Stabilimento Tecnico and the Danubius.

Navalists in Austria-Hungary were greatly heartened by a resolution of the Reichsrat introduced during debate on the naval budget for 1908 that called upon the common government to see to it that 'the Navy received all the means to reach its required strength for the defence of the coast and if necessary in the future to urge approval of the special credit for ship construction'.[25]

In February 1908 Admiral Montecuccoli explained to the Delegations that the increase in naval expenditures (to the tune of about 12 million crowns) was justified because previously appropriations for the Navy were too low, while the construction costs for ships had considerably increased. He requested from the Delegations a new 127-million-crown special credit for ship construction to be spread over five years (1907–11). Montecuccoli proposed that the annual instalments of the special credit be 10, 23, 31, 39, and 23 million crowns respectively.[26] However, no decision on Montecuccoli's request was made at that time.

Strengthening of sea defences

By the spring of 1907 the Dual Monarchy also began to strengthen her defences along the border with Italy. In addition, the Army allocated in its budget about 2.5 million crowns for the modernization of defences of Sebenico's naval base. However, Cattaro ceased to be officially a fortress in July 1907 because of its vulnerability to Montenegrin batteries on Mount Lovcen overlooking the city.[27]

By the spring of 1908 Austria-Hungary took additional steps to improve the defences along her south-western border and in the littoral area. The Pola garrison was reinforced by eight fortress artillery companies and one engineer company, doubling the total strength of the fortress. One fortress artillery company was redeployed to Lussin Island (approximately 30 miles south-east of Pola). This island guarded the entrance to the Quarnero Channel and because of its proximity to Pola could be used as a base to blockade that main naval base. In addition, seven companies of the fortress artillery deployed in the Bay of Cattaro were reinforced by an additional two companies.[28]

Italy's response

The Dual Monarchy's steps in the spring of 1908, her defences along the south-western border and the troops in the naval bases caused a great uproar in Italy. The Italians thought that these measures were primarily directed against Italy.[29] Hence, the Italian government announced that the number of submarines and high seas torpedo craft for employment in the Adriatic would be increased, while the expansion and modernization of the landfront and seafront defences in its naval bases on the Adriatic coast, especially Venice, would continue.

Italy's plan to build two dreadnoughts and further strengthen her defences in the Adriatic in turn alarmed Austrian navalists. They argued, among other things, that Dalmatia could be defended only with a strong fleet. Accordingly, the Dual Monarchy had to possess a force sufficiently strong to prevent a potential enemy from blockading her coasts and excluding her commerce from the Straits of Otranto.[30]

The influential General Conrad indirectly supported the arguments of the navalists by urging the common government in September 1908 to strengthen both the Army and the Navy. He thought that the Dual Monarchy should possess a fleet equal to that of Italy.[31]

Fleet expansion

The expansion and modernization of the Austro-Hungarian fleet intensified as more ships were built or entered service. The Navy's personnel totalled about 12,000 men (including 743 line officers) in 1908.[32] By September 1908 the first 14,500-ton battleship (*Erzherzog Franz Ferdinand*) was launched at the Stabilimento Tecnico. The first *Huszar* built at the Danubius and the three *Kaimans* built in Trieste were also completed in 1908, as were two 240-ton *Germania*-class submarines built in Kiel.

By the end of 1908 the two rivals for supremacy in the Adriatic, Austria-Hungary and Italy, had embarked upon naval expansion programmes directed primarily against each other. This naval race continued until the outbreak of the First World War and exercised great influence upon the military and foreign policies of both Italy and the Dual Monarchy. Moreover, the expansion of the Italian and particularly the Austro-Hungarian Navy began to play a critical role in the changing naval balance in the Mediterranean.

Initially, the Italian naval build-up, as exemplified by the Navy Act of 1905, was more ambitious than the Dual Monarchy's. Italy's position in the Mediterranean, her thirst for colonial expansion, and ultimately her continued economic well-being depended considerably on her naval strength. Thus there was strong popular support in Italy for government efforts to strengthen the Navy. As we have seen this was not the case in Austria-Hungary where navalists faced stiff opposition to any large, long-term naval construction programmes. However, after the approval of the 121-million-crown special credit in 1905, the Navy was able to embark on a modest programme of expanding and modernizing the fleet. Proponents of a stronger Navy were now in a more favourable position to advocate additional funds for naval construction in the years ahead.

NOTES

1. 'Unsere neue Turmschlachtschiffe und Kreuzer', *Danzers Armee Zeitung* (7 January 1904) p. 6.
2. 'Neue Flottenvorlage', *Danzers Armee Zeitung* (19 May 1904) p. 4.
3. Friedrich Wallisch, *Die Flagge Rot-Weiss-Rot. Maenner und Taten der Oesterreichischen Marine in vier Jahrhunderten* (Graz: Verlag Styria, 1956) p. 199.
4. The full title was The Association for Advancement of Austrian Shipping: The Austrian Fleet's Association (Verein fuer Forderung der Oesterreichischen Schiffahrt: Oesterreichische Flottenverein). Later on, only the subtitle was commonly used as a designation.
5. Leo Reiter, 'Die Entwicklung der K.u.K. Flotte und die Delegation des Reichsrates' (Vienna University, unpublished Ph.D. dissertation, 1949) p. 168.
6. 'Informazioni e Notizie. Marina Militare', *Rivista Marittima* (Rome) 10 (October 1904) p. 131.
7. Rudolf Kiszling, 'Die Entwicklung der Oesterreichisch-Ungarischen Wehrmacht seit der Annexion Krise 1908', *Berliner Monatshefte* (Berlin) 9 (September 1934) p. 739.
8. 'Rundschau in allen Marinen', *Marine Rundschau* (Berlin) 8 (August 1906) p. 1026.
9. Before 1904–5 torpedo craft were classified as first-class (more than 100 tons), second-class (50–100 tons) and third-class (less than 50 tons).
10. 'Informazioni e Notizie. Marina Militare', *Rivista Marittima* 1 (January 1908) p. 100.
11. 'Rundschau in allen Marinen', *Marine Rundschau* 7 (July 1906) p. 881.
12. 'Informazioni e Notizie. Marina Militare', *Rivista Marittima* 1 (January 1908) p. 100.
13. 'Rundschau in allen Marinen', *Marine Rundschau* 8 (August 1906) p. 1026.
14. *Internationale Revue ueber die Gesamte Armee und Flotte* (Dresden, 1906) pp. 301–2; 'Fortschritte fremder Kriegsmarinen', *Nauticus* (1906) p. 134.
15. *Marine Rundschau* 4 (April 1906) p. 512.
16. 'Rundschau in allen Marinen', *Marine Rundschau* 12 (December 1906) p. 1424; 'Fortschritte in allen Marinen', *Marine Rundschau* 12 (December 1906) p. 1425.
17. Rudolf Kiszling, *Erzherzog Franz Ferdinand von Oesterreich-Este, Leben, Plaene, und Wirken aus Schiksalweg der Donaumonarchie* (Graz/Koeln: Verlag Boehlau, 1953) p. 28; Theodor von Sosnosky, *Franz Ferdinand. Der Erzherzog-Thronfolger. Ein Lebenbild* (Munich/Berlin: Verlag R. Oldenbourg, 1929) p. 113.
18. Kiszling, *Erzherzog Franz Ferdinand*, pp. 67–8.
19. Sosnosky, *Franz Ferdinand*, pp. 113–14.
20. Carl von Bardolff, *Soldat im Alten Oesterreich. Erinnerungen aus meinem Leben* (Jena: Eugen Diedrichs Verlag, 1938) p. 144.
21. 'Fortschritte fremder Kriegsmarinen', *Nauticus* (1907) p. 134.
22. 'Rundschau in allen Marinen', *Marine Rundschau*, 11 (November 1906), p. 1289; Leopold Chlumecky, *Oesterreich-Ungarn und Italien. Das Westbalkanische Problem und Italiens Kampf um die Vorherrschaft in der Adria* (Leipzig/Vienna: Franz Deutizke, 2nd edn, 1907), p. 29.
23. 'Fortschritte fremder Kriegsmarinen', *Nauticus* (1907) pp. 124–6 and (1908) p. 138.
24. 'Informazioni e Notizie. Marina Militare', *Rivista Marittima* 1 (January 1908) p. 102.
25. 'Der Ausbau der oesterreichisch-ungarischen Flotte', *Marine Rundschau* 4 (April 1911) p. 461.
26. 'Informazioni e Notizie. Marina Militare', *Rivista Marittima* 3 (March 1908) p. 555.
27. *Internationale Revue ueber die Gesamte Armee und Flotte* (1907) pp. 30–1; 'Rundschau in allen Marinen', *Marine Rundschau* 11 (November 1907) p. 1338.
28. 'Rundschau in allen Marinen', *Marine Rundschau* 5 (May 1908) p. 558.
29. Ibid., p. 558.
30. Reiter, 'Die Entwicklung der K.u.K. Flotte', p. 168; 'Italian new construction', *Naval League Annual* (1908) p. 30.
31. Franz Conrad von Hoetzendorf, *Aus meiner Dienstzeit 1908–1918*, 5 vols (Vienna: Rikola Verlag, 1922–25) Vol. 1, p. 273.

32. *Jahresberichte der K.u.K. Kriegsmarine fuer das Jahr 1908*, p. 27; 'Informazioni e Notizie. Marina Militare', *Rivista Marittima* 6 (June 1908) p. 470.

4

The Bosnian crisis of 1908–9

After 1900 there was no great crisis in the Balkans because of Russia's preoccupation with the Far East and the Dual Monarchy's policy of preserving the status quo in the area. However, all that began to change in the aftermath of the Russo-Japanese War in 1905. Then the new Austro-Hungarian Foreign Minister, Baron Alois Lexa von Aehrenthal, began a more active policy in the Balkans. Serbia on her part initiated a policy of seeking closer relations with Russia and her ally France. Russia responded by increasing her attention toward the Balkans. Thus, the stage was set for a new crisis in the Balkans.

By 1906 the growing tensions between Vienna and Belgrade resulted in an economic war. Austria-Hungary forbade all imports from Serbia, intending to severely damage the Serbian economy. The latter was heavily dependent on the export of pigs, cattle and poultry to the Dual Monarchy. This conflict, known as the 'pigs war', had unexpected results for Vienna because Serbia eventually found new markets for her exports and attracted more foreign investment, principally from France. More ominous from Vienna's standpoint was Serbia's intensified efforts to acquire an outlet to the Adriatic to avoid being dependent on the Dual Monarchy for her trade.

The new crisis came in January 1908 when von Aehrenthal announced that Austria-Hungary planned to build a railway line through the Sanjak of Novibazar to Mitrowitza and ultimately to link it with Salonika. Russia immediately charged that this project would violate the *status quo* in the Balkans and supported Serbia's plan to construct a railway along the Danube River via Nish–Mitrowitza to the Albanian port of San Giovanni di Medua. However, Vienna strongly opposed any railway that would allow Serbia to acquire a direct link with the Adriatic. Yet, Italy favoured Serbia's plan because it would enable her to develop trade with Serbia and other small Balkan states. In the end Vienna abandoned her plan; and Serbia's own plan was not realized because of the opposition by the Dual Monarchy. However, the diplomatic furore over the Austro-Hungarian railway scheme served a warning to Vienna of what might happen if she tried to advance southward. Yet, this warning went unheeded by von Aehrenthal.

Vienna's plans

The 'Young Turk' revolution of July 1908 (that led to the overthrow of the Hamidian regime and the inauguration of constitutional government) triggered the first major crisis in the Balkans after 1900. Von Aehrenthal thought that internal turmoil in Turkey provided an opportunity for the Dual Monarchy finally to annex the provinces of Bosnia and Herzegovina. He believed that annexation would have the positive effect of thwarting Serbia's attempts to acquire the province for herself. Vienna also calculated that permanent possession of Bosnia and Herzegovina would greatly strengthen the defence of Dalmatia's littoral.

Von Aehrenthal's intention to annex Bosnia and Herzegovina came seemingly at an opportune time because Russia needed the support of the great powers to realize her long-standing designs on the Straits and feared that the 'Young Turk' regime might lead to a revival of Turkish strength. Russian Foreign Minister A. P. Isvolsky knew that it would be very difficult to win British acquiescence to open the Straits to the Russian warships, though he was certain of French support. His immediate aim was to reach an understanding with the Dual Monarchy before seeking the support of the other great European powers.

Von Aehrenthal and Isvolsky met secretly in Buchlau in September 1908. As the price for Russian acceptance of Vienna's annexation plans, Isvolsky asked von Aehrenthal to agree that warships belonging to the Black Sea riparian states (that is, primarily Russian) be allowed to pass through the Straits in both directions as long as Turkey was not at war and no more than three naval vessels of one flag were en route between the Black Sea and the Mediterranean at the same time. Isvolsky promised von Aehrenthal that Russia did not desire to seize Constantinople. However, he requested that the Turkish Straits should remain closed to the warships of all other states. Von Aehrenthal for his part (rather unwisely) renounced the Austro-Hungarian rights in the Sanjak of Novibazar.

At the same meeting, Isvolsky asked von Aehrenthal to ease some restrictions on Montenegro concerning Article 29 of the Berlin Treaty. However, von Aehrenthal rejected that proposal, arguing that 'although the Dual Monarchy had no fear of Montenegro, she must prevent Montenegrin ports from becoming naval bases of foreign fleets'. He added that the Austro-Hungarian policy 'must be directed to maintain her freedom in the Adriatic and links with the Mediterranean'.[1]

A written memorandum of the meeting at Buchlau was considered but not drawn up. This omission caused controversy when Vienna announced on 6 October the annexation of Bosnia. Isvolsky, who was then in London, disavowed any agreement with von Aehrenthal. Also, Vienna did not inform her two allies of the action taken.

Belgrade's reaction

Not surprisingly, the most violent reactions to the annexation of Bosnia came from Serbia and Turkey. The Serbian Skupstina (Parliament) voted for war measures, while the Serbian public, incited by the press, clamoured for war even without Russia's help. The Serbs wanted an autonomous Bosnia or, failing that, a slice of the Sanjak of Novibazar as compensation. Russia's reaction was strong and threatening: she was prepared to fight the Dual Monarchy, but her army was not ready so soon after the disastrous war with Japan. Italy's reaction to the annexation was also negative. However, throughout the crisis Italy pursued a vacillating and irresolute course.

Austria-Hungary declares partial mobilization

In the wake of the annexation pronouncement, Vienna asked Belgrade to recognize the annexation and to abandon its hostile attitude toward Austria-Hungary. Serbia's response was to mobilize her army. Encouraged by Great Britain and Russia, she also demanded autonomy for Bosnia under a guarantee by the great powers, and a port for herself in the Adriatic.

Because of Serbia's warlike measures, the Dual Monarchy partially mobilized her Army and Navy in October 1908. The Navy was ordered to concentrate its *Active Eskadre* in the Gulf of Cattaro. The Danube flotilla in Budapest was fully mobilized and made ready for eventual action against Serbia. Both the *Active Eskadre* and the Danube flotilla remained mobilized throughout the winter of 1908-9 while diplomatic efforts were underway to resolve the Bosnian crisis.

Debate on naval budget for 1909

At the height of the crisis over Bosnia there was a debate in the Delegations on the proposed naval budget for 1909. Admiral Montecuccoli stated on 22 October 1908 that the future Austro-

Hungarian battleships should displace between 18,000 and 19,000 tons. The funds for their construction had to come either from an increase in regular naval expenditures or the special credit. The *Wiener Zeitung* revealed on 1 November that Montecuccoli also proposed to the Delegations a new construction programmeme for 1910 that included the funds to build three 18,000–19,000-ton dreadnoughts, three 3,500-ton *Admiral Spaun*-class scout-cruisers, one torpedo depot ship, two colliers, and two Danube monitors.[2]

Admiral Montecuccoli also explained to the Delegations that the *Radetzkys* were not built as dreadnoughts because plans for their construction had been drawn up three years before they were constructed. However, he emphasized that although the *Radetzkys* were smaller than the modern battleships of other navies, they had thicker armour than French *République*-class battleships.[3]

Montecuccoli's statement on naval construction plans was the first sign that the Dual Monarchy intended to join the ranks of other sea powers in building dreadnoughts, the largest and mightiest ships then afloat. By the end of 1908 nine other navies (Great Britain, Germany, the United States, Japan, France, Russia, Italy, Brazil, and Argentina) had already built or announced plans to build dreadnoughts.[4]

Hungarian complaints

During a debate in October 1908 the Hungarian Delegation raised the question of introducing Hungarian insignias into the Navy and complained of the small share of Navy orders given to the Hungarian industry. The Navy's orders for domestic industries amounted to 59.1 million crowns in 1908, but only about 29 per cent were assigned to Hungarian firms. An additional 9.4 million crowns' worth of naval orders were given to foreign firms.[5] Montecuccoli responded by arguing that the Navy orders for armament and equipment should be based on the needs of the fleet rather than on political considerations.[6]

When the Hungarians complained of the small percentage of Hungarian petty officers in the Navy, Montecuccoli responded that there had been in fact an increase in the number of Hungarian applicants for petty officers in the past two years but that the time had been too short for many of them to reach petty officer rank. By the end of 1908 only 230 petty officers, or 7.9 per cent of the total, were listed as having been born in Hungary.[7] The Hungarian deputies also pressed Montecuccoli to introduce the Hungarian language into the Navy, to increase Hungary's share of the Navy's annual recruiting contingent from 33 to 42 per cent, and to man some naval vessels exclusively with Hungarians. Montecuccoli merely promised that Hungarian demands would be considered by the common government.[8]

Decision to build first dreadnought

The Delegations approved the naval budget of 91 million crowns (31 per cent larger than that of 1908). However, they rejected Montecuccoli's request for shares of the special credit for ship construction. Specifically, the naval budget for 1909 provided funds to complete ships then under construction or approved: to start work on the first 19,000-ton dreadnought, the second *Admiral Spaun*-class cruiser, one *Huszar*-class destroyer (to replace one that had been lost), and to purchase one large merchant vessel (to be used as a torpedo depot ship). The budget also provided funds to add 850 petty officers and seamen.[9]

Austria-Hungary had only two slipways (both at the Stabilimento Tecnico) to accommodate the projected 19,000-ton dreadnoughts. Both slipways were already occupied by the second and the third *Radetzky*-class battleships then under construction. Thus, the work on the first dreadnought was expected to start in October or November 1909, after one of the slipways was vacated, while construction of the second dreadnought could not begin until April 1910.[10]

Growing influence of the heir to the throne

Francis Ferdinand was the strongest force behind the Navy's decisions to embark on the construction of dreadnoughts. Although the Emperor Francis Joseph I was widely loved and revered, the heir apparent was increasingly perceived as the strong leader that the Dual Monarchy needed. The Archduke exercised a great and growing influence on the Army and he was highly esteemed in the Navy for his consistently strong support for increased naval expenditures. He was so popular in Trieste that his portrait was often displayed more prominently than that of the Emperor.[11]

As the influence of Archduke Francis Ferdinand increased, more and more responsibilities were vested in his military aide, Major Alexander Brosch von Aarenau. The Military Chancellery of Archduke Francis Ferdinand (MKFF)[12] was created in November 1908. The reason was that Francis Ferdinand wanted to be promptly informed of any development in the armed forces. Moreover, the MKFF was to serve as the main conduit through which the Archduke exercised his influence on the Army and Navy. Not surprisingly, the Emperor's Military Chancellery (MKSM)[13] strongly opposed the creation of the new office.[14] The situation was made worse by the bad relations which existed between the heads of the MKFF and the MKSM, Major Brosch and General Arthur von Bolfras.

Initially the MKFF did not exercise significant influence, but subsequently became involved in almost all important matters concerning the Army and the Navy. Moreover, Archduke Francis Ferdinand used the MKFF to acquire ever great influence over promotions and appointments in the armed forces. It is indisputable that the MKFF proved to be of great help to the Navy in its quest for ever-larger expenditures for ship construction.

The crisis deepens

The tensions in the Balkans caused by the Dual Monarchy's annexation of Bosnia and Herzegovina continued to rise. The other great European powers remained opposed to Vienna's action. Even Emperor William II thought that Austria-Hungary's move might jeopardize Germany's prestige and her future prospects in Turkey. However, Chancellor Bernhard von Buelow argued that unless Germany firmly supported Vienna it would lose the Dual Monarchy's friendship and stand isolated in Europe. In the end, Berlin promised to support Austria-Hungary but urged her to conciliate Turkey quickly. However, in dealing with the responses of the Triple Entente, Germany encouraged the firm stand taken by von Aehrenthal.

The navy is fully mobilized

By February 1909 the crisis over Bosnia subsided somewhat, after Turkey accepted monetary compensation for the lost territories and in return recognized the Austro-Hungarian action. Serbia soon followed suit, mainly because Russia, her main protector, was not yet ready to risk a wider conflict in Europe. However, Cetigne on its part, demanded that the Dual Monarchy cede the coastal stretch around the Bay of Spizza, that she acquired under the terms of the Berlin Treaty, and also abrogate Article 29 of that treaty. In response, Austria-Hungary announced full mobilization of her Navy on 15 March 1909. A day later, in a demonstration of force, the *Active Eskadre* (three battleships, one armoured cruiser, two destroyers, and six high seas torpedo craft) deployed in southern Dalmatia conducted amphibious landing exercises near the Austro-Montenegrin border in the Bay of Spizza. The *Reserve Eskadre* (three older battleships, one armoured and one protected cruiser, and one old torpedo vessel) in Pola was mobilized within only 24 hours, while the mobilization of the rest of the fleet was completed four days after the order was issued.[15]

The Navy's mobilization was carried out with speed and efficiency. A total of 10,000 naval reservists were called up. The number of reservists who did not respond to mobilization orders were only five per cent of the total, although Navy authorities had feared the figure might reach 20 per cent.[16]

Resolution of the crisis

An agreement was reached between Vienna and Rome on 31 March regarding the abrogation of some parts of Article 29 of the Berlin Treaty concerning Montenegro. The annulled sections dealt with the Austro-Hungarian maritime police duties in Montenegrin ports and the adoption by Montenegro of maritime legislation as enforced in Dalmatia. However, those parts of Article 29 stipulating freedom of navigation on the Boyana River and prohibiting Montenegro from building fortifications there remained in effect. Antivari was to be used only as a commercial port. In return, Vienna agreed to abrogate Article 25 of the aforesaid treaty, which gave her the right to maintain garrisons in the Sanjak of Novibazar.[17]

By the end of April 1909 the Navy was demobilized. Montecuccoli commended the reservists who had been retained for a fifth year of service for their 'exemplary bearing and on the extremely satisfactory way they had performed their duties'.[18]

Agitation of the Austrian navalists

The rich mineral resources of the newly acquired provinces increased the importance of Dalmatia's ports. This in turn made it imperative to protect the Dual Monarchy's maritime trade. Therefore, in the view of the Austrian navalists there was a need for further strengthening the fleet. The slogan 'Vorherrschaft in der Adria' ('Supremacy in the Adriatic') became a rallying cry for those in Austria-Hungary who advocated and agitated for an ever-larger and stronger Navy. Navalists argued that security from attack across the sea would enable the Dual Monarchy to pursue her interests in the Balkans without interference.

The Austrian Navy League, in an appeal to the population distributed throughout the country in the spring of 1909, stressed that although 'the dark clouds of war which for months overshadowed our Fatherland have disappeared', it was necessary to recognize that 'blessings of peace rest' on 'a powerful striking force'. The appeal, while recognizing the need to increase the strength of the Army, urged the Austrians to remember 'what inestimable services our Navy rendered us in the past and what enormous tasks still await it'.

The Navy League also complained that 'the bulk of the Austro-Hungarian people sadly takes little interest in our [Austrian] merchant marine' and pointed out that since the merchant marine depended on naval strength the Dual Monarchy could not develop a significant overseas trade 'unless we take steps to develop our Navy'. The appeal concluded by calling upon the populace to join the Navy League and help establish local chapters in all the large cities. This effort to increase membership of the Austrian Navy League was apparently successful. By mid-1909 the League comprised 25 local chapters with about 3,000 members – or almost twice as many as in 1908.[19]

The Navy League petitioned the Command of the Austro-Hungarian Navy in March 1909 to build an additional squadron of three 18,000–19,000-ton dreadnoughts, as quickly as possible to neutralize Italy's advantage in this category of warships. It also claimed that the Dual Monarchy's financial burden was not heavy when one considered that Italy spent twice as much money on her Navy.[20]

The agitation of the Navy League for higher expenditures was generally supported by the Austro-Hungarian major papers. Moreover, despite differences between Austria and Hungary on purely political questions, the Budapest press also supported the views of the Austrian navalists.[21]

Italy's reaction

Italy reacted to the annexation of Bosnia with a series of military measures including further improvements in the defences of the north-eastern part of the country and along the Adriatic coast. By the autumn of 1908 the government of Prime Minister Giovanni Giolitti appointed a parliamentary commission to examine the state of Italy's military preparedness. In response to the commission's findings the government decided to increase the peacetime strength of the Italian Army from 205,000 to 250,000 men. Parliament thereafter granted an ordinary credit of 425 million lire to expand and modernize land and coastal fortifications. Almost half of that sum was devoted to the build-up of fortifications around Venice and Verona and along the Adriatic coast. Also the peacetime strength of the troops along the Austro-Italian border was increased.

The British are alarmed

Br. Ger, A.H. naval relations

By the spring of 1909 rumours about Austria-Hungary's plans to construct dreadnoughts and the increased agitation of the Navy League caused apprehension not only in Italy, but also in other European capitals. London, which in the aftermath of the annexation of Bosnia came to regard Vienna as a pliable tool of Berlin, was highly suspicious that Germany had persuaded the Dual Monarchy to start construction of dreadnoughts so to force the British Navy to disperse its strength.

The British correspondent of the *Navy* visited the Dual Monarchy in 1909. He observed that in view of her publicly expressed determination to lay down at a near date four dreadnoughts, which 'introduces an extremely important factor into British naval policy, and in face of the remarkable demonstration of allied strength which the Dual Monarchy and the German Empire offered Europe quite recently, it would be the height of impolicy for British statesmen to ignore the powerful and rapidly increasing fleet which is based in Pola'. He also speculated that whether the Austro-Hungarian Navy was destined to play a role in the North Sea 'must be left to the future'. He was obviously impressed by the 'remarkable enthusiasm displayed by every person in Franz Josef's dominions in regard to maritime expansion'.[22]

By the end of April 1909, the British ambassador in Vienna, Fairfax Cartwright, pointedly asked von Aehrenthal what the truth was in the rumours reaching London of the Austro-Hungarian plans to build dreadnoughts. Von Aehrenthal responded that an expansion of the fleet was being considered, but (falsely) denied that he knew the number of dreadnoughts intended to be built or whether the Delegations would approve the programme. He remarked that public opinion in the Dual Monarchy generally preferred a strengthening of the Army rather than the Navy. However, von Aehrenthal justified the Austro-Hungarian naval build-up as necessary to protect her interests in the Mediterranean. He also expressed surprise that a modest increase in the Austro-Hungarian Navy's strength caused such excitement in Great Britain. He assured the British ambassador that the new dreadnoughts were not being built to help strengthen the German fleet.[23] Yet despite von Aehrenthal's denials, the British politicians and public opinion continued to believe that the planned expansion of the Austro-Hungarian Navy was being instigated by Germany.

The British ambassador in Berlin, Sir Edward Goschen, wrote in a letter to Foreign Secretary Sir Edward Grey on 11 April that Germany's public opinion 'hailed the Austrian decision to build dreadnoughts with the liveliest satisfaction'. He reported that although it was admitted in Germany that the Austro-Hungarian dreadnoughts would be of no direct help to the German Navy in case of a conflict in the North Sea, the existence of a strong Austro-Hungarian fleet in the Mediterranean would make it difficult for the British Navy to concentrate its forces in the North Sea. Also the Berlin daily *Tageblatt* asserted that to all intents and purposes, the Italian and Austro-Hungarian fleets were one and expressed doubt whether Britain's programme to lay down eight dreadnoughts in 1909 would be sufficient to maintain the two-power standard.[24]

Naval progress

The growing concern overseas regarding the Austro-Hungarian fleet's expansion was well-founded. By July 1909 the second *Radetzky*-class battleship was launched, followed in October by the launching of the first 3,500-ton turbine cruiser *Admiral Spaun*. The Danubius shipyard also completed the five *Huszars*, last of a projected group of 12 destroyers of the same class. Nine additional *Kaimans* were commissioned, thereby completing the entire programme of 24 craft funded by the 121-million-crown special credit of 1905 (save for four high seas torpedo craft). Also, all the 12 new 110-ton coastal torpedo craft were laid down, while ten obsolete second-class torpedo craft were decommissioned.[25]

The submarine arm also made rapid progress. Two *Germania*-class submarines were commissioned, while two *Lake*-class were completed. In addition, two 236-ton *Holland*-class boats were launched. After the completion of the two *Germania*-class submarines, the first submarine base was established at Pola in January 1909. The base was subordinate to Port Admiralty Pola. Submarine personnel initially comprised 34 officers and men, all volunteers. The Navy also purchased an 8,430 gross register ton (GRT) large Russian merchant ship, *Moskwa* (ex-German *Fuerst Bismarck*), to be modified as a torpedo depot vessel.[26]

The Austro-Hungarian Navy also took the first steps to create a corps of naval aviators in 1909. A few officers were sent to France and Great Britain to acquire basic flying skills and to create the nucleus of a naval

aviator corps. Among the first aviators was Lieutenant Commander
Viktor Klobucar-Rukavina de Bunic who was credited with being the
founder of Austro-Hungarian naval aviation.[27]

Austro-Hungarian–Italian naval balance

By mid-1909 Italy possessed superiority over the Dual Monarchy both
in number of combatants and in tonnage (see Figure 4). The Italian
Navy had in service twice as many cruisers, torpedo craft, and
submarines and three times as many destroyers as the Austro-Hungarian
Navy. Both fleets were approximately equal in battleship strength.
However, Italy had started construction on the first dreadnought, while
the Dual Monarchy had only announced plans to build one and did not
yet have the necessary funding.

FIGURE 4
COMPARATIVE NAVAL STRENGTH OF ITALY AND AUSTRIA–HUNGARY, MAY 1909

Type	Italy		Austria-Hungary		Italy/ Austria-Hungary Tonnage ratio
	No.	Tonnage	No.	Tonnage	
Battleships	10+2*	124,112	9+3	73,836	1.7:1.0
Armoured cruisers	8+2	59,869	3	18,992	3.1:1.0
Protected cruisers	6+1	14,605	6	16,727	0.9:1.0
Torpedo vessels	6	3,110	6	2,730	1.1:1.0
Destroyers	17+2	5,698	8+4	3,200	1.8:1.0
High seas torpedo craft	8+8	5,936	17+7	3,400	1.7:1.0
Coastal torpedo craft	59	5,254	28+14	2,410	2.1:1.0
Submarines	7+5	1,155	2+6	474	2.4:1.0
Total	121+20	219,759	79+34	121,769	1.8:1.0

Note: *Ships under construction or on order
Source: René Greger, *Austro-Hungarian Warships of World War I* (London: Ian Allen, 1976),
pp. 19-71; *Nauticus* (1909), pp. 516–21, 530–3.

The Italian ships class for class were still superior in armament,
displacement, and steaming range to Austro-Hungarian ships. However,
it was the changing character of the Austro-Hungarian fleet that caused
much concern in Italy. While the Italians had always maintained a Navy
capable of operating in the Mediterranean, the Austro-Hungarian fleet
had been primarily a coastal defence force. The building of the
Habsburgs and *Erzherzogs* indicated that the Dual Monarchy planned to
use her Navy beyond the confined waters of the Adriatic if necessary.
Moreover, it was the trend in Austro-Hungarian naval expansion that

caused the greatest apprehension in Italy. The *Radetzky* class was considered to be the beginning of a fleet of 16 battleships, all dreadnoughts. That was the main reason for Italy's new Navy Act that led to an intensified naval race between Italy and the Dual Monarchy.

Key to
naval policy

Intensified agitation of the Austrian Navy League

The Italian Navy Act was only one sign of growing anti-Austrian sentiment in Italy in the aftermath of the Bosnian crisis. Because the Dual Monarchy did not offer Italy territorial compensation in the Balkans as stipulated by Article 7 of the Triple Alliance Treaty, a new wave of irredentist agitation broke out in Italy. A veritable flood of chauvinistic articles led by the *Preparazione* appeared in the press, rekindling Italy's old suspicions and fears of the Dual Monarchy.

For the Italians the Adriatic was *il mare nostro* (our sea), in which Austria-Hungary was not to be allowed to obtain supremacy. Though the Italians viewed their naval build-up in the Adriatic and the strengthening of their fortifications along the north-eastern frontier as defensive in nature, the Dual Monarchy did not. Memories of the wars of 1848 and 1859, when Austrian naval weakness made it impossible for her to prevent blockades of her coasts, still lingered in the minds of many in Austria. Yet, *Tegetthoff's* victory off Lissa in 1866 proved that a strong Navy can offset defeats on land.

Austrian navalists argued that the annexation of Bosnia made possession of a stronger fleet imperative. The fleet had to be so strong that no power would be able to blockade Austria-Hungary's coast, cut off her trade, or land troops. If Italy closed the Strait of Otranto and blockaded the Dual Monarchy's ports and naval bases in the northern Adriatic, Austria-Hungary would be unable to resist. Therefore, it was not surprising that Italy's announced plans to build four dreadnoughts and strengthen her torpedo flotillas and submarine arm caused great concern in Austro-Hungarian naval circles.

Italy's new Navy Act and the growing irredentist agitation in that country led to intensified efforts by the Austro-Hungarian navalists to hasten the expansion of the fleet. A large number of pamphlets critically viewed Austro-Hungarian naval policy. For example, Max Schloss, a well-known writer on naval matters, in a pamphlet entitled *Oesterreich-Ungarns Wacht zur See* (Austria-Hungary's Watch At Sea) appealed for the establishment of a strong Navy, which he considered a matter of life or death for the Dual Monarchy. He warned his countrymen that Italy might establish a naval blockade, occupy the Dalmatian Islands, and by seizing centrally located Lissa obtain control of the Adriatic. The only recourse for Austria-Hungary was to possess a strong fleet, even more so because in his view Great Britain might support any Italian action against the Dual Monarchy.[28] The latter charge did not make much sense at the time but perhaps it reflected the disillusionment of the author with British opposition to the Austro-Hungarian annexation of Bosnia. The editor of the influential *Reichspost*, Anton von Moerl, in his pamphlet *Tod oder Leben fuer Unsere Kriegsmarine* (Death or Life for Our Navy) also strongly urged that the Dual Monarchy be required to possess a strong Navy.

Debate on the fleet's size

By the summer and autumn of 1909 there was a lively debate as to how large a fleet Austria-Hungary needed. Navalists urged a large expansion of the fleet to allow the Dual Monarchy to obtain undisputed supremacy in the Adriatic. For example, Mr Schloss in a pamphlet entitled *Wem sind Oesterreich-Ungarns Seeinteresse anvertraut* (To Whom Are Entrusted Austria-Hungary's Maritime Interests) sharply criticized Admiral Montecuccoli for the supposed inadequacies of the Austro-Hungarian fleet expansion programme. He claimed that the Dual Monarchy required a fleet comprising 32 22,000–26,000-ton dreadnoughts, 12 15,000–18,000-ton battle-cruisers, 26 scout-cruisers, one cruiser for foreign service, 26 30-knot destroyers, and 70 28-knot high seas torpedo craft.[29] Such a large fleet was not only unnecessary for Austria-Hungary but clearly beyond her financial capacity. Those who urged a more modest naval expansion programme claimed that because of her advantageous position in the Adriatic with regard to Italy, the Dual Monarchy required a Navy only two-thirds the size of her neighbour's.

There were some rumours in 1909 that after the completion of the first four dreadnoughts in 1913 or 1914, Austria-Hungary planned to build three others to replace the *Monarchs*, three more to replace the *Habsburgs* and eventually to possess a battle fleet of 16 dreadnoughts. The influential Viennese daily *Die Zeit* also revealed in October 1909 that the new Austro-Hungarian naval construction programme contemplated a fleet of 16 dreadnoughts. The paper argued that only a powerful Navy could guarantee peace with Italy and effectively protect the Dual Monarchy's commercial interests in the Mediterranean.[30]

Plans for the new dreadnought construction

The article in *Die Zeit* was in fact based on inside knowledge of the programme that Montecuccoli had presented to a meeting of the Ministerial Council in mid-September 1909 during a debate on the naval budget for 1910. Montecuccoli had proposed a new construction programme spread over four years. Among other things, he called for the construction of four more dreadnoughts, three scout-cruisers, and a number of destroyers, high seas torpedo craft, and submarines, as well as for speedier construction of the *Radetzky*-class battleships. However, that programme could only be carried out by the approval of a special credit that would entail a two-fold increase in annual naval expenditures. Montecuccoli wanted the Austro-Hungarian fleet to comprise 16 battleships, each to be automatically replaced after 18 years in service. However, the Finance Ministry rejected Admiral Montecuccoli's programme because of the government's inability to assume any new financial commitments at that time because of the costs incurred by the annexation of Bosnia, the mobilization of the Army and Navy, and the supplementary Army expenditures of 1909. The proposed expenditures totalled 217.5 million crowns, a substantial sum for that time. They were divided as follows: 39 million crowns were paid to Turkey as an indemnity for the annexation of Bosnia, 120.7 million crowns were expended on the mobilization of the Army and Navy, and the Army's supplementary credit amounted to 57.8 million crowns.[31]

Nevertheless, Admiral Montecuccoli's proposal was not entirely rejected because it was returned to the ministers for revision and subsequent approval. The Delegations could not vote on the Navy Commander's proposal because of the political crisis in Hungary, where for many months 'moderates' and 'radicals' in Parliament were engaged in a bitter conflict, disrupting the work of Parliament and making it impossible for the Delegations to consider any new proposal for common expenditures.

In the end the regular naval budget for 1910 amounted to only 67 million crowns. The 19 million crowns allocated for ship construction included funds for completion of the *Radetzky* battleships, the *Admiral Spaun* cruiser, and a dozen 110-ton coastal torpedo craft. However, the naval budget did not include supplementary funds for new ship construction. By then, the Navy was in arrears for about 19 million crowns to domestic shipbuilders as a result of its inability to pay for all the ships then under construction.[32]

Another problem caused by the lack of supplementary expenditures for the ship construction was that the Stabilimento Tecnico shipyard (where three *Radetzkys* were being built) faced a dilemma to dismiss a number of its skilled workers because of the lack of the Navy's orders for battleships. This situation arose because after the launching of the second *Radetzky* in July 1909, the second slipway was vacated, while the third slipway for the battleship construction was to be vacant in January 1910 (after the launching of the third 14,500-ton battleship *Zrinyi*). Faced with the prospect of so much idle capacity, the Stabilimento Tecnico offered to start preliminary work on one or two of the projected dreadnoughts at its own risk. The ships were to be built according to plans approved by the Navy. Admiral Montecuccoli accepted the Stabilimento Tecnico's proposal, which was subsequently approved by all three ministers of the common government.[33] However, formal Navy orders had not been given to the Stabilimento Tecnico shipyard by the end of 1909.

The final settlement of the Bosnian crisis undoubtedly represented a great diplomatic victory for Austria-Hungary and Germany. For the first time the German aims in the Balkans were clearly identified with those of the Dual Monarchy. Afterwards the German policy was designed to preserve Austria-Hungary as a great power against any challenge that might arise. Russia on her part was determined for the time being to avoid further humiliation by Germany or the Dual Monarchy even at the risk of a general European war. Although Russia was forced by the crisis to abandon her plans in regard to the Turkish Straits, she hoped to reopen this question at an opportune time in the future. Great Britain and France concluded that henceforth the Triple Entente had to follow a common course of action if challenged again by the Triple Alliance.

The annexation of Bosnia further poisoned relations between Belgrade and Vienna. Moreover, the Dual Monarchy's violent overthrow of the *status quo* made a similar action against Turkey by Serbia, or Montenegro, or other small Balkan states more likely in the future. Nevertheless, the Dual Monarchy's incorporation of Bosnia and Herzegovina enhanced her geostrategic position against Montenegro and Serbia. The defence of Dalmatia, especially her narrow southern part, against a possible enemy landing was significantly enhanced.

NOTES

1. Von Aehrenthal memorandum on his conversations with Isvolsky in Buchlau, 16 September 1908, no. 79, Ludwig Bittner and Hans Uebersberger, eds, *Oesterreich-Ungarns Aussenpolitik von der Bosnischen Krise 1908 bis zum Kriegsausbruch 1914* (Diplomatische Aktenstuecke des Oesterreichisch-Ungarischen Ministerium des Aeussern) 9 vols (Vienna/Leipzig: Oesterreichischer Bundesverlag, 1930) Vol. 1, p. 90.
2. 'Rundschau in allen Marinen', *Marine Rundschau* 11 (November 1908) p. 1338; ibid., 12 (December 1908) p. 1469; 'Informazioni e Notizie. Marina Militare', *Rivista Marittima* 12 (December 1908) p. 517.
3. 'Rundschau in allen Marinen', *Marine Rundschau* 11 (November 1908) p. 1335.
4. 'Comparative naval strength', *Navy League Annual* (1909) p. 107.
5. *Die Flagge* (Vienna, 1 January 1912) p. 1.
6. 'Rundschau in allen Marinen', *Marine Rundschau* 11 (November 1908) p. 1335.
7. 'Appendix 18: Nachweisung ueber die Heimatzustaendigkeit der Unteroffizieren des Friedenspraesenzstandes mit Ende 1908', *Jahresberichte der K.u.K. Kriegsmarine fuer das Jahr 1908*, p. 124.
8. 'Rundschau in allen Marinen', *Marine Rundschau* 12 (December 1908) p. 1469.
9. 'The Austrian Navy', *Navy League Annual* (1909) pp. 82–3; René Greger, *Austro-Hungarian Warships of World War I* (London: Ian Allan, 1976) p. 42; 'Rundschau in allen Marinen', *Marine Rundschau* 2 (February 1909) p. 469.
10. 'The Austrian Navy', *Navy League Annual* (1909) p. 82.
11. Ibid., p. 87.
12. MKFF (Militaer Kanzlei des Thronfolgers Erzherzog Franz Ferdinand).
13. MKSM (Militaer Kanzlei Seiner Majestaet des Kaiser und Koenigs) was created in 1867 instead of the existing Military Aide Office (General Adjutantur).
14. Carl von Bardolff, *Soldat im Alten Oesterreich. Erinnerungen aus meinem Leben* (Jena: Eugen Diedrichs Verlag, 1938) pp. 118, 121.
15. 'Informazioni e Notizie. Marine Militare', *Rivista Marittima* 3 (March 1909) p. 391.
16. 'Rundschau in allen Marinen', *Marine Rundschau* 1 (January 1909) p. 110; ibid., 3 (March 1909) p. 480; ibid., 5 (May 1909) p. 618; *Journal of the Royal United Service Institution* (London), 5 (May 1909) pp. 648–9; 'Informazioni e Notizie. Marina Militare', *Rivista Marittima* 5 (May 1909) pp. 277–8.
17. All the other great European powers recognized this agreement on 24 May 1909.
18. 'Naval notes', *Journal of the Royal United Service Institution*, 5 (May 1909), p. 649.
19. 'The Austrian Navy', *Navy League Annual* (1909) p. 86; Leo Reiter, 'Die Entwicklung der K.u.K. Flotte und die Delegation des Reichsrates' (Vienna University, unpublished Ph.D. dissertation, 1949) p. 168. Other sources claimed that at the end of April 1909 the Navy League had only 1,966 members. 'Rundschau in allen Marinen', *Marine Rundschau* 7 (July 1909), p. 876.
20. Unsigned, 20 March 1909, Kriegsarchiv, Praesidial Kanzlei, Marinesektion-SV-7/4, 1909.
21. 'The Austrian Navy', *Navy League Annual* (1909) p. 87.
22. Ibid.
23. Alfred F. Pribram, *Austria-Hungary and Great Britain, 1908–1914* (London: Oxford University Press, 1951) p. 149.
24. Sir E. Goschen to Grey, 11 April 1909, no. 171, *British Documents on the Origins of the War 1898–1914*, ed. G. P. Gooch and Harold Temperley, 11 vols (London: HMSO, 1926–38) Vol. 6, p. 262.
25. *Jahresberichte der K.u.K. Kriegsmarine fuer das Jahr 1909*, pp. 20–1.
26. 'Informazioni e Notizie. Marina Militare', *Rivista Marittima* 2 (February 1909) p. 384; ibid., 3 (March 1909) p. 600.
27. German Air Transport Ministry, *Die Militaerluftfahrt bis zum Beginn des Weltkrieges 1914*, 2 vols (Berlin: Ernst Siegfried Mittler und Sohn, 1941) Vol. 1, p. 460.
28. John Leyland, 'The Command of the Adriatic', *The Naval Annual 1910*, edited by T.A. Brassey (London: J. Griffin and Co., 1910), p. 147.
29. *Army and Navy Gazette* (London) 31 July 1909, p. 723.
30. John Leyland, 'The Command of the Adriatic', p. 152; *Army and Navy Gazette*, 6 October 1909, p. 987.
31. 'Die fremden Kriegsmarinen', *Nauticus* (1910) pp. 208–9.

32. 'Budget des K.u.K. Kriegsmarine fuer das Jahr 1910', *Mitteilungen aus dem Gebiete des Seewesens* 1 (January 1911) pp. 152-6; 'Rundschau in allen Marinen', *Marine Rundschau 5* (May 1909) p. 613.
33. Unsigned, 27 May 1910, no. 2153, Kriegsarchiv, Praesidial Kanzlei, Marinesektion-XV-7, 1910.

5

Naval build-up intensifies, 1909–11

The Bosnian crisis led to an intensified naval and military build-up and growing anti-Austrian sentiment in Italy. Rome began to seek closer relations with St Petersburg because Italy and Russia both wanted to prevent the Dual Monarchy from expanding south of her borders. By October 1909 the Italian and Russian sovereigns and foreign ministers met at Racconigi and concluded an agreement to co-ordinate their policies in the Balkans. Italy and Russia reaffirmed their wish to maintain the status quo there, but agreed that if changes had to be made they should follow the principles of nationality. In other words, Rome and St Petersburg opposed any territorial changes in the peninsula that were advantageous to Austria-Hungary but were willing to accept those that favoured the small Balkan states. Both countries also promised mutual support in case of an Italian action against Tripoli or a Russian move to reopen the Turkish Straits.

The Russo-Italian agreement resulted from the convergence of the national interests of both countries. Both Italy and Russia wanted to expand their influence at Turkey's expense and feared an eventual thrust by Austria-Hungary in the direction of Salonika. They also saw each other as counterweights to Austro-Hungarian expansion in the Balkans.

However, the tensions in relations between Vienna and Rome over the annexation of Bosnia were overcome by December 1909 when both countries reached an agreement concerning their policies in the Balkans. The agreement stipulated, among other things, that if the Dual Monarchy acquired the Sanjak of Novibazar, Italy was entitled to receive territorial compensation. The Dual Monarchy and Italy promised that neither country would enter into any special agreement in regard to the Balkans with a third party without informing the other. Nevertheless, despite the agreement, the Austro-Italian rivalry in Albania and Montenegro continued. The Italians gradually increased their share of the Albanian and Montenegrin commerce and maritime trade to the detriment of Austria-Hungary. The rivalry between the two countries for supremacy in the Adriatic and their conflicting interests in the Balkans determined their naval policies. While the Dual Monarchy strove to catch up with Italy in naval strength, Italy was determined to retain and even improve her position in respect to Austria-Hungary in the Adriatic and the Mediterranean.

Naval base in central Dalmatia

The Dual Monarchy's annexation of Bosnia made it imperative to build a large naval base in central Dalmatia. At the same time, the Austro-Hungarian acquiescence in the use of the hitherto commercial Montenegrin port of Antivari for visits by foreign warships enhanced the value of the Gulf of Cattaro. However, the Bay of Cattaro was too exposed to serve as a large naval base. Therefore, the Austro-Hungarian troops from Cattaro were redeployed to Teodo which was considered less vulnerable to Montenegrin guns on Mount Lovcen. By the spring of 1910 General Conrad urgently requested funds to modernize the obsolete forts overlooking Teodo and the works on the seafront of the Bay of Cattaro. Specifically, this included modernization of Fort Vermac (overlooking Teodo) and the seafront works at Kobila, Kaballa, Lustica, Cape d'Ostro, and Rondoni Island.[1]

Although the Austro-Hungarian ships based in the Bay of Cattaro could be deployed in the southern Adriatic, it was too far away to offer help to the fleet based in Pola. Therefore, there was an urgent need to establish a large naval base in the central part of Dalmatia. A fleet deployed there was to be capable of operating offensively, especially against an enemy force trying to seize the strategically located island of Lissa. The Navy and Army agreed that a new naval base should be built in central Dalmatia. However, they disagreed over whether to expand the existing advanced naval base in Sebenico or to build a new one elsewhere in Dalmatia.

Montecuccoli was in favour of expanding the existing naval base in Sebenico, but the Army wanted a new base to be established at the Bay of Trau (north of Spalato). The Army's position was strongly supported by the Inspector of Engineer Troops, General Leuthner. General Conrad urged the Emperor on 15 February 1910 to build up Sebenico as an advanced base to the tune of about 150 million crowns. He thought that besides six fortress artillery battalions, an additional infantry division should be deployed in the Sebenico area. However, Conrad eventually changed his mind about Sebenico. He argued that, although Sebenico was sufficiently large to accommodate a great number of ships, the narrow San Antonio Channel was vulnerable to an enemy attack by sea.

He also thought that transforming Sebenico into a large naval base would require considerable funds to strengthen the defences of a number of the offshore islands guarding its approaches.[2]

Admiral Montecuccoli (who reconnoitred the Bay of Saldun and Sebenico in the spring of 1910) found that the former, by virtue of its proximity to Cape Planka and the open sea, was favourably located to serve as a base for the defence of the island of Lissa and the coastal sector between Spalato and the Narenta River estuary against possible enemy landings. The Bay of Saldun would afford good protection for any fleet based there. It was roomy and deep throughout and the approaches to the bay were accessible even to large ships. The approaches to the Bay of Saldun could be defended by coastal batteries mounted on the islands of Bua and Zirona Grande. However, Montecuccoli emphasized that the greatest shortcoming of Val Bossigliana as a prospective naval base was the lack of any naval facility and, more seriously, the absence of any railway link with the interior of the country. He strongly opposed construction of a naval base in the Bay of Saldun as long as the projected Lika railroad was not completed.[3] Thus, the question of building a large naval base in Sebenico or the Bay of Saldun was left unresolved.

Montecuccoli's memorandum to the Emperor

Admiral Montecuccoli resumed his efforts to obtain support from the Emperor and the common government for the fleet expansion programme that he had presented in the previous September. In a rather long memorandum to the Emperor in May 1910 he strongly urged the need for rapid expansion of the Austro-Hungarian fleet. He pointed out that Italy, Spain, and Turkey had made great efforts to strengthen their fleets, but singled out Italy as the primary reason for the 'significant' shift in the naval balance against Austria-Hungary. Specifically, Montecuccoli cited Italy's planned construction of 'not less than four 19,000–20,000-ton dreadnoughts, three 3,000-ton cruisers, 13 destroyers, 50 high seas torpedo craft and six submarines'. Italy's ultimate goal was to obtain significant political and economic advantages, to the detriment of the Dual Monarchy, in the not-so-distant future. He foresaw that when the contemplated Italian and Austro-Hungarian naval construction programmes were completed, the Italian fleet would have four dreadnoughts and six first-class battleships, or twice the strength of the Austro-Hungarian fleet in both categories. In addition, the Italian Navy would have a completely modernized torpedo flotilla.

In the same memorandum, Montecuccoli informed the Emperor that in no circumstances could he take responsibility 'for defence of our (Austro-Hungarian) coast', unless there was 'the urgent and quickest possible completion' of his proposed fleet construction programme. He specifically wanted to raise the strength of the Austro-Hungarian fleet to 16 battleships, 12 cruisers, 24 destroyers, 72 torpedo craft, and 12 submarines. However about 40 per cent of 135 combat vessels in 1910 were obsolescent and had to be replaced (see Figure 5). To reach the proposed strength, the Dual Monarchy had to build four dreadnoughts, three scout-cruisers, six destroyers, 12 high seas torpedo craft, six submarines, and four Danube monitors. This programme would be completed in five years (1911–15) at the cost of about 330 million crowns.[4] Eventually, the Emperor approved Montecuccoli's proposal in principle.

Dreadnought construction

The Navy did not formally order the shipyard to start construction on the two 20,400-ton dreadnoughts until January 1910. The guns and armour plates for these ships were ordered from the Skoda Works and the Vitkovice Steel Works, respectively. The orders were given despite the fact that the Delegations had not granted funds for dreadnought construction. Montecuccoli wanted to have these ships completed at an early date without waiting for approval by the Delegations. The Stabilimento Tecnico also did not want to dismiss many of its skilled workers for the lack of Navy orders. The shipyard assumed the dreadnoughts would be taken by the Navy. There were reports that the Stabilimento Tecnico planned to sell the dreadnoughts to a foreign navy if Montecuccoli could not secure approval from the Delegations for their construction.[5]

Montecuccoli's decision to proceed with the dreadnought construction was a shrewd move designed to force the Delegations to grant the necessary funds, which were reportedly advanced by Baron Albert Rothschild after a personal appeal by Archduke Francis Ferdinand.[6] Rothschild had controlling interests in the Skoda and Vitkovice Steel Works as well as the Stabilimento Tecnico. The shares of the Skoda Works doubled in price in two weeks after the orders for guns were given. The newspaper *Arbeiter Zeitung* reported that the value of the Skoda Works shares on the Vienna Stock Exchange amounted to 252 crowns in 1907, 260 in 1908, and 249.5 in 1909. However, after the announcement of dreadnought construction the value of these shares rose to 395 crowns in 1910.[7]

In a note sent in May 1910 to von Aehrenthal and the presidents of the Austrian and Hungarian governments, Admiral Montecuccoli reminded them that he had requested the funds for the expansion of the fleet in 1908. He also explained that the agreements with Stabilimento Tecnico, Skoda, and Vitkovice to initiate preliminary work on the two dreadnoughts had been reached, provided that approval of the necessary funds by the Delegations would follow.[8]

The first Austro-Hungarian dreadnought was laid down in July 1910 and the second two months later. These 20,400-ton ships (then rumoured to be named *Franz Joseph I* and *Tegetthoff*) were designed by the Navy's chief engineer Popper. They were to carry twelve 12-inch guns in four triple centreline turrets. In this respect the Austro-Hungarian dreadnoughts were unique because only the Italian dreadnought *Dante Alighieri* then under construction was to have the same main armament arrangement.

FIGURE 5

ACTUAL v. REQUIRED STRENGTH OF THE AUSTRO-HUNGARIAN NAVY, 1911–15

Type	Obsolete	Combat ready	In service	Planned in completion 1911–15 construct. program.	Upon of 1911–15 program.	Required strength	Required construction in 1916
Battleships	3*	9	12	4	13	16	3
Cruisers	5	6	11	3	9	12	3
Destroyers	7	12	19	6	18	24	6
Torpedo craft	37§	36	73	12	48	72	24
Submarines	-	6	6	6	12	12	-
Danube monitors	4	2	6	-	2	8	6
Danube patrol craft	1	7	8	-	7	12	5
Total	57	78	135	31	109	156	47

Notes: *Monarch*-class;§ Built 1886–92.
Source: Montecuccoli to the Emperor, 'Ausgestaltung der Flotte', 30 May 1910, Vienna, *Kriegsarchiv Operations Kanzlei, Marineseltion – XV-78, 1910.* (Hereafter cited as MKSM.)

By June 1910 the first 14,500-ton semi-dreadnought *Erzherzog Franz Ferdinand* was completed. This class strongly resembled the British *King Edward VII* class. The *Radetzkys* were reportedly built to counter the Italian 10,400-ton *Pisa*-class armoured cruisers and the 17,700-ton French *Danton*-class battleships. The most notable feature of the *Radetzkys* was a specially constructed hull bottom designed to lessen the effects of a mine explosion.

By November 1910 the first of the new 3,500-ton *Admiral Spaun* turbine cruisers was commissioned. All but one 110-ton coastal torpedo craft of the new class built at the Danubius and the Stabilimento Tecnico shipyards were completed by the end of 1910. The Whitehead shipyard in Fiume completed two 236-ton *Holland*-class submarines. Another boat of the same class was laid down at the Whitehead shipyard, built as a private venture.[9]

Changes in naval programme

By the summer of 1910 the Austro-Hungarian naval construction programme underwent some revisions. Although the number of ships to be built remained unchanged, the total estimated cost was scaled down to 312.4 million crowns and the programme spread over six years (1911–16) rather than five. Montecuccoli presented the revised programme to the Delegations in October 1910, explaining that the Dual Monarchy needs a strong fleet to protect the sea routes along her coast against any enemy action. This problem became more acute because of the annexation of Bosnia. Montecuccoli justified the Navy's decision to build dreadnoughts because of the 'widespread recognition that they are the only fully combat worthy ships'. He claimed that building dreadnoughts would enable Austria-Hungary with relatively small financial expenditures to increase her naval strength to the level dictated by her commercial and military interests.[10]

Von Aehrenthal also defended the new naval construction programme in the Hungarian Delegation against strong criticism by Count Batthanny, who asserted that the programme was instigated by Germany. He countered that Batthanny's charge was 'a legend invented by the British press, but now even the latter does not believe it'. He further criticized Batthanny's claim that the Austro-Hungarian naval build-up was directed 'against our ally Italy'. Von Aehrenthal noted that the Dual Monarchy lagged behind other powers in naval strength and was faced with the prospect 'either to modernize the fleet or not to have a fleet at all'. He assured the deputies that the Austro-Hungarian fleet expansion was 'absolutely not aimed against anybody'. Count Aehrenthal also pointed out that regardless of Austria-Hungary's satisfactory relations with other powers, 'it was necessary for the government to think of the future when complications might arise, because we have to bear the responsibility for our own security ourselves'.[11]

Dreadnought controversy

Admiral Montecuccoli provided the long-awaited explanation of the 'unofficial' construction of two dreadnoughts at the Stabilimento Tecnico in October 1910. He informed the Delegations that this action had been approved by all the ministers of the common government. He also revealed that no governmental funds had been spent on the ships. Therefore, he claimed that the budgetary rights of the Delegations had been fully respected. Montecuccoli added that the Navy was 'more or less obliged to take over these two ships'. Nevertheless, the deputies in the Delegations were sharply critical and considered the Navy's decision a violation of their constitutional prerogatives. Afterwards, Montecuccoli on his part promised that this would not happen again.[12]

Admiral Montecuccoli also requested the construction of four dreadnoughts and proposed the expenditure of 312.4 million crowns over a period of five years (1911–15). The revised programme was discussed at a session of the common Ministerial Council on 10 November 1910. The ministers complained that 'while Admiral Montecuccoli earlier requested three dreadnoughts, now suddenly he asks for four dreadnoughts and a number of auxiliary vessels'. The Finance Minister, Leon von Biliński, agreed that four dreadnoughts should be built but only three could be proposed to the Delegations. He rejected Montecuccoli's request that the Navy receive a one-time financial obligation amounting to 82 million crowns, and agreed to secure only 55 million crowns for this purpose. However, Montecuccoli requested an increase in naval expenditures from the planned 123 million crowns in 1911 to 145 million crowns in 1916. Hence, between 1917 and 1920 the ship construction programme was to be entirely funded from the regular Navy budget and without recourse to special credits.[13]

Debate in the Delegations

During the debate in the Delegations on naval appropriations in December 1910, Admiral Montecuccoli justified the increases in the budget by citing the greatly increased cost of ship construction. He noted that while a battleship in the past cost about 19 million crowns, 'now they cost three times as much'. He also claimed that the domestic steel used in naval construction cost between 30 and 80 per cent more than British-produced steel, while the productivity of domestic shipyards was far less than that of British ones.[14]

During a debate in the Austrian Delegation on the naval budget, a

Socialist deputy requested that the Dual Monarchy initiate negotiations with Italy on a mutual halt to the naval race. However, the majority of deputies rejected that proposal on the grounds that 'such agreement was possible only by common action on the part of all powers. Besides, the commercial and political interests of Austria-Hungary at that time required strengthening the fleet.' At the same time, the Austrian Delegation advised the common government to take advantage of any opportunity to achieve agreement on naval disarmament. However, a Croatian deputy urged that in view of Italy's policies in the Balkans, Austria-Hungary had to act with caution. Senior Commander Karl Lucich, who defended the programme in the Hungarian Delegation, asserted that the Dual Monarchy required 'a fleet that would be prepared for the outbreak of a war and whose attack would be feared by the enemy'. A fleet intended solely for defence and which had to withdraw before the enemy was useless.[15]

The debates on the new five-year naval construction programme in the common Ministerial Council and the Delegations showed that there was significant support in 1910 for a rapid expansion of the Austro-Hungarian fleet. Therefore, approval of the programme by the Delegations appeared almost assured. Also the start of the 'unofficial' construction of the first two dreadnoughts at the Stabilimento Tecnico was a clever ploy by Admiral Montecuccoli. His action was strongly supported by the heir to the throne and his friends in the Austrian financial and industrial circles. The Navy in effect forced the Delegations to approve funds for dreadnought construction.

The naval construction programme is presented

Admiral Montecuccoli formally presented the common Ministerial Council with the final version of his long-expected naval construction programme on 5 January 1911. His plan envisaged the construction of four 20,000-ton dreadnoughts, three 3,500-ton scout-cruisers, six 800-ton destroyers, 12 250-ton high seas torpedo craft, six submarines, and two Danube monitors. The entire programme was to be completed by 1916 at a cost of 312.4 million crowns (see Figure 6). Upon completion of the programme the Austro-Hungarian fleet was to consist of four dreadnoughts and nine other battleships (three *Habsburgs*, three *Radetzkys*, three *Erzherzogs*), nine cruisers, 18 destroyers, 68 torpedo craft, and 12 submarines.[16]

Admiral Montecuccoli explained to the Delegations that the Navy decided to build dreadnoughts because they had the greatest

Why build dreadnoughts

concentration of offensive and defensive power. The number of battleships and cruisers depended on the size of the probable theatre of operations and the nature of the tasks to be accomplished. Therefore, scout-cruisers were considered as the most suitable ships for the employment in the Adriatic. Montecuccoli also asserted that even if the probable war theatre were larger, scout-cruisers would be able to carry out their tasks successfully. He argued that the Austro-Hungarian Navy did not require battle-cruisers. Montecuccoli also explained that construction of the proposed large destroyers and high seas torpedo craft was necessary to replace older ships then in service. He also claimed that the six submarines included in the programme were urgently required for defence of important Austro-Hungarian ports.[17]

During debate on the naval budget in the Delegations some deputies expressed concern that the proposed 20,000-ton dreadnoughts were too small and under-armed given that other powers already planned to build 30,000-ton ships carrying 13.5-inch guns. Montecuccoli responded that the 20,000-ton dreadnoughts were large enough because they did not need to carry great reserves of fuel as dreadnoughts in service with the blue-water navies. Also, Austro-Hungarian dreadnoughts would remain

FIGURE 6

STRUCTURE OF NAVAL CONSTRUCTION PROGRAMME, 1911–15
(IN MILLIONS OF CROWNS)

Type	Number of Ships/Craft	Year						Total
		1911	1912	1913	1914	1915	1916	
Dreadnoughts								
'IV' (Donau)[1]	} 4	19	20	10.6	11	–	–	60.6
'V' (Erzherzog Friedrich)		16	20	15.6	9	–	–	60.6
'VI' (Dandolo)		5	9	11.6	20	15	–	60.6
'VII' (Saida)		5	9	11.6	20	15	–	60.6
Cruisers								
'G' (Frundsberg)	} 3	3	3	3	–	1	–	10
'H' (Aurora)		3	3	3	–	1	–	10
'J' (Zrinyi)		2	3	3	2	1	–	10
Destroyers	6	2	–	5	5	5	3	18
High Seas Torpedo Craft	12	3	2	3	2	5	2	12
Submarines	6	–	–	2	2	6	–	10
Total	31	58	69	68.4	68	49	5	312.4

Source: Montecuccoli to the Emperor, 5 January 1911, Vienna, *MKSM, 51-1/3-1, 1911.*

Note: [1] Indicates name of ship to be replaced.

dependent to a large degree on the country's naval bases. He admitted that although 13.5-inch guns had between 6,600 and 7,700 yards greater range than 12-inch guns, this distance had little practical value as there were limits to the guns' range-finding equipment. In his view there was also little difference between the destructive power of a 13.5-inch and a 12-inch gun shell.[18]

Montecuccoli informed the Delegations that he was more interested in obtaining funds for new construction and the replacement of older ships within the regular naval budget than in securing the enactment of a Navy Bill. His opposition to a bill stemmed from his belief that rapid technological changes would require frequent revision, and that would lead in turn to constant delays in the naval construction programme. However, he assured the deputies that the Navy would prepare a Navy Act containing several short-term construction programmes (each no longer than five years), provided the Delegations passed a resolution to this effect.[19] Finally, Montecuccoli requested the Delegations to allow the Navy to start construction on the proposed dreadnoughts and cruisers in 1911 and the destroyers and submarines in 1912 and 1913, respectively.

Approval of extraordinary expenditures

The common Ministerial Council made a decision on 8 January that upon approval of the new Defence Bill (*Wehrgesetz*) the Navy would receive as a part of the regular budget, between 1911 and 1915, a total of 40 million crowns for extraordinary expenditures, provided the Navy reached an agreement with the Army. Although Montecuccoli requested that at least 6.5 million crowns for these purposes be transferred to the Navy annually, and although the Finance Ministry promised him 4.5 million crowns, the Navy subsequently received only 1.5 million crowns because of the opposition to its request by the War Minister, General Franz von Schoenaich. Montecuccoli pointed out that the 1.5 million crowns in supplementary expenditures were inadequate to cover the cost of the increase of 800 draftees planned in 1911. He also noted that more money for these purposes was needed because of the increased cost of maintaining in commission the new dreadnoughts then built. For example, while maintaining one *Erzherzog*-class battleship in commission cost 1.1 million crowns per year, the new 20,000-ton dreadnought cost two million crowns.[20]

Regular naval budget of 1911

Montecuccoli presented to the Delegations the new naval budget amounting to 68 million crowns, an all-time high, in January 1991.[21] He also submitted the first instalment of the proposed five-year fleet expansion programme amounting to 55 million crowns. Thus, the total naval outlays for 1911 were 123 million crowns, or twice the amount for 1904. The Navy Commander informed the Delegations that the regular naval budget would amount to 80 million crowns in 1915, or 145 million crowns if the instalment of the special credit was included. Afterwards, and until 1920, naval expenditures were to remain constant. He thought it unwise to use the special credit for naval construction because this always caused much concern both abroad and within the Dual Monarchy. Hence, it would be much better to obtain an adequate increase in the ordinary naval budget. Montecuccoli also announced that expanding the fleet would require a steady increase in naval personnel from 14,000 men in 1911 to 17,000 in 1916 and to 21,000 in 1920.[22]

The Hungarian Delegation approved the budget for 1911 without changes on 28 February after only a four-day debate, the Austrian Delegation having approved it earlier. A Hungarian reporter on the budget, Julius Rosenberg, wrote that the Austro-Hungarian Navy planned to deploy her ships only in the Adriatic and Levant. He dismissed rumours that the new construction programme was inspired by Germany and asserted that 'though the strength of the Navy affects the value of a state as an ally, it is not this point of view but the needs of her own national security that came into consideration'.[23]

Criticism of the navy's practices

During debate in the Austrian Delegation there was renewed criticism of the high construction costs of naval vessels in domestic shipyards. Montecuccoli claimed that the difference in the cost of building warships at home and abroad was about 10 per cent. He blamed the Austrian steel cartel for this. Not only were Austrian steel prices for ship hulls higher than in Great Britain and Germany, but so were the armour plates and guns produced by the Skoda and Vitkovice Steel Works. A subcommittee of the Austrian Delegation on the Army's industrial orders calculated that the cost of building a dreadnought domestically was about 4.3 million crowns, or 8.5 per cent higher than in Great Britain, primarily because of the low productivity of workers in the Dual Monarchy. For instance, the total cost of the projected 20,000-ton dreadnought (without ammunition) was estimated to be 50.4 million crowns. If built in a British shipyard the cost would be 46.1 million crowns.[24]

Controversy on the share of naval orders

Another problem to be resolved before the new five-year fleet expansion
programme could begin was to determine the shares Austrian and
Hungarian industries were to have in it. By a secret agreement reached
on 31 January 1911 between the War Minister and the Hungarian Trade
Minister, Hungarian industry was to receive orders amounting to 113.7
million crowns, or 36.4 per cent of the total. Specifically, Hungarian
shipyards were to build one dreadnought, two scout-cruisers, six
destroyers, and six submarines. Montecuccoli was obliged to promise
these orders to the Hungarians to ensure their support for the entire
construction programme. The problem was that the Danubius shipyard
in Hungary had no slipway for dreadnought construction and no
experience in building naval vessels larger than destroyers. The
Hungarian government subsequently took steps to enlarge the Danubius
shipyard and announced the establishment of a gun factory at Diosgyör.

Austrian deputies learned of the secret protocol through a debate in
the Hungarian Delegation. They were angry that Hungary received
orders for ammunition amounting to 30 million crowns (or 75 per cent
of the total) instead of their normal share of 15 million crowns. Admiral
Montecuccoli justified his decision by noting that Hungary did not
receive any orders for armour plates, therefore larger orders for
ammunition were awarded to her as compensation.[25] However, the
Austrian deputies were not satisfied with Montecuccoli's response and
charged that the decision would lead to the dismissal of workers in
Austrian ammunition plants. While Hungary then had only four such
plants with a total of 10,000 workers, Austria had 21 plants with about
30,000 workers.

Montecuccoli was so harshly criticized that it appeared he might lose
considerable support that he hitherto had enjoyed among the deputies
in the Austrian Delegation. The Christian-Democratic deputies offered
a resolution which disavowed any agreement reached without the
approval of the Delegation that contravened the 1906 agreement
between Austrian and Hungarian industries. Moreover, the Austrian
Trade Minister refused to accept the validity of the agreement reached
with the Hungarians and threatened to cancel the 1904 agreement on
ammunition as well as to revise the agreement of 1906.

The negative attitude of the Austrian Delegation toward the
agreement of 31 January was so strong that a serious conflict with the
Hungarians seemed likely. The Austrian deputies were not mollified
until a representative of the Navy Commander, Captain Eugen von

Chmelarz, declared in the Delegation that the Hungarian share of naval orders (113 million crowns) was a provisional estimate only. He promised that the agreement on the share of Hungarian industry in naval orders would be drawn up in the form of a supplementary protocol that would be liable to change if necessary. Montecuccoli and the Hungarian Trade Minister gave similar assurances to the Delegations, but these proved to be illusory because the Navy subsequently adhered to the original agreement with the Hungarians.

Approval of special credit

The 312.4 million crown special credit for naval construction was approved in February by large majorities in both Delegations. The main feature of the 1911–15 fleet expansion programme was the projected increase in the number of battleships to 13 by 1916, of which seven were to be modern classes. The build-up of the torpedo force was to allow cruisers and destroyers to operate beyond the Adriatic if necessary. Admiral Montecuccoli indicated that his next goal was to obtain approval for an additional four dreadnoughts so that the Navy would have two battle squadrons of four dreadnoughts each.[26]

During the debate in the Delegations on the new fleet expansion programme, Montecuccoli gave an interview to the *Magyar Figyelo* (Hungarian Observer) to solicit Hungarian support for a stronger and larger Navy. In that interview, he pointed out that strengthening the fleet would benefit Hungary economically by preventing enemy blockade of the Adriatic and the Danube estuary. He argued that a strong Austro-Hungarian fleet could also be of great service to the Army by obviating the need to deploy large numbers of troops along the coast and by shifting a war to enemy-held shores. He demanded that although 'for the near future Austria-Hungary seeks to exercise her influence only in the Adriatic and the Levant', the fleet should be strengthened to complement the Army's strength. Montecuccoli emphasized that 'we could avoid making the Navy's sacrifices valueless only if we strengthen our fleet in such a way that it would have every prospect of success in war'.[27]

Debate on the Navy Act

To achieve Admiral Montecuccoli's goal to rapidly strengthen the fleet, a long-term naval construction programme accompanied by a ship age scheme was needed. Hence, by January 1911 the Austrian Delegation offered a resolution to pass a Navy Act (*Flottengesetz*) similar to Germany's.[28] Four months later, the President of the Austrian government solicited Montecuccoli's opinion on the matter. Montecuccoli called attention to the fact that the Hungarian Delegation at the last session had declined to approve a Navy Act. Therefore, he thought that bringing up the question of a Navy Act in the Reichsrat was not worth the effort, unless the Hungarian Parliament did the same. Montecuccoli also suggested that the President inquire as to the position of the Hungarian government before he decide to support such a move.[29]

By July Montecuccoli, in a memorandum to the President of the Austrian government, expressed his views regarding the eventual enactment of a Navy Act. He stated that such a bill would perhaps favour the steady development of the Navy and end the present situation in which inadequate funds had been allocated in the naval budget for ship construction and replacement. While a Navy Act would enable the Austro-Hungarian fleet to replace obsolete ships speedily, there were also several strong reasons against a Navy Bill. Montecuccoli reminded the President that nowhere had a long-term Navy Act remained unchanged, because a number of individual types of ships were always dependent on the force structure of potential naval opponents. Moreover, a Navy Act should envisage necessary ship strength (*Sollbestand*), material reserve, and a ship's age scheme, as was the case in the German Navy Act.

Admiral Montecuccoli, in his report on the naval budget for 1912, explained to the Delegations that strength in ships depended on tactical and strategic considerations, the comparative strength of other fleets, and the need to adequately protect the Dual Monarchy's coast against enemy assault from across the sea. The planned strength of the Austro-Hungarian Navy was not 'sufficient for the conduct of offensive operations in distant seas or cruiser warfare'. Montecuccoli thought the Dual Monarchy should possess a fleet of 16 battleships, 12 cruisers, 24 destroyers, 72 high seas torpedo craft, 12 submarines, eight Danube monitors, and 12 patrol craft – with a 'material reserve' of two battleships, three cruisers and destroyers each (see Figure 7).[30]

Montecuccoli's proposed ship age scheme (which was not approved) stipulated that battleships, cruisers, and monitors were to be replaced after 20 years in service, destroyers and submarines after 15 years, and high seas torpedo craft and Danube patrol craft after 12 years. Any ships lost for whatever reasons were to be immediately replaced. However, in contrast to the German Navy Act (in which replacement was reckoned

FIGURE 7

ACTUAL v. REQUIRED STRENGTH OF THE AUSTRO-HUNGARIAN NAVY, 1914–24

Type	In Service	Obsolete	Modern	Built or approved by June 1914	In Service end 1915	Montecuccoli's construction programme	Under construction or approved 1915–19	Modern ships in service end 1919	Required to be built 1920–24
Battleships	15	9	6	1	16	16+2*	4	11	3
Cruisers	12	9	3	1	13	12+3	3	7	9
Destroyers	18	-	18	-	18	24+3	6	24	17
High seas torpedo craft	25	-	25	26	51	72	24	51	21
Submarines	6	-	6	6	12	12	5	6	-
Danube monitors	6	4	2	4	10	8	2	8	2
River patrol craft	3	-	3	-	-	12	-	3	-
Total	85	22	63	38	120	156+8	44	115	52

Source: Montecuccoli to President of Austrian government, 'Material zum einen Flottengesetz', 5 July 1911, no. 2248, PK/MS–XV–7, 1911
Note: * Denotes ships in 'material reserve'

from the time of approval of the first instalment of the ship to be replaced until approval of the first instalment for the new ship) Montecuccoli's scheme counted the time between the ship's launchings. In other words, it offered the advantage of having ships in commission for a time when their combat value was highest. Prior to 1914 the construction of large naval vessels, especially dreadnoughts, between laying down and launching took too long a time in all but a few navies. Consequently, the ships were often already obsolescent soon after being commissioned.

Conflict with the Army

By the spring of 1911 a serious conflict had developed between the Army and the Navy over the Delegations' approval of the Navy's 312.4 million crown special credit. At the same time the Army's request for additional funds was reduced 'to only 200 million crowns'.[31] The Navy also resented Army opposition to increases in the extraordinary expenditures of the regular budget to cover the cost of keeping modern battleships in active service.

General Conrad agreed that the development of the Navy and the build-up of an efficient and strong fleet was highly welcome, but not at the expense of the Army. He emphasized a war would be decided on land and that the greatest naval victory would not offset defeat on land. Conrad tried to cancel the fourth dreadnought, planned to be built at Fiume, and thereby effect savings of about 60 million crowns to be transferred to the Army budget. However, General Conrad failed to do that because of the determined opposition on this issue by Archduke Francis Ferdinand.[32]

The Archduke's attempt to re-establish the Navy Ministry

Although Francis Ferdinand's influence grew steadily, there was still a good deal of friction between the MKFF and MKSM because of the lack of clearly delineated authority for the former and the personal animosity between their chiefs. However, after Colonel Carl von Bardolff succeeded Major Brosch in February 1911, co-operation between the MKFF and MKSM was improved because of the mutual trust between General Bolfras and Colonel Bardolff.

Francis Ferdinand tried through the MKFF to enhance the Navy's status by re-establishing the Navy Ministry. Although the Austro-Hungarian Navy enjoyed in practice a great degree of independence from the Army, the Navy Section was viewed as an appendage of the War Ministry where the Navy's interests were sacrificed to those of the Army. There were also recurring conflicts between Montecuccoli and succeeding War Ministers over budgetary matters. These were the main reasons for the proposal by the MKFF to create a separate Navy Ministry, presented to the Emperor in 1911. The MKFF's rationale to re-establish the ministry was that the influence of the War Minister on naval budgetary matters had to be removed. In addition, by having its own ministry, the Navy influence and prestige would be greatly strengthened because it would then have the same standing as the other three ministries of the common government.[33]

However, concerns were expressed that re-establishing the Navy Ministry was bound to cause political problems because an increase in the number of the common ministries to four would lead to a demand by the Hungarians that two of the ministries be transferred from Vienna to Budapest. Therefore, either the War Ministry or the Navy Ministry would most likely be relocated to Budapest and be headed by a Hungarian. If the Hungarians demanded that a Hungarian naval officer head the Navy Ministry, another problem would arise because at that time there was no flag officer of Hungarian nationality.

The MKFF memorandum urged that the Navy Ministry be headed by an active flag officer appointed by the Emperor, and it called for the rejection of any Hungarian demand for the post. The MKFF also argued that the Navy Ministry should be in Vienna because both the seat of the common government and the Emperor were there, thereby allowing easy access and communication between them. However, the proposal to re-establish the Navy Ministry was never realized largely because of political difficulties with the Hungarians.

Implementation of the 1911–15 programme

The approval of the new naval construction programme reinvigorated Austrian and Hungarian shipyards, as reflected on the Vienna stock exchange in the large increases in the values of shares of the shipbuilding and naval armament industries. For example, the value of shares of the Skoda Works jumped from 525 crowns to 837 crowns between the end of February and 20 April 1911.[34]

The Stabilimento Tecnico received orders for the construction of three dreadnoughts, while the Cantiere Navale Tecnico shipyard at Monfalcone was to build one 3,500-ton improved *Admiral Spaun*-class scout-cruiser. By April 1911 the Danubius shipyard was awarded a contract to build one dreadnought, two 3,500-ton scout-cruisers and six new 800-ton *Tatra*-class destroyers. The implementation of the 1911–15 construction programme proceeded rapidly. The first dreadnought, *Viribus Unitis*, was launched on 24 June 1911 at the Stabilimento Tecnico in the presence of Francis Ferdinand, whose sister, Archduchess Maria Annunziata, was the ship's sponsor. The Emperor wrote a letter to the heir apparent congratulating him on that event and praising his 'successful activity in the maritime field'.[35] By the autumn of 1911 two scout-cruisers (*Saida* and *Helgoland*) were laid down, one at Monfalcone and the other at Fiume, as were two *Tatras* at the Danubius shipyard in Porto Rè. The last 14,500-ton battleship (*Zrinyi*) was commissioned in 1911, as were two *Lake*-class submarines and the last of 12 new 110-ton coastal torpedo craft. By the beginning of 1911 the second destroyer (*Huszar*) was completed. All three *Habsburg*-class battleships were partly reconstructed to reduce their superstructure, while ten 78-ton *Schichau*-class torpedo craft were taken out of service and gradually converted into minesweepers. The process of decommissioning obsolescent torpedo-craft ended. By then a total of 36 torpedo-craft had been stricken from the list. Also, an ex-merchant vessel, the 12,200-ton *Gaea*, was converted into a destroyer depot ship; and the 2,420-ton *Pelikan*, a former torpedo-boat depot ship, was converted into a submarine tender.[36]

The year 1911 also saw great progress in the development of the Austrian Navy League. Between June 1910 and 1911 the League's membership grew from 4,500 to 12,600 and its local chapters rose from 31 to 72.[37] The Navy League was by then practically established among all classes and strata of the population. It had chapters overseas in almost every country where the Dual Monarchy's citizens lived. More important, the Navy League made its influence felt among a large part of the Austrian population. Nevertheless, it did not have nearly as large a membership as its counterpart in Germany.[38]

Foreign views

The Dual Monarchy's naval progress continued to interest foreign observers. There were many observers in Great Britain who saw the Dual Monarchy's determination to establish a position of prominence upon the seas as a subtle move by Germany. It was suggested that Germany and Austria-Hungary hoped to divide the British battle fleet between the Mediterranean and the North Sea. The British apparently admired how much value the Austro-Hungarians had obtained for the relatively small amount of money they had spent on their Navy and they compared the steady Austro-Hungarian progress to the German Navy's development. They feared that the Dual Monarchy might emerge as the foremost among the Mediterranean sea powers. The British did not regard the Austro-Hungarian Navy as a negligible force either in the number of ships or the quality and training.

Some British observers perceived that the gulf dividing Austria-Hungary and Italy was assiduously broadened and that neither country would tolerate the supremacy of the other in the Adriatic. In their view the Triple Alliance represented a greater menace on the sea for Great Britain with the Dual Monarchy and Italy mutually antagonistic than if these two countries were on friendly terms. However, the fact was that their naval build-ups were primarily directed against each other and, without this incentive, no pressure from Germany for naval expansion would be sufficient to divert for very long the funds Austria-Hungary badly needed for internal social development.[39]

NOTES

1. 'Rundschau in allen Marinen', *Marine Rundschau* 1 (January 1910) p. 137; Eduard Ritter von Steinitz, 'Die Reichsbefestigung Oesterreich-Ungarn zur Zeit Conrads von Hoetzendorf', *Militaerwissenschaftlichen Mitteilungen* 12 (December 1936), pp. 923–39, at p. 930.
2. Steinitz, 'Die Reichsbefestigung', p. 937; Franz Conrad von Hoetzendorf, *Aus meiner Dienstzeit 1908–1918* 5 vols (Vienna: Rikola Verlag, 1922–25), Vol. 2, p. 701 and Vol. 1, p. 438.
3. 'Vortrag d.Marinekommandant ueber das Resultaet einer Rekognoszierung in Mitteldalmatien hinsichtlich d. Einschaffung eines neuen Flottenstuetzpunkt', 15 April 1910, no. 712, Kriegsarchiv Operations Kanzlei, Marinesektion-VI-1/3, 1910 (hereafter OK/MS).
4. Montecuccoli to the Emperor, 'Ausgestaltung der Flotte', 30 May 1910, OK/MS-XV-7/8, 1910.
5. 'Rundschau in allen Marinen', *Marine Rundschau* 5 (May 1910) pp. 656–7.
6. 'The progress of foreign navies', *Navy League Annual* (1911) p. 29.
7. Arthur J. May, *The Habsburg Monarchy 1867–1914* (Cambridge, MA: Harvard University Press, 1951) p. 452; 'Informazioni e Notizie. Marina Militare', *Rivista Marittima* 5 (May 1911) p. 288.
8. Montecuccoli to the Emperor, 27 May 1910, no. 2153, Kriegsarchiv, Praesidial Kanzlei, Marinesektion-XV-7, 1910 (hereafter PK/MS).
9. René Greger, *Austro-Hungarian Warships of World War I* (London: Ian Allan, 1976) p. 71.
10. 'Der Ausbau der oesterreichisch-ungarischen Flotte', *Marine Rundschau* 4 (April 1911) p. 462.
11. Ibid.
12. 'Rundschau in allen Marinen', *Marine Rundschau* 12 (December 1910) p. 1589; 'The progress of foreign navies', *Navy League Annual* (1911) p. 29.
13. 'Auszug aus dem Protokolle des Ministerrates fuer gemeinsamen Angelegenheiten von 11.10.1910', 20 November 1910, no. 26, PK/MS-XV-7/1, 1911.
14. 'The progress of foreign navies', *Navy League Annual* (1911) p. 30; 'Rundschau in allen Marinen', *Marine Rundschau* 12 (December 1910) p. 1589.
15. 'Rundschau in allen Marinen', *Marine Rundschau* 12 (December 1910) p. 1590.
16. Montecuccoli to the Emperor, 5 January 1911, Kriegsarchiv, Militaer Kanzlei Seiner Majestaet-51-1/3-1, 1911 (hereafter MKSM).
17. 'Die fremden Kriegsmarinen', *Nauticus* (1911) p. 156; 'Der Ausbau der oesterreichischen-ungarischen Flotte', *Marine Rundschau* 4 (April 1911) p. 466.
18. 'Der Ausbau der oesterreichischen-ungarischen Flotte', *Marine Rundschau* 4 (April 1911).
19. Ibid., pp. 464–5.
20. Montecuccoli to Berchtold, 10 July 1912, MKSM-25-1/5, 1912; Unsigned, 5 January 1911, MKSM-51-1/3-1, 1911.
21. 'Budget der K.u.K. Kriegsmarine fuer das Jahr 1911', *Mitteilungen aus dem Gebiete des Seewesens* 3 (March 1911) pp. 563–8; 'Der Ausbau der oesterreichischen-ungarischen Flotte', *Marine Rundschau* 4 (April 1911) p. 470.
22. 'Der Ausbau der oesterreichischen-ungarischen Flotte', *Marine Rundschau* 4 (April 1911) pp. 468–9.
23. 'The progress of foreign navies', *Navy League Annual* (1911) p. 31.
24. 'Der Ausbau der oesterreichischen-ungarischen Flotte', *Marine Rundschau* 4 (April 1911) pp. 470–1.
25. Ibid., p. 473; Unsigned, 2 June 1911, no. 960, PK/MS-XV-7/5, 1911.
26. 'Die fremden Kriegsmarinen', *Nauticus* (1911) p. 160; 'Der Ausbau der oesterreichischen-ungarischen Flotte', *Marine Rundschau* 4 (April 1911) pp. 474–5.
27. 'Rundschau in allen Marinen', *Marine Rundschau* 2 (February 1911) p. 258.
28. The German Navy Acts embodied three principles: fixing a definite number of ships and personnel to be reached and maintained; automatic regulation of obsolescence and replacement of ships; and the so-called 'Risikoprinzip', that is, the German fleet should be so strong that no enemy could attack it without risk. 'Die fremden Kriegsmarinen', *Nauticus (1911)* p. 160.
29. Unsigned, 16 May 1911, Kriegsarchiv Militaer Kanzlei des Erzherzog Franz Ferdinand Mm/63,1911 (hereafter MKFF).
30. Montecuccoli to President of Austrian government, 'Material zum einen Flottengesetz', 5 July 1911, no. 2248, PK/MS-XV-7,1911. Also in MKFF Mm/63, 1911.

31. Montecuccoli to Berchtold, 10 July 1912, MKSM-25-1/5,1912.
32. Conrad, *Aus meiner Dienstzeit*, Vol. 2, p. 132; Rudolf Kiszling, 'Die Entwicklung der oesterreichisch-ungarischen Wehrmacht seit der Annexionkrise 1908', *Berliner Monatshefte 9* (September 1934), pp. 735–49, at p. 743.
33. Unsigned, n.d., MKFF Mm 15-7/1,1911.
34. 'Informazioni e Notizie. Marina Militare', *Rivista Marittima 5* (May 1911) p. 788.
35. 'Rundschau in allen Marinen', *Marine Rundschau 8* (August 1911) p. 1046.
36. Greger, *Austro-Hungarian Warships*, pp. 21, 60; *Jahresberichte des K.u.K. Kriegsmarine fuer das Jahr 1911*, pp. 20–23; Harald Fock, *Schwarze Gesellen*, 1, Torpedoboote b.s. 1914 (Herford: Koehlers Verlagsgesellschaft, 1979) p. 152.
37. Leo Reiter, 'Die Entwicklung der K.u.K. Flotte und die Delegation des Reichsrates' (Vienna University, unpublished Ph.D. dissertation, 1949) p. 168.
38. 'The German Navy', *Navy League Annual* (1910) p. 76.
39. 'The progress of foreign navies', *Navy League Annual* (1911) pp. 47–8.

6

The Mediterranean problems, 1911–12

The situation in the Mediterranean began to change drastically in the summer of 1911 because of the outbreak of the Italo-Turkish War, the Agadir crisis and the resulting political rearrangements among the great powers in the area. By the summer of 1911 Italy decided to achieve her long-standing ambitions to acquire the two Turkish provinces of Tripolitania and Cyrenaica by using force. The alleged reason for Italy's action against Turkey was the need to restore the balance of power in North Africa because of the French expedition against the Moroccan capital of Fez in the spring of 1911. Another reason was the Agadir crisis in July 1911 when the Triple Entente's determined stand led to Germany's diplomatic retreat. The prospect of a peaceful settlement of the Franco-German conflict over Morocco alarmed the Italian government because it feared that it might lead to the loss of Triple Entente support for the then planned Italian action in North Africa. Therefore Italy decided to resolve this issue by force as soon as possible lest she lose the opportunity to acquire Tripolitania and Cyrenaica by default.

The outbreak of hostilities between Italy and Turkey

By the summer of 1911 the Italian government encouraged the country's press to conduct a campaign concerning the alleged mistreatment of Italian nationals by Turkish authorities in Tripoli. Rome also tried to ascertain the attitudes of the other great European powers regarding the possible Italian military action against Tripoli. Berlin wanted a peaceful resolution of the issue and warned Rome that war would weaken Italy and jeopardize Germany's friendship with Turkey. Vienna in contrast was not sorry to see a war between Italy and Turkey and took no action on a Turkish request early in September 1911 to use its good offices with Rome to prevent the outbreak of hostilities. In von Aehrenthal's view, war with Turkey would divert Italy from the South Tyrol and the Balkans.[1]

After laying the diplomatic groundwork and completing her military preparations, Italy began action against Tripoli on 28 September. Rome issued a 24-hour ultimatum to Turkey demanding the admission of Italian troops into Tripoli. After the ultimatum expired with no reply from Turkey, Italy opened hostilities. In one of the first naval actions of the war, Italian ships on 29 September opened fire on two Turkish torpedo craft between the islands of Corfu and Prevesa (at the entrance the Gulf of Arta) in the Ionian Sea. One of the Turkish vessels was driven ashore while the other escaped to Prevesa. The following day, two Italian destroyers sank two Turkish torpedo craft lying in Prevesa harbour; and further northward, the Italians captured two Turkish transports.

Austria-Hungary reacts

Vienna's reaction to Italy's action at Prevesa was immediate. The Austro-Hungarian fleet was placed in a higher state of combat readiness and Army troops deployed along the Italian border were alerted. Because of the outbreak of the Turco-Italian War the Austro-Hungarian Navy on 1 October decided to retain in service all seamen drafted in 1908, so that the ships of the *Reserve Eskadre* could be fully manned.[2] Von Aehrenthal informed Italian Ambassador Giuseppe Avarna that Italy's action at Prevesa flagrantly violated her promise to localize the war in the Mediterranean. He threatened grave and unspecified consequences if Italy continued hostilities in the Adriatic and Ionian Seas.[3]

Because of the Dual Monarchy's opposition, Rome ordered the Italian fleet commander not to extend any action in the Ionian Sea and the Adriatic until further notice, and informed von Aehrenthal of this confidentially on 2 October. In fact, von Aehrenthal had by then advised the Turkish government to withdraw its warships from the Adriatic upon receiving information that the Italians had blockaded Prevesa.[4] British Ambassador Cartwright learned from a person close to the Ballhausplatz (the site of the Foreign Ministry in Vienna) that Austria-Hungary would not view with indifference Italy's parading her flag within sight of the Albanian population, as this might increase her prestige in Albania.[5] Berlin wanted to keep Italy and the Dual Monarchy on friendly terms and therefore advised Rome on 3 October not to bombard or land troops on the Albanian coast. Berlin urged quick action by Italy in Tripoli, hinting that Great Britain might intervene.[6]

Vienna became alarmed by Rome's intentions on 4 October when it learned of an Italian threat to bombard Prevesa unless all the Turkish ships there surrendered. Von Aehrenthal again threatened grave but unspecified consequences if Italy took any military action in the vicinity of the Adriatic. Italy finally promised that she would not bombard Prevesa, but stated that several of her warships would remain in the Ionian Sea and attack Turkish ships if they dared to leave Prevesa.[7]

Germany and Austria-Hungary jointly approached Turkey with an Italian proposal for an agreement to localize the war. Italy was ready to suspend military actions along the Albanian coast and the Ionian Sea from the Boyana River to the island of Zante. However, Turkey wanted the agreement to include the coasts of the Red Sea. The Italian government on 12 October formally submitted a plan to von Aehrenthal to establish a neutral zone in the Adriatic and Ionian Sea extending from Antivari in the north to the southernmost part of the Albanian coast. Italy, while reserving the right to conduct a naval action against Turkey elsewhere, promised not to attack Turkish ships within the proposed neutral zone if they remained in port. Despite the support Italy's plan received from the Triple Alliance and Great Britain, Turkey refused to accept it.[8]

Rome also refused to reassure Vienna concerning future Italian actions in the Adriatic and Ionian Seas so as to keep Turkey in suspense. However, Italy did not want to offend the Dual Monarchy's sensibilities. Therefore Marquis San Giuliano formally promised von Aehrenthal that the Italian government would not conduct any action in the Adriatic unless Turkey sent more naval vessels there. In return, he asked Aehrenthal to keep Italy's promise secret and requested Vienna to support Italy diplomatically if other powers attempted to restrict her naval actions against Turkey elsewhere in the Mediterranean. Von Aehrenthal accepted San Giuliano's assurances and did not insist on a formal agreement because he also was unwilling to promise anything to Italy.[9]

After consulting with San Giuliano, von Aehrenthal informed the Delegations that Italy would restrict her naval activities to the Mediterranean and would not do anything that might endanger peace in the Balkans.[10] After this statement was publicly announced in both the Reichsrat and Parliament on 24 October, the tone of the press in the Dual Monarchy became visibly friendlier toward Italy.

Conrad's memorandum of November 1911

Despite this apparent relaxation of tensions between Vienna and Rome, the 'war' party in Vienna urged that Austria-Hungary take advantage of Italy's preoccupation with Turkey to declare war upon her. General Conrad, in a memorandum sent to Archduke Francis Ferdinand on 15 November 1911, asked him to support such a course of action. Among the advantages of a war with Italy, Conrad claimed, would be the reacquisition of the province of Veneto, which would secure supremacy in the Adriatic for the Dual Monarchy, guarantee the security of her territories, and eventually enable her to acquire the Italian fleet. However, neither Vienna nor Budapest was ready for vigorous action against Italy at that time. The troublesome Conrad was removed from his post at the urging of von Aehrenthal and appointed Inspector General of the Army to keep him away from Vienna.[11]

By the end of October 1911 the Italian campaign in Libya, which had begun successfully, started to bog down in the face of strong native resistance. Because the war in Libya appeared to be protracted regardless of Turkey's ultimate fate, the Italian government started to look for ways to fight Turkey elsewhere. Italy was unable to undertake military actions on land against Turkey in the Balkans or Anatolia because the great European powers would not condone such actions. Von Aehrenthal informed San Giuliano that he would oppose any Italian landing on the mainland of European Turkey.

Italian intentions alarmed the other European powers. Rumours that the Italians might bombard Salonika prompted the German ambassador in Turkey, Adolf Marschall von Bieberstein, to urge his government to join the Dual Monarchy in opposing the extension of the war into the Aegean. Von Aehrenthal warned Italy on 27 October that she would cause complications and lose the support of the great powers if she waged war outside Libya.[12] That same day San Giuliano directed Ambassador Avarna to inquire as to Vienna's attitude to possible Italian naval actions in the Aegean and temporary occupation of the islands there. Specifically, San Giuliano wanted to know if in such a case Article 7 of the Triple Alliance would be applied.[13] In his view it did not apply if the occupation of the Aegean Islands was only temporary and did not lead to permanent territorial changes to Italy's advantage. San Giuliano remarked that if necessary Italy would forego actions along the coast of the Ionian and Adriatic Seas, but would reserve liberty of action elsewhere and seek the Dual Monarchy's consent.[14]

Von Aehrenthal informed Avarna that Italian actions in the Aegean would violate the terms of the Triple Alliance. He also told British Ambassador Cartwright that if the Italian fleet took a similar action in the Dardanelles 'it would be a real European catastrophe and might lead

excellent background to problems up to WWI

to the most serious consequences'. Von Aehrenthal's threat to abrogate Article 7 of the Triple Alliance apparently led Rome to promise on 16 December that she would take no action in the Aegean for the time being without the approval of the Dual Monarchy.[15]

Russia's threat to open the Straits

The crisis in the eastern Mediterranean was heightened by a parallel Russian move in October 1911 to open the Straits to her warships and secure dominant influence in Turkey. In fact Russia became alarmed by the Turkish naval build-up and considered opening the Straits Question as early as May 1911. Russia sought permission from Turkey to reinforce the Black Sea fleet from the Baltic in return for Russian consent to the building of a new Turkish railroad. Turkey was sympathetic to the Russian approaches but wanted to extract as many concessions as possible by playing off Russia and Germany.

The attitudes of the other powers to Russia's initiative on the Straits Question ranged from full support to disapproval. Von Aehrenthal told Cartwright on 7 December that it would be 'unfortunate if Russia raised the question [of the Straits] now, as this would open the door to other powers coming forward with demands; Greece would probably raise the Cretan question again'. He added that if Turkey acceded to these demands 'she would emerge so weakened from the present crisis that it would be absurd for the powers to assert that they wanted to maintain the status quo in the Balkans'. Von Aehrenthal expressed the hope that Great Britain and France would restrain Russia from raising the question. He took a strong stand against Russia's ambitions by arguing that the eventual opening of the Straits would bring her warships into the Mediterranean and thereby strengthen the Triple Entente.[16] This represented a great change from the position von Aehrenthal had taken on the Straits Question in 1908.

go back & check this

Tensions between Berlin and Vienna

The Straits Question also became a source of friction between Germany and the Dual Monarchy. German Foreign Minister Alfred von Kiderlen-Waechter thought that the Russian initiative offered an excellent opportunity for the Triple Alliance to sow discord between Russia and Great Britain while at the same time keeping the status of the Straits unchanged. But Ambassador Marschall thought otherwise, pointing out that support for Russian ambitions in the Straits might give Russia

imp of Straits Question   *intra-alliance diplomacy*

control over Constantinople and thereby affect the future of the Baghdad railway (that passed through the city). He also thought that Russia might decide to move her entire Navy to the Black Sea and thus make Turkey the Tsar's vassal.[17] In short, Marschall wanted Germany and Austria-Hungary to maintain the status quo in the Straits Question.

Turkey's moves

By the autumn of 1911 Turkey was ready to conclude a secret entente with the Dual Monarchy, Germany, and Rumania to preserve the status quo in the Balkans. Although von Aehrenthal refused to enter into any agreement with Turkey while she was at war with Italy, he was attracted by the prospect of blocking Russia's ambitions and thereby offering greater protection for Austria-Hungary from the south. Then Vienna would be in a better position to influence railroad construction in the Balkans and have a free hand in Albania. Therefore von Aehrenthal urged Turkey to reject Russia's proposal concerning the Straits. At the same time he sought to win over Germany and Great Britain to his view and to make clear to Russia that she could expect no blank cheque from the Dual Monarchy on the Straits Question.[18]

The policy of entente with Russia was very unpopular in Great Britain and thus London opposed Russia's scheme and so informed Constantinople. Although Turkey had initially favoured the Russian idea, she rejected it in December 1911 when she realized that Britain wanted no part of the scheme and that accepting it would not save Tripoli from falling into Italy's hands.[19]

Vienna's diplomacy may have played a crucial role in Turkey's refusal to accommodate Russia's wishes. Von Aehrenthal advised the Turkish government to maintain the *status quo* in the Straits, advice that Turkey followed.[20] Vienna's influence at Constantinople was never greater than at the end of 1911.

Italy warms toward the Triple Alliance

By early 1912, despite her uneasy relations with the Dual Monarchy, there was evidence of renewed interest and favour in Italy toward the Triple Alliance. The reason was the animosities between Italy and France as well as a more sympathetic German attitude toward Italy. Franco-Italian relations deteriorated mainly because the French allowed free passage through Tunisia to Turkish soldiers and war matériel. Tensions between the two countries escalated sharply following the Italian capture on the high seas of two French merchant vessels, the *Carthage* and the *Manouba*, in January 1912. Both ships and their crews were eventually released following a strong protest by the French government, but the Italian action made a very bad impression in France where the press took an extremely hostile attitude toward Italy. The end result was a serious worsening of relations between Rome and Paris that made Italy aware of the need to improve ties to her Triple Alliance partners.

Even before the *Carthage* and the *Manouba* incidents there were some influential people in the Dual Monarchy who urged the need for greater Austro-Italian naval co-operation in the Mediterranean. For example, Anton Chiari, a retired admiral and former President of the Austrian Navy League, argued in the *Neue Freie Presse* on 9 January that a strong Italian fleet was in the interest of the Triple Alliance. The Italian parliamentary deputy De Palma wrote in the *Rivista Nautica* in February 1912 that the combined fleets of Italy and Austria-Hungary should equal in strength those of the Triple Entente in the Mediterranean. He argued that in case of a war against the Triple Alliance the French could concentrate their entire battle fleet in the Mediterranean and thus have 26 battleships as opposed to only 17 in the combined Austro-Italian fleet. De Palma estimated that if the trend continued, France would have 22 dreadnoughts by 1920 in contrast to only ten for the Dual Monarchy and Italy combined. In his view, Italy should build 15 dreadnoughts and Austria-Hungary ten. Curiously enough, De Palma had previously been one of the chief critics of the Austro-Hungarian plan to build dreadnoughts. However, he came to view France as a greater threat to Italian sea power than the Dual Monarchy.[21]

An article in the *Wiener Blatt* agreed with the Italian press that the debate in the French Parliament on the new Navy Act revealed that France was intent on securing a dominant position in the Mediterranean to the detriment of the Triple Alliance. Therefore the paper urged the Austro-Hungarian and Italian fleets to become so strong that they could offset the Triple Entente fleets in the Mediterranean. By mid-February the French Parliament approved a new Navy Act that among other things provided for the construction between 1910 and 1917 of 17 dreadnoughts and between 1917 and 1919 of six battle-cruisers. The main purpose of this Act was to enable the French fleet to obtain sea superiority in the western Mediterranean. The French Navy was to face the Austro-Italian fleet and, with the help of the British Mediterranean fleet, secure the transport of French troops from North Africa to France.[22]

Admiral Montecuccoli's new construction programme

In the midst of the Turco-Italian War, Admiral Montecuccoli drew up a new naval construction programme intended to go into effect upon completion of the 1911–15 programme. He was unimpressed by the apparent change in Italy's attitude toward the Triple Alliance and still viewed Italy as the principal threat to the Dual Monarchy in the Adriatic and as her most likely opponent in a war.

Montecuccoli proposed the new naval construction programme in a memorandum to the Emperor in March 1912. He explained in great detail his views on naval balance in the Adriatic. The Navy Commander claimed that Italy's ultimate aim was to obtain superiority in the Adriatic, a goal she was bent on pursuing with 'more energy as her trade and industry developed and the financial possibilities of the country grew'. However, Italy's interest in the Adriatic collided with that of the Dual Monarchy. Control of the Adriatic was far more important for Austria-Hungary than for Italy, because without freedom of maritime trade the Dual Monarchy would become a landlocked country dependent on other great maritime nations. Montecuccoli thought that the *irredente* might expand the areas of friction between the two countries and bring the political situation into an 'uneasy balance'. Montecuccoli believed that the only hope of preventing war with Italy was to maintain a fleet equal in strength to Italy's and supported by secure bases of operations. Thus the Italian fleet was to be the yardstick by which the strength of the Austro-Hungarian Navy was measured.[23]

Unlike General Conrad, Montecuccoli did not believe that the Army alone could accomplish decisive results in a war against Italy. He thought that the Austro-Hungarian troops were 'barely capable of a quick advance through the numerous fortifications and obstacles in the Italian border area'. Montecuccoli contended that in the meantime the Italians could decisively defeat the Austro-Hungarian fleet, thereby threatening the Army's maritime flank. With that, supremacy in the Adriatic would be lost and then even a decisive success on land was to result in a peace with Italy on the basis of the *status quo ante*. In other words, the Dual Monarchy would lose her fleet without any compensating gain on land.

Montecuccoli analysed in some detail Italy's steps to modernize her existing naval bases and to build new ones in the Adriatic. He also described the state of the coastal defences of both Italy and Austria-Hungary. In the same memorandum, Montecuccoli compared the actual and projected naval strength of both navies. He was certain that the

Italian Navy Act of June 1909 was directed against Austria-Hungary. He warned that unless the Austro-Hungarian fleet was rapidly strengthened the Italian Navy could start hostilities in the Adriatic with no great risk.

Montecuccoli urged the Emperor to include in a minimal ship construction programme an additional four 24,500-ton dreadnoughts, five scout-cruisers, 12 destroyers, 24 high seas torpedo craft, six submarines, three colliers, and one 35,000–40,000-ton floating dock. This programme was to require expenditures to the tune of 464 million crowns. Montecuccoli also pressed the Emperor to approve plans to expand Sebenico into a main naval base in central Dalmatia. He emphasized that this plan depended on the completion of a normal-gauge railroad between Sebenico and the country's interior. However, the work on Sebenico's fortifications could begin immediately and be completed by 1917, that is, simultaneously with the planned opening of the projected Lika railway.[24]

In another memorandum to the Emperor in April 1912, Montecuccoli requested the approval of 464 million crowns for naval construction to be used not as a new dreadnought credit, but as a part of standing increases in the Title VII of the regular Navy budget. This part of the budget was to increase from 20 to 50 million crowns per year beginning in 1913. Montecuccoli thought that the proposed expansion of the fleet could be accomplished by 1918 and would not require any increase in the Navy recruiting contingent.[25] However, the Emperor did not approve any of Montecuccoli's new proposals for expanding the fleet, largely because of the prevailing unfavourable financial situation in the country. He suggested instead that the matter be postponed to more propitious times.[26]

Dispute with the War Minister

A serious dispute arose between Montecuccoli and the War Minister over proposed naval expenditures for ship construction. During preliminary discussions on the naval budget for 1913, the Navy Commander tried to enlist the support of Archduke Francis Ferdinand for an increase in naval expenditures totalling 25 million crowns. He justified his request for additional funds because of the planned expansion of naval personnel by 1,600 officers and men. Therefore, the funds for Title VII of the regular naval budget should be increased from 14.5 million to about 25 million crowns in 1913. The Navy's expenditures for 1912 (including the second instalment of the 1911–15 construction programme) amounted to 101 million crowns. Of this sum

63.6 million crowns were allocated for ship construction.[27] Montecuccoli also planned to allocate provisionally about 30 million crowns for preliminary work on a new 24,500-ton dreadnought (*Ersatz Monarch*), nine 250-ton high seas torpedo craft, and one 1,000-ton minelayer.

However the War Minister, General Moritz Ritter von Auffenberg, opposed any increase in naval expenditures for 1913. He argued that the defence budget had already been fixed and there was no money available because of the requirements of the new Defence Reform Act (*Wehrreform*) then under discussion.[28]

By the spring of 1912 Montecuccoli's unauthorized raising of loans at various banks and shipyards engaged in naval construction led to further conflict with the War Ministry. General Auffenberg sharply reminded the Navy Commander of his responsibilities as War Minister in naval matters. Moreover, he warned Montecuccoli never again to assume without the War Minister's prior approval any financial obligation that would exceed the regular budget or involve expenditures not specifically approved by the Delegations.[29]

Italy's relations with France continue to worsen

The Austro-Hungarian naval policy was also affected in the spring of 1912 by Italy's actions against Turkey. Italy annexed Tripolitania and Cyrenaica on 5 November 1911. However, faced with continued stubborn native resistance in the newly conquered provinces and Turkey's refusal to end the war, Italy decided to intensify naval activities in the Red Sea and in the Levant. However, the Dual Monarchy, which sympathized with Turkey and had extensive commercial interests in the Levant, was duty-bound to oppose any warlike act by Italy.

In the first action of the war, two Italian cruisers on 24 February blockaded Beirut, where a Turkish coastal defence ship and a destroyer had found refuge. After the Turks refused the summons to surrender, Italian cruisers opened fire at short range, sinking both Turkish warships, damaging many buildings in the city, and causing some loss of life among civilians. The Viennese government and press were highly critical of that action because of concerns for the Dual Monarchy's trade in the Levant. However, Rome thought that only the threat to extend naval actions to the Aegean and the Straits would force Turkey into submission. By March 1912 San Giuliano asked a high German Foreign Ministry official, Gottlieb von Jagow, for his country's help in persuading Vienna to give Italy a free hand in dealing with Turkey. A week later San Giuliano approached Leopold von Berchtold with an ambiguous proposal to limit Italy's naval activities in the Mediterranean in return for a Turkish withdrawal from Libya.[30] However, Vienna remained adamantly opposed to any Italian action against Turkey in the Aegean.

Germany for her part tried to exploit the opportunity offered by Italy's worsening relations with France to strengthen the Triple Alliance. Berlin had occasion to do this during the visit of Emperor William II to Venice between 24 and 26 March 1912. Also the Italian press praised Italian–German friendship and stressed the need of the Triple Alliance for Italy. The German Emperor, clearly affected by Italian cordiality, promised diplomatic support for the planned Italian actions in the Aegean. The German Emperor also tried to persuade Archduke Francis Ferdinand during their meeting at Brioni Island that Vienna should take a more favourable attitude toward Italian action in the Aegean. However, the heir to the throne remained unmoved because he doubted Italy's loyalty to the Triple Alliance.[31]

The Austro-Hungarian Foreign Minister Berchtold, apparently convinced by German arguments, reluctantly agreed to open talks on 13 April with Ambassador Avarna concerning the problem of eventual Italian occupation of the Aegean Islands. However, he stood firm on the interpretation of Article 7 of the Triple Alliance Treaty. Berchtold made a conciliatory gesture to Italy by agreeing not to regard Rhodes and two nearby islands as being in the Aegean, but in return wanted a public declaration by Italy that her occupation would be temporary. San Giuliano secretly assured Berchtold that the Italian occupation of these islands would be temporary but refused to make any public commitment.[32]

Italian action v. Dardanelles

During the talks between Berchtold and Ambassador Avarna, Rome decided that the only way to force Turkey to sue for peace was to threaten Turkey's Anatolian coast and occupy some Turkish-held islands in the Aegean. First, Italian warships bombarded two outer forts guarding the western entrances to the Dardanelles on 18 April. The aim was to force the powers to exert pressure on Turkey to conclude peace. However, Turkey remained adamant and on 19 April closed the Straits with mines and announced that this waterway would be reopened only if there was no immediate threat of a new Italian attack. The closure of the Straits greatly affected neutral trade because an average of 60 steamers passed through the waterway each day.[33]

The reaction of the great powers to Italian naval action against the Dardanelles was uniformly negative. The Viennese press accused Italy of threatening peace in the Balkans by reopening the Eastern Question. Foreign Minister Berchtold was especially incensed because the Italian action took place during his discussions with Ambassador Avarna. He declared that Vienna would reserve the right to freedom of action in case Italy occupied the Aegean Islands.[34]

Because the Austro-Hungarian shipping companies also suffered losses, Vienna joined London and Paris in advising Turkey to reopen the Straits to neutral commerce. Russia threatened to reopen the entire Straits Question if Turkey did not comply.[35] Consequently Turkey announced on 1 May that she would reopen the Straits as soon as the mines were removed. The latter was done on 19 May 1912.[36]

The Dodecanese Question

Between 6 and 20 May Italian troops occupied the Turkish-held island of Rhodes and a dozen islands in the Dodecanese group, thus producing fears among the great European powers as to Italy's future course of action in the war with Turkey. Berchtold was determined to demand compensation for the Dual Monarchy in case Italy occupied any other Aegean island and so informed Berlin on 18 May. Three days later Rome assured Berlin that it did not plan to seize other islands because of Vienna's objections. However, Italy clearly hoped that Germany might persuade Austria-Hungary to allow her to occupy the island of Chios, a request Kiderlen-Waechter refused to forward to Berchtold during the latter's visit to Berlin on 24–26 May. In fact, at that point Berlin was in complete agreement with Vienna. Italy finally decided not to occupy Chios because of Vienna's opposition.[37]

After May 1912 the ultimate fate of the Dodecanese Islands preoccupied the great powers for some time. Negotiations between Rome and Vienna to enable Italy to return the island to Turkey started in June but ended in failure. Italy in fact wanted to use the Dodecanese Islands to extract recognition by the other powers of her annexation of Libya.

The question of the Dodecanese Islands was discussed among the powers in the summer of 1912; all of them agreed that the islands should be turned over to Turkey at the end of the war. Nevertheless, there were apprehensions of possible complications because the Greek population on the islands would almost certainly object to reverting to the rule of the much despised Turks. By September 1912 Great Britain and France agreed that the Dodecanese Islands should be returned to Turkey at the conclusion of peace, provided the Turks gave guarantees for the Greek population. However, Berchtold and Kiderlen-Waechter refused to support the Anglo-French proposal because they considered it an attempt by the Triple Entente to return the Dodecanese Islands unconditionally to Turkey. Afterwards, Berlin exerted pressure upon Turkey to conclude peace with Italy, for otherwise it would be impossible for her to regain the Dodecanese Islands.[38]

The Turco-Italian War ends

The outbreak of the First Balkan War brought Turkey speedily to the conference table. The peace treaty that ended the Turco-Italian War was formally signed at Lausanne on 18 October 1912. By its terms Italy acquired *de facto* Libya. She promised to withdraw her troops from the Aegean Islands as soon as Turkey evacuated Libya, a promise Italy never kept. By 25 October all the other great European powers had recognized the peace agreement between Italy and Turkey.

Changing naval balance

While the Turco-Italian War was in progress, it became clear that it was to result in a momentous change in the balance of power in the Mediterranean. Italy's acquisition of Libya and occupation of the Dodecanese Islands greatly improved her strategic position: by controlling both shores of the central Mediterranean, the Italian fleet was able to interrupt the sea traffic of her potential opponents there. Control of the Dodecanese Islands allowed the Italian Navy to endanger the security of the shipping routes to the southern approaches of the Straits and the Suez Canal. Moreover, the British naval base at Malta became more vulnerable to a possible Italian attack.

Even more important were the political consequences of the Turco-Italian War in the Mediterranean. The relations between Italy and France suffered a severe setback as a result of French attitudes and policy during the war. That in turn led Rome to seek to improve its ties with the Triple Alliance. Italy was also offended by what she perceived as the French decision to expand her fleet so as to obtain supremacy in the western Mediterranean. Hence, influential people both in Italy and the Dual Monarchy argued that the only way to prevent France from becoming mistress of the Mediterranean was through close Austro-Italian naval co-operation.

British decision to reorganize the fleet

No European power was more unfavourably affected by the new situation in the Mediterranean than Great Britain. Her problem was compounded by her inability to maintain a sufficiently strong fleet both in home waters and the Mediterranean in the face of Germany's large and unprecedented naval build-up in the North Sea. In the aftermath of the failure of the British Secretary of War Viscount Haldane's effort in February 1912 to reach an agreement with Germany on reducing naval construction, First Lord of the Admiralty Winston Churchill announced in the House of Commons on 18 March 1912 a plan to organize three fleets. The largest and most important, the First fleet in home waters, was to consist of four fully commissioned battle squadrons. The Atlantic fleet (previously based in Gibraltar) was to be redesignated the Third Battle Squadron and redeployed to home waters. The Fourth Battle Squadron would be stationed at Gibraltar instead of Malta and was to be employed either to reinforce the squadrons at home or re-enter the Mediterranean as circumstances might dictate.[39]

The Admiralty's decision in effect weakened the British position in the Mediterranean. So it was not surprising that the Foreign Office was alarmed at what effect the proposed reorganization of the fleet might have upon the British international position. Under-Secretary of State for Foreign Affairs Sir Eyre Crowe drafted a memorandum (revised by Foreign Secretary Sir Edward Grey) which was presented to the Committee of Imperial Defence on 8 May. Sir Eyre argued that the withdrawal of the British fleet could possibly lead Italy away from half-hearted co-operation with the Triple Alliance and toward friendship with Great Britain. However, he thought that might happen only if Rome knew that Paris was assured of British support in case of war between the Triple Alliance and the Triple Entente. At the same time Great Britain could not expect France to check a combined Austro-Italian fleet in the Mediterranean unless she could rely on British assistance to protect her Atlantic coast against the German fleet.[40]

The Committee of Imperial Defence, at its meeting in Malta on 2 June 1912, decided that a definite agreement should be made with France to have the British fleet defend the French Atlantic coast. It also sought to ensure that the French fleet in the Mediterranean and the British ships deployed there could successfully face the combined Austro-Italian fleet in case of the outbreak of war with the Triple Alliance.[41]

The Admiralty proposed to maintain permanently in the Mediterranean two and preferably three battle-cruisers with a four-ship cruiser squadron. A squadron of eight battleships based in Gibraltar was to patrol the Mediterranean. This force (though it would be available to reinforce the fleet in home waters in case of war with Germany) was not to be redeployed in peacetime except in case of some contingency. The squadron was to be designated the Mediterranean Battle fleet (Fourth Battle Squadron).

Churchill, in a 15 June memorandum on the naval situation in the Mediterranean, stated that Great Britain could not afford to keep six battleships there in full commission. In his view it was a waste of the country's limited resources to use full complements to man inferior ships. Churchill argued that it would be unwise to maintain a battle squadron at Malta because Great Britain was not in a position to face a combined Austro-Italian fleet. He envisioned that by January 1915 the Austro-Hungarian and Italian fleets together would have ten dreadnoughts in commission against the four *Duncans* and two *Swiftsures* based at Malta. The 14,200-ton *Duncans* were armed with four 12-inch and 12 5.9-inch guns and were capable of attaining a speed of 19.5 knots, while the 12,000-ton *Swiftsure* class (built in 1903) carried four 10-inch and 14 7.5-inch guns and had a maximum speed of 19 knots.[42] He thought that as soon as the two Austro-Hungarian dreadnoughts entered into service by April 1913, they, plus the three *Radetzkys*, would be stronger than the six British battleships stationed at Malta – even without taking into account Italian battleships.

Churchill strongly opposed a policy aimed at maintaining British naval supremacy in home waters as well as the Mediterranean. To achieve superiority in the Mediterranean, Great Britain had to be ready to build an additional squadron of dreadnoughts. This meant in effect that Great Britain, while maintaining 60 per cent greater strength than the German fleet, would in addition have to adopt a two-power standard against the Austro-Hungarian and Italian fleets in the Mediterranean. Churchill warned that there was neither time nor money to build a special dreadnought squadron for the Mediterranean. He gloomily concluded that whatever action Great Britain might take, control of the Mediterranean was rapidly passing from her hands to those of her potential enemies.

As a solution to this problem, Churchill proposed that the British position could be improved only with the help of France. The French fleet, supported by an adequate British naval force and enjoying the protection of well-fortified bases, would be superior to any Austro-Italian combination. Moreover, a combined Anglo-French fleet would not only protect the interests of both countries in the Mediterranean but allow continued British superiority over the German fleet in the North Sea. Finally Churchill urged that a definite naval agreement be made with France without delay.[43]

In the same memorandum Churchill went on to say that one of the most important British aims in the Mediterranean should be to make sure that France was strong enough with British aid to overcome the combined strength of the Triple Alliance's fleets in the area. By then, French fleet in the Mediterranean was considered slightly stronger than the Austro-Italian combination. However, the French Navy was expected to have eight dreadnoughts compared with a combined total of nine for the Italian and Austro-Hungarian navies in 1913–14. Only by late 1915 was it projected that France's superiority in dreadnoughts would surpass the combined Triple Alliance's fleets.

In a new draft proposal for disposition of British naval forces in the Mediterranean in peacetime and attached to the memorandum of 15 June, Churchill proposed the deployment of two and preferably three battle-cruisers and a four-ship armoured cruiser squadron, all based at Malta. In addition, a destroyer flotilla was to remain at Malta, while a submarine flotilla plus one old battleship was to be stationed at Alexandria. The Fourth Battle Squadron of eight battleships and a cruiser was to remain at Gibraltar as previously announced. This squadron would be available for deployment elsewhere if necessary.[44]

Berlin considered the proposed redeployment of the British fleet as a triumph of its own naval policy. German navalists believed that their naval build-up had forced Great Britain to hand over to France guardianship of the waters she had once ruled supreme.

Undoubtedly the Austro-Hungarian dreadnought construction played an important role in British calculations of their position in the Mediterranean. Both London and Paris were suspicious of the Dual Monarchy's motives for building dreadnoughts. During a debate in Parliament on British policy in the Mediterranean in the summer of 1912, for example, Arthur James Balfour took note of the Austro-Hungarian relatively short coastline and implied that her decision to construct dreadnoughts meant that she 'was acting as an agent of German policy'. Other observers believed that Germany welcomed the naval race between her two allies because it increased the strength of the Triple Alliance in the Mediterranean. The French naval attaché in Vienna, Commander Viscount de Faramond, thought that the Austro-Italian naval rivalry might one day lead to a rapprochement between those two countries. Moreover, the steady expansion of the Austro-

Hungarian and Italian fleets would make the Triple Alliance supreme in the Mediterranean.[45]

The British ambassador in Berlin, Sir Edward Goschen, thought that the redistribution of the British fleet might persuade Germany's allies, Italy and Austria-Hungary, to push their naval construction to the utmost limit. The problem was that the British fleet stationed in Gibraltar could not go both ways at once. If circumstances drew it northward, the Italian and Austro-Hungarian fleets, which in a few years would be superior to the French Toulon fleet in respect of numbers, quality of ships, and personnel, had a fair chance of becoming masters of the Mediterranean. Goschen worried that if the redeployment of the British fleet from Malta to Gibraltar was carried out, it would lead to increased naval construction not only by Germany but also by Italy and the Dual Monarchy. In his view, Austria-Hungary would always be influenced by Germany in the development of her naval strength. At the same time rivalry between the Dual Monarchy and Italy would continue so that increased naval construction by one side would be countered by the other side. All Germany had to do was encourage Austria-Hungary to expand her fleet and Italy was certain to respond in kind.[46]

Search for the new Mediterranean agreement

The Turco-Italian War prompted Great Britain and France to bind Italy to some kind of new Mediterranean agreement and thereby prevent the Triple Alliance from obtaining predominance in the area. The British ambassador in Rome, Sir J. Rennell Rodd, was one of the staunchest proponents of the policy of friendship with Italy. As early as October 1911 he propounded the idea of persuading Italy to come to an agreement with Great Britain and France regarding the maintenance of the *status quo* in the Mediterranean. The French ambassador in Rome, Camille Barrere, sought to bring Russia to Italy's aid in the Adriatic in the event of an attack by the Dual Monarchy. French Ambassador Paul M. Cambon and British Permanent Under-Secretary of State for Foreign Affairs Sir Arthur Nicolson discussed how to woo Italy away from her allies in February 1912. However, because of Franco-Italian tensions they decided the matter could not be pursued further at that time.[47]

Twice in April 1912 Rodd wrote private letters to Grey, raising anew the question of an entente among Italy, Great Britain, and France. Ambassador Cambon informed Nicolson on 18 May that the French Prime Minister and Foreign Minister, Raymond M. Poincaré, had in mind a proposal by which an arrangement was to be made with Italy to maintain the status quo in the Mediterranean. Under that plan Great Britain, France and Italy were to promise to respect and maintain the territorial integrity of each other's possessions in the area extending from the Strait of Gibraltar to the Suez Canal.

Although Grey agreed to the French proposal in principle, he thought that no agreement was possible before the conclusion of peace between Italy and Turkey. However, all the efforts to conclude a new Mediterranean agreement with Italy were abruptly halted on 9 July when a British newspaper revealed that negotiations to that effect were under way. This disclosure prompted all three governments involved to assure the Dual Monarchy and Germany that no negotiations of that nature were being conducted.[48]

After the British and French failure to conclude a Mediterranean agreement with Italy, an article appeared on 24 July in the Hungarian newspaper *Pester Lloyd*, suggesting that Austria-Hungary cease her naval build-up in return for a British promise not to attack her coast. The article, written by the paper's correspondent in Paris, was in fact a 'feeler' by Grey as to Vienna's attitude to an eventual agreement with Great Britain on the matter. The Ballhausplatz, however, quickly disavowed any such idea, announcing through the *Neuer Wiener Tageblatt* on 31 July that the article in the *Pester Lloyd* did not represent the views of the Viennese government. Subsequently, Berchtold instructed Vienna's embassy counsellor in London, Count Karl Trauttmansdorff, to inform the British government that the Dual Monarchy's naval build-up was not specifically aimed against any other power, including Great Britain. He tried hard to convince London that Vienna's policies in the Mediterranean were intended to further her own interests, not Germany's, and that they were not designed to run counter to those of Great Britain.[49]

Dispute over naval budget

While the Dual Monarchy's diplomats were busily involved with Mediterranean problems in the summer of 1912, a serious dispute arose between the Austrian and Hungarian members of the common Ministerial Council over the increase in the funds in Title VII of the regular naval budget for 1913 (proposed by Admiral Montecuccoli in May 1912). This request was bitterly opposed at a session of the common Ministerial Council held on 8 July by the President of the Hungarian government and his Finance Minister. The Hungarian President reminded the Austrian ministers that the naval construction programme for 1911–15 had been approved by the Hungarian Delegation on condition that no new increases for the Navy's budget would be requested. Hungarian Finance Minister Dr Johann Teleszki also was opposed to the request because the Delegations had approved a 250-million-crown special credit for the Army. He explained that Hungary required the same amount to cover its own financial obligations and was concerned that the announcement of a new naval construction programme might lead to closure of the French money market to the Dual Monarchy's government bonds and industrial loans.[50]

However, the common Finance Minister, Biliński, disagreed with Teleszki on this issue. He was supported by Berchtold, who pointed out that the proposed increase in the Navy budget was warranted because of the then existing international tensions. Nevertheless, both Hungarian ministers remained unconvinced and argued that no new naval appropriations had to be discussed until 1916 (that is, until the completion of the then current five-year naval construction programme). They asked for cancellation of the first instalment for the proposed building of the new dreadnought. Yet, they agreed in return to approve construction of two colliers. The Austrian members finally supported (though reluctantly) the requested increase in the naval budget.[51]

Admiral Montecuccoli tried to convince Archduke Francis Ferdinand to persuade the ministers to discuss the entire question of the budget for 1913 before the Delegations session in the autumn of 1912. He also sent a letter to Berchtold on 10 July, explaining that during the discussion at the common Ministerial Council four million crowns were approved at his request as the first instalment for the construction of the second collier, which the Navy had considered necessary for a long time.

Montecuccoli requested 30 million crowns in Title VII of the proposed budget for 1913, but the Ministerial Council approved only one-third of that sum. He then complained to Berchtold that the reduction of Title VII of the budget represented a great obstacle to the continued strengthening of the Navy. Moreover, Montecuccoli stated that as the official 'responsible for the effectiveness of the fleet', he could not defend the budget for 1913 as altered by the common Ministerial Council. He praised the Emperor for his steady support for strengthening the Navy and appealed to the 'government of Your Majesty to urge the new session of the council to approve a larger share of funds for the Navy, including Title VII'.

Berchtold, on his part, responded that because of growing tensions in the Balkans at that time he could not make a final decision. Nevertheless, he raised the possibility that the Austrian and Hungarian governments still might respond favourably to the Navy's requests in 1912 or at the beginning of the following year. The regular naval budget for 1913 was eventually approved but was higher than in the preceding year by a mere 1.5 million crowns.[52] Afterwards, Archduke Francis Ferdinand directed Admiral Montecuccoli to prepare a report for the Emperor describing in detail the military-political consequences for the Dual Monarchy of a reduction in the naval budget.

Montecuccoli's memorandum of 27 July

The Navy Commander submitted a memorandum to the Emperor on 27 July in which he proposed to start construction on replacements for all three old *Monarch*-class battleships. He explained that the Stabilimento Tecnico would have one slipway vacant after launching the dreadnought *Tegetthoff*, and another by early 1914 after launching the *Schlachtschiff VI*. Because of intensified dreadnought construction by all the great powers and the long lead time required for their construction, the building would have to start soon.[53] Montecuccoli warned that any delay in the construction of dreadnoughts would lead to a dangerous imbalance between Austria-Hungary and Italy and would require concurrent construction of a larger number of dreadnoughts. Moreover, an on-and-off naval construction programme would have a deleterious effect upon shipbuilding industries, forcing them to dismiss their idle labour force. The lack of a systematic, long-term construction programme would also cause late orders for ships and costly overruns. Montecuccoli complained that his proposed 1913 budget of 24 million crowns for Title VII as the first instalment for a projected 24,500-ton dreadnought (*Schlachtschiff VIII*) was deleted at the session of the common Ministerial Council. He then requested that these funds be reinstated because as he stated 'in recent times all great states spend larger financial means for the Navy's purposes than the Monarchy'.[54] However, a decision on the request was postponed until the common Ministerial Council met in the autumn of 1912.

Defence Reform Act of 1912

Another event which had repercussions in the Navy was the Defence Reform Act that went into effect on 5 July 1912 after a long, acrimonious debate in the Delegations. The Act increased the annual recruiting contingent for the common armed forces and changed the duration of military service for all the categories of draftees. Conscription in Austria-Hungary was introduced after the new National Defence Act (*Wehrgesetz*) was adopted in December 1868. The recruiting contingent was granted annually by the Reichsrat and the Hungarian Parliament according to each part of the Dual Monarchy's share of the total peacetime strength of the common armed forces as fixed by respective Austrian and Hungarian National Defence Acts. Also, separate recruiting contingents for the territorial forces (the Austrian *Landwehr* and the Hungarian *Honvéd*) were approved.

In later years, despite many efforts by military leaders, supported by the Reichsrat, to raise the peacetime strength of the common armed forces, they were all unsuccessful because of stubborn Hungarian opposition. Not until 1911 were the long-awaited reforms of the armed forces seriously considered by both legislative bodies. The Defence Reform Act increased the peacetime strength of the common Army and the Navy from 294,000 to 344,000 men and raised the annual recruiting contingent for both parts of the Dual Monarchy from 103,100 to 159,500 men.[55]

In regard to the Navy, the Defence Reform Act allowed it to increase in size from 5,500 men in 1913 to 7,000 men by 1916. From then on and until 1920 the Navy's recruiting contingent was to be kept at a constant level.[56] Thus the planned expansion of the Austro-Hungarian fleet could be carried out without having recourse to the Delegations for periodic approval of increases in naval personnel.

Calls for a closer naval co-operation

By mid-1912 there were new calls in Italy for a larger naval build-up by the Triple Alliance in the Mediterranean to match France's. Deputy De Palma wrote in the June issue of *Rivista Nautica* that the combined Austro-Italian fleet should equal in strength the French fleet. By June 1912 the Italian Parliament approved a new Navy Bill which extended the Navy Act of 1911 by four years until fiscal year 1921–22. During this 11-year period 550 million lire (518 million crowns at the then current exchange rate) were to be spent on ship construction. Besides the completion of ships approved by the Navy Acts of 1909 and 1911, two new *Duilio*-class dreadnoughts, two 2,600-ton scout-cruisers, two submarines, an undetermined number of destroyers and torpedo craft, and five auxiliary ships were to be built.[57]

De Palma thought that the British would withdraw their battleships from the Mediterranean, so that the only opponent of the Triple Alliance there would be the French fleet based in Toulon. He asserted that strengthening the Italian fleet was necessary to ensure control of Libya and the Dodecanese Islands, to cope with the possibility that Russia might become a Mediterranean power, and to increase Italy's value to the Triple Alliance. However, he contended that the ratio of naval strength between Italy and the Dual Monarchy in terms of tonnage should be three to two.[58]

German Chancellor Theobald von Bethmann Hollweg also advocated closer naval co-operation between Austria-Hungary and Italy. In a conversation on 2 July with the Austro-Hungarian ambassador in Berlin, Count Ladislas Szögyèny-Marich, the German Chancellor urged that Vienna should view Italian policies in the Mediterranean with sympathy. However, Szögyèny replied that Italy's greatly strengthened position in the Mediterranean was bound to aggravate Austro-Italian rivalries in the Adriatic. Bethmann Hollweg maintained that the extension of Italy's interests in the Mediterranean would actually reduce Italy's rivalry with the Dual Monarchy in the Adriatic. He also added that he envisaged co-operation between the Italian and Austro-Hungarian fleets in the Mediterranean.[59]

The Anglo-French rapprochement in the Mediterranean

By mid-1912 France and Great Britain believed that the expected renewal of the Triple Alliance would cover the Mediterranean and that Germany might obtain a coaling station in Tripoli as her price for supporting Italy's interests in the Mediterranean. The French ambassador in London, Cambon, suggested to Grey on 6 June that the time had come to admit Russia into the Mediterranean. He suggested that although French superiority over the combined Austro-Hungarian and Italian fleets would not be lost until 1915, the deployment of a significant German naval force in the Mediterranean would change the balance of power to France's disadvantage. Therefore his government thought it would be desirable for Russia to play a role in the Mediterranean.[60]

In fact, France had by then begun negotiations with Russia that led to the signing of a naval convention in Paris on 18 July 1912. The agreement stipulated that the naval forces of the two countries were to co-operate whenever there was combined action by their armies on land. Russian Foreign Minister Sergey Dmitriyevich Sazonov informed Grey that the principal aim of the naval convention was to have the

French fleet protect Russian interests in the southern war theatre 'by preventing the Austrian fleet from penetrating the Black Sea'.[61]

After Great Britain and France were forced to postpone their efforts to reach a Mediterranean agreement with Italy, they resumed negotiations with each other for an understanding on the division of responsibilities for protecting their interests in the Mediterranean. British First Sea Lord Admiral Sir Francis Bridgeman presented a draft Anglo-French naval agreement on 23 July. The document called for France to deploy almost her entire fleet in the Mediterranean while leaving the defence of the Atlantic coast to torpedo flotillas. Great Britain wanted to concentrate her main strength in home waters while maintaining a strong 'containing force of battle-cruisers and armoured cruisers and torpedo craft' in the Mediterranean. The proposed agreement also envisaged the British fleet to protect Anglo-French interests east of Malta and the French fleet defend them west of it.[62] However, the draft clearly stated that neither France nor Great Britain would be fully committed to come to each other's aid in case of war with the Triple Alliance. This led Ambassador Cambon at a meeting with Sir Arthur Nicolson on 24 July to remark that requiring the French Navy to concentrate nine-tenths of her battle strength in the Mediterranean would leave the country's Atlantic and Channel coasts open to German attack with no guarantee that Great Britain would come to her assistance.[63]

The French government wanted an exchange of notes between London and Paris to define the joint interests of both countries and stating explicitly that in case any of these interests were endangered both governments should consult on the means to defend them. If this was unacceptable to the British, the French would be satisfied with a simple exchange of declarations that both governments would enjoy complete freedom of action, notwithstanding any arrangements signed by their experts.[64]

Churchill in a memorandum to Grey opposed any binding commitment to France. He believed that British freedom of action would be seriously endangered if the French could claim that they had weakened their defences in the north in order to concentrate their forces in the Mediterranean. In his view, the French decision to concentrate in the Mediterranean was the correct one because their fleet in that area would be superior to a combination of their potential opponents. He denied that the French fleet was in the Mediterranean to protect British interests and added that 'if France did not exist we should make no other disposition of our forces'.[65] Despite disagreements as to what form an Anglo-French naval convention should take, discussions between London and Paris continued during the summer of 1912 without reaching a final agreement.

In September 1912 the long-awaited redistribution of the French fleet was carried out. Three battle squadrons were deployed in the Mediterranean along with some older battleships. The first battle fleet was to be based at Toulon. The Third Battle Squadron of six battleships was transferred to the Mediterranean in October 1912 and was to be based either at Toulon or Bizerte. Six modern armoured cruisers and 38 destroyers were also deployed in the Mediterranean. Another cruiser squadron with a torpedo craft flotilla and submarine flotillas remained along France's Channel and Atlantic coasts.

The French at first insisted that concentrating their fleet in the Mediterranean was a temporary measure to allow certain battleships based on the Atlantic coast to participate in the Mediterranean manoeuvres. Apparently the French wanted to ascertain Great Britain's real intentions before making the deployment of their fleet permanent.[66]

Renewed calls for closer naval co-operation

News of the Franco-Russian naval convention and rumours of the on-going negotiations for an Anglo-French naval agreement strengthened the hands of those in Italy and the Dual Monarchy who urged close naval co-operation between the two powers. The publication in *Le Matin* on 10 September of France's decision to concentrate her battle strength in the Mediterranean provoked a strong reaction in Italy, where public opinion was especially incensed by the tone of the French press, that openly called for French mastery in the Mediterranean.

The Austro-Hungarian ambassador in Rome, Count Ludwig Ambrozy, informed Berchtold on 14 September that the situation was so serious that both Italy and the Dual Monarchy had to 'take care of their Navy's development to be ready to face any eventuality'. Count Ambrozy observed that the French could not have done a greater service for the cause of the Triple Alliance. The official Italian paper *Tribuna* noted on the same day that 'Italy ought to respond to the French fleet concentration in the Mediterranean and in this new situation be ready to change either alone or in co-operation with her two allies'.[67]

Numerous chauvinistic articles in the French press in the autumn of 1912 further inflamed anti-French sentiment in Italy and convinced Rome that the French naval concentration in Toulon was directed against her. The end result was that Italy's trust in France was severely shaken. There was a growing feeling in Rome, strongly supported by public opinion, that closer co-operation with Italy's partners in the Triple Alliance was highly desirable.

NOTES

1. William C. Askew, *Europe and Italy's Acquisition of Libya 1911–12* (Durham NC: Duke University Press, 1942) p. 58; Kolossa to Aehrenthal, 25–26 September 1911, no. 3659, *Oesterreich-Ungarns Aussenpolitik von der Bosnischen Krise 1908 bis zum Kriegsausbruch 1914. Diplomatische Aktenstuecke des Oesterreichisch-Ungarischen Ministeriums des Aeussern,* ed. Ludwig Bittner, Alfred Francis Pribram, Heinrich Srbik, and Hans Uebersberger, 9 vols (Vienna: Oesterreichischer Bundesverlag fuer Unterricht, Wissenschaft und Kunst, 1930) (hereafter *OuA*) Vol. 3, pp. 357–8.
2. Askew, *Europe and Italy's Acquisition of Libya*, p. 79; 'Rundschau in allen Marinen', *Marine Rundschau* 12 (December 1911) p. 1625.
3. Francesco Malgeri, *La Guerra Libica (1911–1912)* (Rome: Edizione di Storia e Letteratura, 1970) p. 302.
4. R. Rodd to Grey, 1 October 1911, no. 261, *British Documents on the Origins of the War 1898–1914*, ed. G. P. Gooch and Harold Temperley, 11 vols (London: HMSO, 1926–38) (hereafter *BD*) Vol. 9(1), pp. 294–5.
5. Fairfax Cartwright to Grey, 2 October 1911, no. 263, *BD*, Vol. 9(1), p. 295.
6. Bethmann Hollweg to Tschirschky, 3 October 1911, no. 1086, *Die Grosse Politik der Europaeischen Kabinette 1871–1914*, ed. Johannes Lepsius, Albrecht M. Bartholdy, Friedrich Thimme, 40 vols (Berlin: Deutsche Verlagsgesellschaft fuer Politik und Geschichte, 1927) (hereafter *GP*) Vol. 30(1), pp. 87–8.
7. Aehrenthal to Ambrozy, 4 October 1911, no. 2706, *OuA*, Vol. 3, p. 392; Ambrozy to Aehrenthal, 5 October 1911, no. 2714, ibid., p. 399.
8. Aehrenthal to Nemes, 5 October 1911, no. 2710, ibid., pp. 394-5; Aehrenthal to Pallavicini, 7 October 1911, no. 2726, ibid., p. 409; Avarna memorandum, 12 October 1911, no. 2747, ibid., pp. 427–8; Kiderlen-Waechter to Marschall, 14 October 1911, no. 10886, *GP*, Vol. 30(1), pp. 106–7.
9. Merey to Aehrenthal, 8 October 1911, no. 2731 and 10 October 1911, no. 2739, *OuA*, Vol. 3, pp. 414–15, 421–2; Aehrenthal to Merey, 12 October 1911, no. 2746, ibid., pp. 425–7.
10. Aehrenthal to Merey, 19 October 1911, no. 2786, ibid., p. 454; Aehrenthal to Embassy in Berlin, 20 October 1911, no. 2789, ibid., pp. 456-8.
11. Franz Conrad von Hoetzendorf, *Aus meiner Dienstzeit 1908-1918*, 5 vols (Vienna: Rikola Verlag, 1922–25) Vol. 2, p. 346.
12. Marschall to Foreign Ministry, 29 October 1911, no. 10931, *GP*, Vol. 30(1), pp. 172-3; Askew, *Europe and Italy's Acquisition of Libya*, p. 112.
13. That article of the 1902 Triple Alliance treaty provided that 'if in the case of these events Italy and Austria-Hungary feel the need to modify the status quo by temporary or permanent occupation on their side, the occupation will not take place except after these two powers reach an agreement based on the principle of reciprocal compensation for any advantage territorial or otherwise resulting from the change of the status quo' (*GP*, Vol. 18(1), p. 549).
14. Francesco Malgeri, *La Guerra Libica (1911–1912)* (Rome: Edizione di Storia e Letteratura, 1970) pp. 316–17.
15. Merey to Aehrenthal, 4 November 1911, no. 2872, *OuA*, Vol. 3, p. 512; F. Cartwright to Grey, 22 November 1911, no. 315, *BD*, Vol. 9(1), p. 326; Tschirschky to Bethmann Hollweg, 9 December 1911, no. 10968, *GP*, Vol. 30(1), p. 199; Kiderlen-Waechter to Tschirschky, 16 December 1911, no. 10969, ibid., p. 200.
16. Cartwright to Grey, 7 December 1911, no. 343, *BD*, Vol. 9(1), p. 848; Aehrenthal to V. Nemes, 20 November 1911, no. 2955, *OuA*, Vol. 3, p. 567.
17. Marschall to Foreign Ministry, 1 December 1911, no. 10978, *GP*, Vol. 30(1), pp. 212–13.
18. Cartwright to Grey, 7 December 1911, no. 343, *BD*, Vol. 9(1), p. 348.
19. Askew, *Europe and Italy's Acquisition of Libya*, p. 135.
20. Pallavicini to Aehrenthal, 14 December 1911, no. 3096, *OuA*, Vol. 3, p. 671.
21. 'Rundschau in allen Marinen', *Marine Rundschau* 3 (March 1912) p. 390; 'Die fremden

Kriegsmarinen', *Nauticus* (1912) pp. 179-80.
22. Ibid., pp. 122–7.
23. Montecuccoli to the Emperor 'Promemoria ueber die militaerisch-maritime Vorsorgen Oesterreich-Ungarn und Italien in der Adria', 12 March 1912, No. 700, *MKSM 25-1/2, 1912.*
24. Ibid.
25. Montecuccoli to the Emperor, 'Maritimen Vorsorgen in der Adria', 13 April 1912, Kriegsarchiv Militaer Kanzlei des Erzherzog Franz Ferdinand Mm/45, 1912 (hereafter MKFF).
26. Bolfras to Montecuccoli, 11 April 1912, Kriegsarchiv Operations Kanzlei, Marinesektion-VI-1/3 1912 (hereafter OK/MS).
27. 'Die fremden Kriegsmarinen', *Nauticus* (1912) p. 182.
28. Auffenberg to Archduke Francis Ferdinand, 10 May 1912, MKFF, Mo/47, 1912.
29. Walter Wagner, *Die Obersten Behoerden der K.u.K. Kriegsmarine 1856–1918* (Vienna: Druck und Verlag Ferdinand Ber, 1961), p. 87.
30. Jagow to Bethmann Hollweg, 15 March 1912, no. 11047, *GP*, Vol. 30(2), pp. 318–20; Berchtold's memorandum, 3 June 1912, no. 3551, *OuA*, Vol. 4, pp. 196-8.
31. Jenisch to Bethmann Hollweg, 28 March 1912, no. 11085, *GP*, Vol. 30(2), pp. 364-5.
32. Berchtold's report on meeting with Avarna, 13 April 1912, no. 3436, *OuA*, Vol. 4, p. 93; Berchtold to Nemes, 15 April 1912, no. 3440, ibid., p. 98.
33. W. H. Beehler, *The History of the Italo-Turkish War. September 29, 1911 to October 18, 1912* (Annapolis, MD.: The Advertiser-Republican, 1913) p. 71.
34. Berchtold to Embassy in Rome, 20 April 1912, no. 3455, *OuA*, Vol. 4, pp. 110–11; Berchtold to Embassies in Berlin, St Petersburg, London and Paris, 22 April 1912, no. 3465, ibid., pp. 119–20.
35. Grey to R. Rodd, 22 April 1912, no. 397, *BD*, Vol. 9(1), pp. 388–9; G. Lowther to Grey, 1 May 1912, no. 402, ibid., p. 391.
36. Pallavicini to Berchtold, 5 May 1912, no. 3509, no. 3510, *OuA*, Vol. 4, pp. 149–51.
37. Berchtold to Szögény, 18 May 1912, no. 3524, *OuA*, Vol. 4, pp. 163–4, Jagow to Bethmann Hollweg, 21 May 1912, no. 11116, *GP*, Vol. 30(2), pp. 400-1; Jagow to Foreign Ministry, 25 May 1912, no. 11117, ibid., p. 402; Jagow to Bethmann Hollweg, 29 May 1912, no. 11119, and 11 June 1912, no. 11123, ibid., pp. 403, 407.
38. Kiderlen-Waechter to Wangenheim, 10 October 1912, no. 11193, *GP*, Vol. 30(2), p. 475.
39. E. W. R. Lumby (ed.), *Policy and Operations in the Mediterranean 1912–14* (London: William Clowes & Sons, Ltd, 1970) p. 3.
40. Crowe to Grey, 'Memorandum on the effect of the British evacuation of the Mediterranean on questions of foreign policy', 8 May 1912, no. 386, *BD*, Vol. 10(2), pp. 586–9.
41. Kitchener to Grey, 2 June 1912, ibid., pp. 594-5; Bensen to A. Nicolson, 8 June 1912, ibid., pp. 595–6.
42. 'Liste der Kriegschiffe der groesseren Seemaechte', *Nauticus* (1912) pp. 512–13.
43. Lumby (ed.), *Policy and Operations in the Mediterranean 1912–14*, pp. 23–8.
44. Ibid., pp. 29–31.
45. Paul G. Halpern, *The Mediterranean Naval Situation (1908–1914)* (Cambridge, MA: Harvard University Press, 1970) pp. 164, 174.
46. Goschen to A. Nicolson, 11 June 1912, no. 394, *BD*, Vol. 10(2), pp. 596–7.
47. R. Rodd to Grey, 6 October 1911, no. 309, *BD*, Vol. 10(1), pp. 309-10; and 5 February 1912, no. 368, ibid., pp. 365–6.
48. Lumby (ed.), *Policy and Operations in the Mediterranean, 1912–14*, p. 21; Grey to F. Bertie, 24 May 1912, no. 391, *BD*, Vol. 10(2), p. 593; Zimmermann to Marschall, 17 July 1912, no. 11577, *GP*, Vol. 31, pp. 516–17.
49. Berchtold to Trauttmansdorff, 8 August 1912, no. 3674, *OuA*, Vol. 4, p. 324.
50. 'Protokoll des Ministerrates fuer gemeinsame Angelegenheiten', 8 July 1912, Haus-Hof und Staatsarchiv, Politische Archiv-XL-310 (hereafter HHSA) p. 423; Rudolf Kiszling, *Erzherzog Franz Ferdinand von Oesterreich-Este. Leben, Plaene und Wirken am Schicksalweg der Donaumonarchie* (Graz/Koeln: Verlag Bohlau, 1953) p. 171; Protokoll des Ministerrates fuer gemeinsame Angelegenheiten, 9 July 1912, HHSA-XL-310.
51. Ibid.
52. Berchtold to Montecuccoli, 23 July 1912, Kriegsarchiv, Praesidial Kanzlei, Marinesektion-XV-7/8, 1912 (hereafter PK/MS); Montecuccoli to Berchtold, 10 July 1912, Kriegsarchiv, Militaer Kanzlei Seiner Majestaet-25-1/5 1912 (hereafter MKSM).

53. MKFF to Montecuccoli, 17 July 1912, PK/MS-XV-7/8, 1912; Montecuccoli to the Emperor, 27 July 1912, no. 3073, PK/MS-XV-7/8 1912; Montecuccoli to the Emperor, undated, MKSM 25-1/5, 1912.
54. Montecuccoli to the Emperor, 27 July 1912, no. 3073, PK/MS-XV-7/8, 1912.
55. 'Rundschau in allen Marinen', *Marine Rundschau* 12 (December 1912) p. 1683; 'Die fremden Kriegsmarinen', *Nauticus* (1912) p. 182.
56. 'Die fremden Kriegsmarinen', *Nauticus* (1913) p. 161; Unsigned, n.d., no. 642, PK/MS-II-2/3, 1913.
57. 'Die fremden Kriegsmarinen', *Nauticus* (1913) p. 131; 'The progress of foreign navies', *Navy League Annual* (1913) p. 46.
58. 'Rundschau in allen Marinen', *Marine Rundschau* 7 (July 1912) p. 1000.
59. Szögyèny to Berchtold, 2 July 1912, no. 3600, *OuA*, Vol. 4, p. 295.
60. Grey to F. Bertie, 6 June 1912, no. 408, *BD*, Vol. 10(1), pp. 396–7.
61. George B. Manhart, *Alliance and Entente 1871–1914* (New York: F. S. Crofts, & Co., 1932) p. 54.
62. Lumby (ed.), *Policy and Operations in the Mediterranean, 1912–14*, p. 92.
63. Minutes by A. Nicolson, E. Grey, Asquith, and Churchill, 24 July 1912, no. 401, *BD*, Vol. 10(2), p. 603.
64. Lumby (ed.), *Policy and Operations in the Mediterranean, 1912–14*, p. 101.
65. Bertie to Grey, 30 July 1912, no. 404, *BD*, Vol. 10(2), pp. 605–7.
66. Grey to Bertie, 19 and 21 September 1912, no. 401 and 411, ibid., pp. 611–12.
67. Ambrozy to Berchtold, 14 September 1911, no. 3784, *OuA*, Vol. 4, p. 427; 'Rundschau in allen Marinen', *Marine Rundschau* 10 (October 1912) p. 1386.

7

The naval convention of 1913

Almost simultaneously with the start of negotiations for the renewal of the Triple Alliance in the autumn of 1912, the German General Staff initiated unofficial talks among the three partners on the subject of military co-operation. Because of the changes that took place in the aftermath of the Turco-Italian War and the concentration of the French fleet in the Mediterranean, the Germans thought the time propitious to encourage Italy and Austria-Hungary to revive the almost forgotten naval convention of 1900.

The first concrete step that eventually led to increased military and naval co-operation among the Triple Alliance partners came in October 1912 when the Chief of the German General Staff, General Helmuth von Moltke, the Younger, privately invited his Italian counterpart, Lieutenant General Alberto Pollio, to exchange ideas on co-operation between their two armies in case of war.[1] General Pollio, an uncritical admirer of Germany, accepted von Moltke's invitation enthusiastically, thereby opening the way for confidential official talks between representatives of the German and Italian General Staffs.

General Pollio sent his personal representative, Colonel Vittorio Zuppeli, to Berlin early in December. Zuppeli informed von Moltke, as Germany already suspected, that in case of war between France and Germany, Italy's need to maintain a strong troop contingent in Libya would prevent her from deploying her Third Army on the Upper Rhine as provided by the Italo-German military convention of 1888. Zuppeli tried to mollify von Moltke by telling him that the Italians would be able to tie up considerable French forces with an offensive thrust across the Franco-Italian border. Then after Italy obtained supremacy in the western Mediterranean, the Italian Army would land in Provence and advance to the Rhône valley. However, Zuppeli was non-committal when von Moltke the Younger asked whether Italy would unequivocally support Germany if war broke out.

In a letter to von Moltke on 21 December, Pollio confirmed Zuppeli's promise that Italy in the event of war with France would honour her treaty obligations with Germany by starting an offensive across the Franco-Italian north-western frontier and mobilizing her fleet. Although von Moltke had few illusions about the value of Italian promises, he was encouraged by Pollio's loyalty and his willingness to support Italy's treaty obligations to Germany. Thereafter von Moltke tried to exploit Italy's apparent willingness to co-operate militarily with Germany and Austria-Hungary.[2]

Negotiations to reach a naval agreement between Paris and London continued in the autumn of 1912. The turning point came on 30 October when the British Cabinet agreed that if either government had cause to expect an unprovoked attack by a third power or a threat to the general peace, it should immediately consult the other on how to prevent aggression and preserve peace. A week later Poincaré accepted this British statement sent to him by Ambassador Cambon.[3]

In an exchange of letters between Grey and Cambon on 22 and 23 November, the British and French governments stated that although consultations between military and naval experts were not to restrict either country's freedom of action, they would consult whenever either country felt itself in danger of unprovoked aggression by a third party and discuss measures to deter aggression and keep the peace. If the aforementioned measures involved military action, the plans of the General Staffs would be taken into consideration and the governments would then decide what effect to give to them.[4] Great Britain thereby assumed a moral obligation to come to France's aid in case of a German attack.

During January 1913 experts worked out the details of Anglo-French naval co-operation in the Channel, the Mediterranean, and the Far East. The final text of the naval convention was presented to both governments for approval on 10 February 1913. The agreement stipulated that it applied only to a war in which Great Britain was allied with France against the Triple Alliance. The North Sea was considered to be the principal theatre of operations where Great Britain was to preserve the freedom of action necessary to defeat the German fleet. She was not obliged to maintain her fleet in the Mediterranean at a predetermined strength but was free to move any ship from that area to home waters should the exigencies of war demand it. However, the British wanted to keep a fleet in the Mediterranean capable of fighting with a reasonable chance of success should the Austro-Hungarian fleet dare to leave the Adriatic.[5]

The British in fact successfully insisted on obtaining the maximum freedom of action to face the German threat in the North Sea. In other

as much other empires' naval policy as A-H

words, the British policy in the Mediterranean was to maintain the one-power standard, that is, to have a fleet strong enough to face the next strongest with the exception of the French fleet.

Von Moltke's fear that General Conrad's anti-Italian sentiment might jeopardize Italy's inclination toward military co-operation within the Triple Alliance led him to explain his views to Conrad in a letter written on 2 January 1913. Von Moltke assured Conrad that Italy would employ her entire Army and Navy on the side of her two partners in the event of war; thus the Dual Monarchy could deploy all of her available forces against Russia without fear of an Italian attack in its rear. Although Italy's Third Army would not be employed in Alsace, von Moltke denied that this was to influence German troop dispositions against Russia. In other words, Germany would not reinforce her troops along the French border by withdrawing forces deployed against Russia.

Von Moltke also informed Conrad of Italy's expressed willingness to revise the existing naval convention of the Triple Alliance. He believed that in case of a general European war, Great Britain was certain to be actively allied with France. Because the major part of the Royal Navy would remain in the North Sea, British forces in the Mediterranean would be weakened. Von Moltke (who had a low opinion of the combat effectiveness of the French fleet) thought that it would be relatively easy for a combined Austro-Italian fleet to obtain command in the Mediterranean. This would be of great value for Germany because it would prevent the transport of the French 19th Army Corps from Algeria and Morocco to metropolitan France. A successful action by a combined Austro-Italian fleet would make possible a projected Italian amphibious landing in Provence and thereby weaken French pressure on the northern frontier against Germany. Hence, the faster the decision on the western front was obtained, the sooner German troops could be transferred to the east to aid the Austro-Hungarian Army against Russia.[6]

Conrad responded that only a surprise action against the French by the combined Italian and Austro-Hungarian fleets in the Mediterranean had any chance of success and informed von Moltke that Admiral Montecuccoli agreed with him on that point. He thought that the concentration of the Italian and Austro-Hungarian fleets could best take place in the Ionian Sea. Only a few torpedo craft would be needed in the Adriatic to defend the coast. Conrad assured von Moltke that he favourably viewed the Italian initiative, although he did not know what attitude Archduke Francis Ferdinand would take.[7]

Subsequently Colonel Bardolff informed Archduke Francis

Ger. trying to orchestrate Aus-H.
naval cooperation

Ferdinand of Conrad's exchange of views with von Moltke and his position on the revision of the naval convention of 1900. Bardolff reiterated Conrad's belief that Balkan problems could not be resolved soon, that the Dual Monarchy should co-operate with Italy without sacrificing her vital interests, and that 'paper co-operation' ('*papierne liaison*') with Italy in a war at sea would justify an Austro-Hungarian decision to embark on a programme of dreadnought construction. In Conrad's view, Austro-Italian naval co-operation would cease when it was no longer in the interest of each party.[8]

By 3 January 1913 Colonel Erich Ludendorff of the German General Staff met with the Chief of the German Naval Staff, Vice-Admiral August von Heeringen, and presented a staff study on the strategic situation in the Mediterranean. Von Heeringen thought the study was over-optimistic about the position of the Triple Alliance in the area because he had little faith in Italy's ability to conduct a large-scale landing operation in Provence in case of war with France. Although Ludendorff apparently agreed with von Heeringen's criticism, he still thought the Germans had to bring the Italians and Austria-Hungarians closer together so that their fleets would co-operate in the Mediterranean.[9] General von Moltke told the Italian military attaché in Berlin on 9 January that Italy must take the initiative in reaching an agreement with Austria-Hungary concerning eventual joint action against French troop transports from North Africa.[10]

Emperor William II directed Vice-Admiral von Heeringen to meet the Austro-Hungarian naval attaché in Berlin, Commander Count Hieronymus Colloredo-Mansfeld, to encourage the Austro-Hungarians to respond favourably to a pending Italian initiative on naval co-operation in the Mediterranean. After meeting with Heeringen on 13 January, Colloredo-Mansfeld informed Montecuccoli that the Italians wanted a revision of the naval convention of 1900. The reason behind Italy's changed position in the Mediterranean was her acquisition of Libya and the considerably increased strength of the Austro-Hungarian fleet. Admiral von Heeringen thought that a revision of the naval convention was unnecessary. He believed that although the Italian and Austro-Hungarian fleets were to operate in designated zones under the terms of the convention of 1900, they had sufficient room to conduct joint operations. Von Heeringen concluded that it would be wise to wait until the Italian Admiral Staff produced a concrete proposal on the subject.[11]

Vice-Admiral von Heeringen informed Colloredo-Mansfeld that the German General Staff believed transport of the 100,000 French troops in North Africa to France must be prevented in case of a general European war. He argued that the deployment and recent manoeuvres of the French fleet showed that protection of these troop transports was to be the principal mission of the French Navy in the Mediterranean. A joint action by the Austro-Hungarian and Italian fleets was necessary to stop the transports because the British fleet would be tied up by the German fleet in the North Sea. Von Heeringen stressed that the German Naval Staff placed great importance on close co-operation among the fleets of the Triple Alliance in the Mediterranean.

Vice-Admiral von Heeringen apparently did not present conclusions or advice to the Austro-Hungarians but only offered the German Naval Staff's views on the situation in the Mediterranean. He thought that the Italian fleet based in La Spezia and the Austro-Hungarian fleet in Pola represented two detachments of a single fleet. In his view the principal strategic problem at the outbreak of war would be how to concentrate the Triple Alliance fleets in the Mediterranean so that they would not be attacked separately by superior forces. The Admiral thought that both fleets should concentrate at Messina or Tarent. Afterwards, they could operate along the North African coast in the western Mediterranean against French troop transports. This would lead the French fleet to seek a decisive battle far away from its main base at Toulon. He ruled out the possibility that the British could reinforce the French fleet in the Mediterranean.

An alternative course of action for the combined Austro-Italian fleet, in the German view, would be for the Italian fleet to remain in La Spezia, thereby tying down the major part of the French fleet in Toulon, while the Austro-Hungarian fleet swept the waters along the North African coast in search of French troop transports. However, this course of action would be risky, because the Austro-Hungarian fleet might find itself in a dangerous situation because of the lack of an adequate number of cruisers.

The German Admiral Staff regarded the destruction of French troop transports as a very important task. Von Heeringen concluded that the presence of the Austro-Hungarian fleet outside the Adriatic would signify the great political importance of that force and also be of the utmost importance for the entire European theatre.[12]

The first concrete steps the Austro-Hungarians took concerning the eventual employment of the fleet in the Mediterranean occurred in January 1913. By 18 January the Emperor directed Admiral Montecuccoli to start preliminary discussions on the question of eventual joint action with the Italian fleet in the Mediterranean.[13]

1 Emperor Franz Joseph in 1910

2 Franz Conrad von Hotzendorf

3 Archduke Francis Ferdinand

4 Admiral Anton Haus

5 *Ersatz Monarch*-class super dreadnought

6 *Viribus Unitis* dreadnought

7 *Prinz Eugen* dreadnought

8 *Radetzky*-class pre-dreadnought

9 *Erzherzog Karl*-class pre-dreadnought

10 *Habsburg*-class pre-dreadnought

11 *Sankt Georg* armoured cruiser

12 *Admiral Spaun*-class scout cruiser

13 *Saida*-class scout cruiser

14 *Tatra*-class destroyer

Thereupon Montecuccoli convened a meeting with Fleet Inspector Admiral Haus and the Commander of Port Admiralty Pola to discuss the problems associated with the eventual employment of the Austro-Hungarian fleet beyond the Adriatic. Montecuccoli informed the Emperor on 23 January that the conference had decided that the Austro-Hungarian fleet should strengthen its train with six to seven colliers with a total capacity of approximately 30,000 tons of coal, a steamer to serve as a victualling vessel, and the tanker *Vesta*. He urged the Emperor to approve the steady procurement of the required number of steamers from domestic shipping companies. Thereafter the Navy would keep ready in the Pola naval base two fully laden large colliers. In addition, one ammunition ship for use in case of mobilization was to be made available to the fleet in peacetime.[14]

All these measures were considered necessary if the Austro-Hungarian fleet was to be employed with the Italian fleet in the Mediterranean. Although Archduke Francis Ferdinand was informed of the intended measures, he chose not to become involved.[15] The Emperor approved Montecuccoli's proposal on 30 January. By the spring of 1913, the Navy actually chartered temporarily from the Austrian Lloyd company the 6,500-ton steamer *Nippon* and the 5,300-ton steamer *Francesca* from the Austro-Americana shipping company to serve as naval auxiliaries. Early in May 1913, however, both vessels were returned to their respective shipping companies.[16]

By the end of January General von Moltke sent his deputy, General Georg von Waldersee to Rome on a confidential mission. After meeting with General Pollio, von Waldersee was to visit Vienna and inform General Conrad of the results of his conversations. He was instructed to emphasize in his talks with Pollio the participation of the Italian Army in a war with France and to deal with naval matters only if the Italians brought up the subject. He was also provided with the necessary background material to deal with the question of eventual co-operation between the Triple Alliance fleets in the Mediterranean. Von Waldersee was authorized to speak for the German Admiralty Staff on these matters and that was highly unusual since the German Army rarely represented the views of the German Navy in important matters and vice versa.

Von Waldersee informed von Moltke on 29 January that General Pollio felt that in case of war the Triple Alliance fleets in the Mediterranean would have to co-operate unconditionally from the outset. In Pollio's view, it would first be necessary to beat the British fleet in the Mediterranean and then the French fleet. Another objective

119

would be to prevent France from transporting troops from North Africa, and then, under the protection of the Italian fleet, to land Italian troops in southern France.[17]

Von Waldersee found Pollio very enthusiastic about the prospects for common action by the Austro-Hungarian and Italian fleets in the Mediterranean and assured Pollio that an Italian initiative for opening talks with the Austrians on the revision of the existing naval convention would be welcomed in Berlin and in Vienna. However, Pollio informed von Waldersee that Italy could not begin direct negotiations soon due to a forthcoming change in the Chief of the Naval Staff. Pollio also held separate conversations with King Vittorio Emmanuelle III and the Italian Chief of the Navy Staff, Admiral Rocca Rey. The King approved the planned talks between Italian and Austro-Hungarian naval representatives.[18]

Von Waldersee proceeded to Vienna where he met with Conrad and Montecuccoli. He explained Italian ideas on joint fleet action in the Mediterranean and found Conrad and Montecuccoli receptive to the Italian initiative. Although Conrad had great confidence in Pollio personally, he was sceptical of Italy's real attitude. Montecuccoli also had difficulty in concealing his mistrust of the Italians.[19] Nevertheless, Conrad and Montecuccoli agreed in principle that at the outbreak of a general European war all available Austro-Hungarian warships would combine with the Italian fleet regardless of whether there was a threat of attack by the Russian fleet against the Dual Monarchy's Adriatic ports. Montecuccoli wanted to reach an arrangement with the Italians concerning the coal supply of Austro-Hungarian ships during joint actions in the Mediterranean.

Von Waldersee later informed von Moltke that Francis Joseph I and Archduke Francis Ferdinand generally agreed on the need for talks between Italian and Austro-Hungarian naval officials on joint fleet action. Nevertheless, Rome and Vienna tacitly recognized that such an arrangement would be valid only in case of a great war between the Triple Alliance and the Triple Entente. Von Waldersee remained cautious about the prospects for early Austro-Italian naval co-operation in the Mediterranean, despite the expressed willingness of both sides. He correctly perceived that latent animosities between the two partners could come into the open at any time. Anti-Austrian sentiment was deeply imbedded among the rank and file of the Italian Army. Also a large segment of Austro-Hungarian military and political leaders, as represented by Archduke Francis Ferdinand, was deeply suspicious of Italian intentions.[20]

By early February General Pollio dispatched his personal representative, Lieutenant-Colonel Carlo Montanari, to Vienna to inform Conrad that he was ready for a comprehensive exchange of views on joint fleet action in the Mediterranean; if Austria-Hungary consented to hold talks, Italy would send representatives to Vienna. Conrad was satisfied with his meeting with Montanari, for in a letter to Pollio on 4 February he expressed readiness for further talks on this subject and assured Pollio of his unconditional loyalty.[21]

The Austro-Hungarian naval attaché in Rome, Prince Johann von Liechtenstein, did not learn of the proposed naval arrangements until 6 February 1913. He was then told by the Chief of Cabinet of the Italian Navy Ministry, Count Tosti di Valminuto, that the time had come for a rapprochement between the two navies. Di Valminuto privately informed von Liechtenstein that discussions of co-operation between the Austro-Hungarian and Italian fleets in case of war were highly desirable. He also hoped that von Liechtenstein would so advise the government in Vienna. Di Valminuto remarked that if war broke out, the Triple Alliance could count on facing not only the entire French fleet but also the British Mediterranean fleet. He noted that while co-operation between the General Staffs was good, this was not the case with the commands of the Triple Alliance's fleet. Therefore, he suggested that a Navy Captain be appointed by each side to discuss wartime co-operation between the Italian and Austro-Hungarian fleets.[22]

The Austro-Hungarian military attaché in Rome, Lieutenant-Colonel Count Stanislaus Szeptycki, was sceptical of the value of closer military ties with Italy. In a report to Conrad on 10 February, Szeptycki expressed doubts about the likelihood of a naval arrangement with Italy against the French and British fleets in the Mediterranean while Italy was simultaneously seeking the consent of Germany and the Dual Monarchy to open the Straits to Russia. He warned that in case of a naval agreement between Italy and Austria-Hungary, 'we have to be very cautious not to disclose everything to the Italians which they perhaps could one day use against us'. He believed that when Italy overcame her military weaknesses, she would again become hostile to the Dual Monarchy.

In another report to Conrad on 29 February, Szeptycki suggested that Italy had renewed the Triple Alliance Treaty because she was militarily weak and needed the Austro-Hungarian support to retain control of the Aegean islands of Rhodes and Stampalia. He argued that Italy required at least six years to overcome her military and naval deficiencies, and afterwards the Dual Monarchy would no longer be able to count on her friendship. Although Szeptycki believed Austro-Italian co-operation would be essentially passive, it would nonetheless enable Austria-Hungary to fight a war with Russia without having to be overly concerned about Italy's attitude.[23]

Relations between Rome and Paris witnessed a serious deterioration in the early months of 1913, while relations between Italy and the Dual Monarchy continued to improve. In a major speech to the Chamber of Deputies on 22 February, San Giuliano praised collaboration between Rome and Vienna in the Mediterranean and asserted that Italy's acquisition of Libya had resolved the problem of the balance of power in the central Mediterranean. San Giuliano claimed that in that respect the interests of Italy and the Dual Monarchy were identical.

In a letter to the Italian ambassador in Paris on 28 February, San Giuliano revealed that there was much resentment in Italy of a recent boast in the French Parliament that the French fleet could destroy the Italian fleet in less than an hour. He argued that France's insistence that Italy turn over the Dodecanese Islands to Greece was calculated to bring about a partition of Turkey for the exclusive benefit of the Triple Entente. He also claimed that the Triple Alliance could not allow the Mediterranean to become an Anglo-French 'lake'. However, he hoped that France would recognize Italy as a great power in the Mediterranean 'while there is still time', thereby avoiding a conflict between the two countries and preparing an eventual entente between them.[24]

The bad state of Franco-Italian relations favoured those who urged closer military and naval co-operation between Italy and her Triple Alliance partners. Prince Liechtenstein informed the operations chancellery (OK/MS) on 25 February that General Pollio was preoccupied with the question of revising the naval convention and wanted the Italian Navy command to open talks as soon as possible. Von Liechtenstein also reported that close co-operation between the two navies would be popular among Italian naval officers.[25]

Montecuccoli informed Austro-Hungarian naval attachés in Rome and Berlin that although talks with the Italians on joint action in the Mediterranean would be welcome, the Italians first had to make formal proposals.[26]

General Pollio informed Conrad on 19 March that the King had agreed to send an Italian representative for talks on military co-operation among the three partners of the Triple Alliance. However, these talks could not begin until the appointment of a successor to the Chief of the Naval Staff, Admiral Rocca Rey. Pollio assured Conrad that Rey's designated successor, Admiral Paolo Thaon di Revel, agreed with the need for the proposed naval talks.[27] The long-awaited change in the Italian Chief of Staff came into effect on 1 April, thus opening the way for preliminary talks on naval co-operation among the Triple Alliance fleets in the Mediterranean.

When Prince Liechtenstein was received by Admiral di Revel on 5 April, he found him less cordial than Rey. Revel said nothing to von Liechtenstein about eventual talks on naval co-operation. This annoyed von Liechtenstein because apparently the German military and naval attachés in Rome knew more about the ongoing preliminary talks on this matter than he did.[28]

Szeptycki informed Conrad on 9 April of a meeting with Pollio in which the general explained the advantages of joint Austro-Italian fleet action in the Mediterranean. However, Szeptycki feared that in case of common action the Austro-Hungarian fleet would serve the interests of Italy and Germany, and not Austria-Hungary. He believed that a naval convention should be delayed and that in the event of war it would be better to deploy the Austro-Hungarian fleet for offensive action in the Black Sea against Russia.[29]

The OK/MS strongly disagreed with Szeptycki's views on the undesirability of a naval convention with Italy. In a letter to Conrad on 13 April, the OK/MS contended that by offering the use of naval bases for the Austro-Hungarian fleet the Italians would disclose far more secrets than the Austro-Hungarians. Nevertheless, the OK/MS stressed that there were too many unknowns that had to be clarified before any agreement with Italy could be reached.[30]

By April 1913 Archduke Francis Ferdinand still opposed naval co-operation with Italy despite efforts by Colonel Bardolff to change his views. In fact, the heir apparent instructed Conrad on 9 April to delay the beginning of naval talks for as long as possible. Berchtold, who was informed of the forthcoming talks, asked Conrad to explain Francis Ferdinand's attitude, but Conrad could not. The Archduke's opposition may have stemmed from his ignorance of the ongoing conversations among the three General Staffs, for there is very little information about them in the documents of his military chancellery.[31]

Between December 1912 and April 1913 Generals von Moltke and Pollio tried to convince the naval authorities of their countries of the need for an agreement on joint fleet action in the Mediterranean. Admiral di Revel took the first step to open preliminary official talks on the subject by sending the former head of intelligence in the Italian Naval Staff, Senior Commander Angelo Ugo Conz, to Berlin and Vienna with Italian proposals for a new naval arrangement. After Conz arrived in Berlin on 26 April he was received by the new Chief of Naval Staff, Admiral Hugo von Pohl. Conz's mission was to win German support for the Italian proposal to enhance his negotiating position in Vienna.

Admiral di Revel instructed Conz to propose that the Austro-Hungarian fleet be deployed in the western Mediterranean; that Germany deploy at least one more Army corps on the Russian frontier than was called for by the terms of the military convention of 1888; and that Italy compensate Germany by landing one or more Army corps in southern France.

During his conversations with Admiral Pohl and his representatives, Captain Paul Behncke and Commander Erich Koehler, Conz obtained their agreement to his proposed course of action. The German Naval Staff emphasized the importance of destroying French troop convoys in the early phase of a war. After command of the sea was obtained, the Germans wanted to conduct war against British shipping in the Mediterranean. Although Conz was unable to meet von Moltke, he conversed with von Waldersee, who was concerned that Italy would suffer if Great Britain cut off her coal imports in time of war. Von Waldersee thought that the Triple Alliance fleets in the Mediterranean should possess coal stocks sufficient to last at least one month under wartime conditions because of the heavy demand for the transport of troops and war matériel in the initial phase of a war.[32]

During Conz's stay in Berlin, Behncke and Koehler asked Commander Colloredo-Mansfeld to explain the Austro-Hungarian views on joint fleet action in the Mediterranean. However, because of the lack of instructions from his superiors, Colloredo-Mansfeld was unable to provide more than a general view of the subject. He informed the OK/MS on 30 April that the German Naval Staff considered joint fleet action highly desirable and wanted to deploy the Austro-Hungarian fleet outside the Adriatic. The Germans thought that it would be most suitable to concentrate the combined fleet in a southern Italian port, in which case the German squadron stationed in the Mediterranean could sail directly to the rendezvous point instead of proceeding to the Adriatic.

By the autumn of 1912 the German Navy had one 'mission ship' (*Lorelai*) permanently deployed at Constantinople; two 6,000-ton training cruisers (*Mineta, Hertha*) were in the western Mediterranean and one 1,700-ton gunboat (*Geier*) was in an Egyptian port. The outbreak of the Balkan War and fears of unrest in Turkey prompted Germany to strengthen her fleet in the Mediterranean. Her two newest and most powerful ships, the battle-cruiser *Goeben* and the light-cruiser

Breslau, were ordered to the Mediterranean on 4 November. Both ships arrived in Malta seven days later. By mid-November 1912 the *Goeben*, the *Breslau* and two training cruisers officially became part of the newly formed Mittelmeerdivision (Mediterranean Squadron) under the command of Rear-Admiral Trummler. Naval Staff planned to employ these ships jointly with the Austro-Hungarian and Italian fleets.

Colloredo-Mansfeld informed the OK/MS that the German Naval Staff believed there existed an agreement between France and Spain concerning the transport of French troops from North Africa to metropolitan France over Spanish territory. In that case the transport route would be shifted farther west and thereby make the task of the Triple Alliance fleets more difficult. At the same time it would delay the arrival of French troops at the northern front for five days.[33]

The Italian Senior Commander Conz proceeded to Vienna for talks with Admiral Haus and General Conrad. In the meantime von Waldersee asked the German military attaché in Vienna, Count Karl von Kageneck, to use his influence with Conrad to make him co-operate with Conz. He also urged Kageneck to make clear to Conrad the great importance von Moltke attached to an arrangement on joint fleet action in the Mediterranean.[34]

Conz met with Admiral Haus on 5 May and outlined the Italian plan for naval co-operation in the Mediterranean. He urged quick acceptance of the plan so that the talks could begin soon. However, Admiral Haus was reluctant to discuss the Italian plan because the political situation in the Balkans remained unresolved. He noted that the question of deploying the Austro-Hungarian fleet outside the Adriatic could be decided only by General Conrad with the consent of the Emperor and Archduke Francis Ferdinand. After Conz assured Haus that he was authorized to present Italian proposals in detail, Haus agreed that Conz should attend the meeting of high-ranking Austro-Hungarian naval officers on the following day. Although Haus and his colleagues were pleased by Conz's presentation of his views, the admiral suggested that Archduke Francis Ferdinand still had to be persuaded.[35]

General Conrad met with Conz on 6 May. He reported that the Italians wanted close co-operation between the two Triple Alliance fleets because of the Italian fleet's superiority in relation to the French Navy. The Italian naval leaders believed that the primary task of the French fleet was to operate in the Ligurian Sea and support amphibious landings near Genoa to divert Italian troops from France's north-west border. Conz presented the Italian proposal to concentrate the Triple Alliance fleets at Messina and then sail to the Bonifacio Straits to seek a decisive battle with the French fleet. The rest of the Italian fleet, based in Tarent, would be employed to protect the Adriatic, while the remainder of the Austro-Hungarian fleet would be concentrated in the Gulf of Cattaro. If the proposed course of action was acceptable to Austro-Hungarians, Conz assured Conrad, Italy would prepare reserves of fuel and food in the operational zone and start to establish a torpedo station in Trapani (Sicily) and an advanced naval base in La Maddalena (Sardinia).

The Italians thought the British fleet in the Mediterranean was roughly equal in strength to the Austro-Hungarian fleet. Conz doubted whether the Russian fleet could reach Corfú before the tenth day of mobilization, that is, after the decisive encounter with the French fleet was to take place. He told Conrad that the German objective of destroying French troop transports from North Africa could be achieved only after the French fleet was paralysed.[36]

Conrad described the views of the Austro-Hungarian General Staff on naval co-operation by the Triple Alliance in the Mediterranean in a report probably drafted on 6 May. He foresaw that the entire Italian and Austro-Hungarian battle fleets and the German *Mittelmeerdivision* would concentrate off Messina, from where they would seek a decisive battle and attack the French or Franco-British fleet. Afterwards, the combined fleet would prevent the arrival of French troop transports from North Africa. The problem of the supreme command could be resolved in two ways. If the Austro-Hungarian and Italian fleets in the operational zone were of approximately equal strength, the overall command would go to the senior ranking flag officer of either Navy. However, if one fleet was superior to the other by a ratio of 1.5 to 1.0, the former would appoint the supreme commander of the combined fleet. The Chief of the General Staff envisaged the concentration of the rest of the Italian and Austro-Hungarian fleets in Brindisi to protect the Adriatic. Only after the combined fleet obtained command of the sea would naval forces be deployed in the Adriatic to convoy Italian troop transports to southern France. The Italian Navy would take responsibility for logistical support of the combined Triple Alliance fleets.[37]

Conrad submitted a proposal for revising the naval convention of 1900 to the Emperor on 9 May, and Francis Joseph I promptly approved the measure.[38] Curiously, Francis Ferdinand was then in the province of Styria, raising suspicions that he was intentionally bypassed by Conrad and Haus in the preliminary talks with the Italians on naval co-operation.[39] Conrad's audience with the Emperor was originally scheduled for 8 May but was postponed a day to coincide with Francis Ferdinand's departure from Vienna. Admiral Haus did not inform the MKFF of the details of his talks with Senior Commander Conz until 9 May. Nevertheless, it appears unlikely that Francis Ferdinand was unaware of Conz's mission before he left for Styria. He probably deliberately chose not to be closely involved in any negotiations with the Italians on a new naval agreement.

Admiral Haus's report to the MKFF on his conversations with Senior Commander Conz provided more details on the Italian proposal for naval co-operation among the Triple Alliance fleets. Haus explained that the Italians envisaged that joint action would be required in the Mediterranean either against the French fleet alone or against the French and British fleets. In the former case the allied fleets were to concentrate as soon as possible in the sea area off Augusta, Messina, and Tarent, preferably before the outbreak of war. The Italians promised to prepare these three naval bases so that a combined Austro-Italian-German fleet could start offensive action against the French fleet to obtain command of the sea and destroy French troop transports sailing from North Africa. Afterwards, the combined fleet was to support the landing of about 100,000 Italian troops in southern France.

In case of war against France and Great Britain, the fleets of the Triple Alliance were also to concentrate in Sicilian waters to prevent the union of the British and French fleets. If the combined fleet was unable to prevent that, it was then to use La Maddalena and La Spezia as bases for attacks on French troop transports and the southern French coast. In the Italian view the principal task of the Triple Alliance fleets was either to prevent the arrival of 100,000 fresh French troops in Europe or to threaten the coast of southern France. In either case enough French troops would be diverted from the Franco-German front to allow Germany to deploy more troops against Russia in support of the Austro-Hungarian army on the eastern front. If war broke out with France alone or with France and Great Britain, the Adriatic would be defended by older Italian and Austro-Hungarian warships.[40]

Admiral Haus observed that Conz's proposals were based on sound strategic principles and had the full approval of leading German military authorities. He informed Archduke Francis Ferdinand that as soon as a naval agreement was accepted in principle, the Germans promised to deploy in the Mediterranean several fast modern scout-cruisers in addition to one battle-cruiser (*Goeben*) already deployed in the area. The Germans also planned to use a large number of merchant vessels as naval auxiliaries in case of war. However, Italy had to take responsibility for storing sufficient reserves of coal and food in advanced bases in Augusta and La Maddalena as well as fuel in the oil depots at Cagliari and Trapani. Augusta was foreseen primarily as a naval base for support of the Austro-Hungarian fleet.

Admiral Haus also informed Francis Ferdinand that details of the proposed naval co-operation, such as plans for various scenarios, norms for joint manoeuvring, signals, use of wireless telegraphy, and supplies of coal and fuel, would be worked out by a special commission composed of representatives of all three navies that was to meet in Vienna by the end of May.

Conrad informed Francis Ferdinand on 10 May that the Italians thought that the new naval convention would be in effect only if the Triple Alliance was to fight a war against the Triple Entente. Then one of the main aims was to defeat the French Mediterranean fleet as quickly as possible before the Russian Black Sea fleet could intervene in time. The Adriatic was to be secured through a decision obtained in the main theatre of operations.[41]

Archduke Francis Ferdinand approved in principle a new naval convention. However, he directed Admiral Haus to instruct the Austro-Hungarian officers involved in the forthcoming talks to be careful not to divulge secrets when dealing with their Italian counterparts.[42]

Because the OK/MS was slow to present proposals for the conversations scheduled for the end of May, Bardolff proposed that the instructions for the Austro-Hungarian delegates at the conference be submitted first to the MKFF. Archduke Francis Ferdinand remarked sarcastically that the secretive OK/MS should 'not treat me as a distinguished foreigner'.[43]

The Navy Section selected Captain Alfred Cicoli (the future Chief of the OK/MS) to be its delegate at the conference on the proposed new naval convention. Captain Cicoli received instructions from the OK/MS on 24 May that were to serve as the basis for the forthcoming conference. The naval convention of 1900 was to remain essentially unchanged. However, the proposed operational plan for the deployment of the Triple Alliance fleets approved by the Emperor was to be added as a separate protocol to the existing naval agreement. The Italians were to be given the initiative in all other matters at the conference.[44] Cicoli was to secure the revision of the common signal book drawn up in 1900 but to keep secret the details of Austro-Hungarian wireless signalling. At the same time he was directed to learn anything he could about Italian methods of wireless telegraphy. The OK/MS was concerned that if it had to draw up a new signal book it

[margin handwritten note: mistrust]

might unwittingly disclose details of Austro-Hungarian signal procedures and manoeuvring norms. Therefore it wanted this task to be assigned to the Italians and Germans.[45]

Admiral Haus personally informed the Emperor of the outlines of the proposed revision of the naval convention. He contended that the aim was not to conclude a new naval agreement but to amend several articles of the 1900 naval convention. Among other things these revisions included: enlargement of the Italian zone of operations; deployment of German naval forces in the Mediterranean; rapid concentration of the Austro-Hungarian and Italian fleets and the German *Mittelmeerdivision* in the Messina-Catania area; and co-ordination of the offensive aims of the combined fleet to defeat the French fleet quickly and the British fleet eventually (see Map 2). Haus also informed the Emperor that the warships stationed in Constantinople or deployed in the Levant should be directed to act as the situation dictated in the event of war. A separate agreement had to be concluded to provide for the attachment of Austro-Hungarian warships deployed in East Asia to the German cruiser squadron in East Asian waters.[46]

Before the opening of the conference in Vienna the Italians and Austro-Hungarians considered the question of supreme command over the combined fleet as one of the most important problems to be resolved. Both sides realized that this issue could frustrate all efforts to achieve naval co-operation in the Mediterranean. Although Italy could claim that the supreme command should be hers because she was making a larger contribution to the combined fleet, Austria-Hungary could counter that she was making a greater sacrifice for the Triple Alliance by deploying her fleet far away from her shores. The only benefit the Dual Monarchy could expect was increased German support on land against Russia, and this was contingent on a successful action against the French fleet. At the same time Admiral Haus (who was a four-star admiral) could not be subordinate to an Italian Commander in Chief who was only a two-star admiral. Admiral di Revel thought it would be a good idea to entrust Haus with the supreme command if in the future the Italians had a four-star admiral to command the fleet. Di Revel hoped that by making such a concession to Austro-Hungarians the Italians would extract greater concessions from her during the conference.[47]

The conference on revising the naval convention of 1900 formally started at the OK/MS in Vienna on 3 June. The German Naval Staff was represented by Commander Koehler and Lieutenant Commander Alfred Saalwaechter; the Austro-Hungarian and Italian navies by Captain

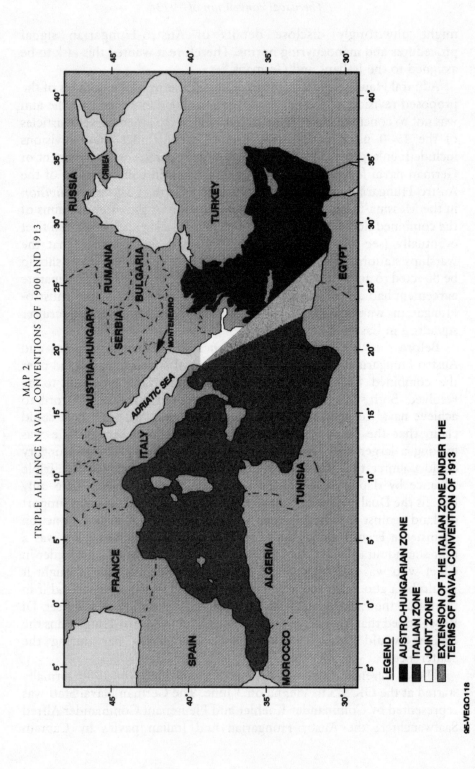

MAP 2
TRIPLE ALLIANCE NAVAL CONVENTIONS OF 1900 AND 1913

LEGEND

AUSTRO-HUNGARIAN ZONE

ITALIAN ZONE

JOINT ZONE

EXTENSION OF THE ITALIAN ZONE UNDER THE
TERMS OF NAVAL CONVENTION OF 1913

95-VEGO118

Cicoli and Senior Commander Conz, respectively. The Deputy Chief of the Navy Section, Rear-Admiral Karl Kailer von Kaltenfels, presided over the first session of the conference. He proposed that the supreme command of the Triple Alliance fleets in the Mediterranean be given to Italian Vice-Admiral Luigi de Savoia, Duke Abruzzi, who enjoyed high prestige in Viennese court circles. Abruzzi's candidacy had in fact been advocated by Haus at a meeting with Conz on 2 June. For reasons that are not clear, Conz opposed the Duke's appointment. Faced with the choice of accepting the Austro-Hungarian proposal or retaining the old arrangement of separate zones of operations, Conz saw no other alternative but to press for the appointment of Admiral Haus as supreme commander. Conz won the support of the Austro-Hungarian and German representatives and Haus was formally appointed supreme commander of the Triple Alliance fleets in the Mediterranean on 9 June.

With the thorniest question resolved, the conference settled into a routine. For most of the remaining 12 sessions Conz was first asked to present the Italian viewpoint on specific questions and then these views were largely accepted by the delegates. In this way the Austro-Hungarians made sure Italians took the initiative. Moreover, Captain Cicoli persuaded the German representatives to draw up a joint signal book, thus fulfilling the directive of the OK/MS.

The OK/MS informed Archduke Francis Ferdinand that the appointment of Admiral Haus as supreme commander of the allied fleet was an undoubted success for the Dual Monarchy. Reflecting its distrust of Italy, the OK/MS pointed out that no concrete plans by the Dual Monarchy had been divulged and that the agreement took full account of Austro-Hungarian interests.[48]

The conference in Vienna ended on 23 June with the signing of a revised naval agreement, approved by the Emperor on 29 June.

After the naval agreement was sent to all three sovereigns for their approval late in June, Admiral di Revel told Rear-Admiral Kaltenfels that some revisions were necessary. Although amendments aimed at enhancing the secrecy of the agreement were made without difficulty, Admiral von Pohl opposed minor verbal changes lest they delay the completion of the agreement.[49] Nevertheless, he felt the supplementary agreement should explicitly mention the British as well as the French fleet. He also proposed that action against the French fleet operating east of Toulon be taken by light forces for local defence of the coast based in Vado.[50]

The proposed changes by Admiral di Revel were formally accepted on 2 August. Thereby, the agreement on naval co-operation in the

Mediterranean among the Triple Alliance fleets in the event of war against France of the Triple Entente was in effect.

NOTES

1. Wolfgang Foerster, 'Die deutsch-italienische Militaerkonvention', *Die Kriegsschuldfrage. Berliner Monatshefte fuer Internationale Aufklaerung* (Berlin) 5 (May 1927) p. 398.
2. Ibid., pp. 398–9.
3. E. W. R. Lumby (ed.), *Policy and Operations in the Mediterranean 1912–14* (London: William Clowes & Sons, Ltd, 1970) p. 104.
4. Grey to Bertie, 30 October, 7 November, 21 November, nos. 413, 414, and Grey to Paul Cambon, 24 November 1912, *British Documents on the Origins of the War 1898–1914*, ed. G. P. Gooch and Harold Temperley, 11 vols (London: HMSO, 1926-38) (hereafter *BD*) Vol. 10(2), pp. 416, 612–15.
5. Lumby (ed.), *Policy and Operations in the Mediterranean 1912–14*, pp. 111–12.
6. Moltke to Conrad, 2 January 1913, *Kriegsarchiv, Generalstab Operationsbüro*, File F89a (hereafter GS/OpB).
7. Conrad to Moltke, 9 January 1913, no. 120, exp. 101, ibid.
8. Bardolff to Francis Ferdinand, 9 January 1913, no. 100, *Kriegsarchiv Militaer Kanzlei des Erzherzog Franz Ferdinand Mb/11-240*, 1912 (hereafter MKFF).
9. Paul G. Halpern, *The Mediterranean Naval Situation (1908-1914)* (Cambridge MA: Harvard University Press, 1970) p. 230.
10. Foerster, 'Die deutsch-italienische Militaerkonvention', pp. 400–1.
11. Colloredo-Mansfeld to Montecuccoli, 'Unterredung mit Chef des Admiralstabes', 11 January 1913, Kriegsarchiv Operations Kanzlei, Marinesektion-I Sonderreihe BV, 1913–15 (hereafter OK/MS). Also in GS/OpB, F89a, 18 January 1913; Kriegsarchiv, Militaer Kanzlei Seiner Majestaet-20-2/1, 1913 (hereafter MKSM); and *Oesterreich-Ungarns Aussenpolitik von der Bosnischen Krise 1908 bis zum Kriegsausbruch 1914. Diplomatische Aktenstuecke des Oesterreichisch-Ungarischen Ministeriums des Aeussern*, ed. Ludwig Bittner, Alfred Francis Pribram, Heinrich Srbik, and Hans Uebersberger, 9 vols (Vienna: Oesterreichischer Bundesverlag fuer Unterricht, Wissenschaft und Kunst, 1930) (hereafter *OuA*) Vol. 5, no. 5333, pp. 418–20.
12. Ibid.
13. Bolfras to Montecuccoli, 18 January 1913, no. 5468, Beilage I, *OuA*, Vol. 5, p. 504.
14. Montecuccoli to MKSM, 23 January 1913, MKSM 20-2-1-2, 1913 and also no. 367, OK/MS-IX-9/3, 1913.
15. Marginal note of Archduke Francis Ferdinand on Bardolff's report of 25 January 1913, MKFF 41-23, 1913; Bolfras to Montecuccoli, 30 January 1913, OK/MS-IX-9/3, 1913.
16. Haus to MKSM, 8 May 1913, OK/MS-IX-9/3, 1913 and Bolfras to Montecuccoli, 9 May 1913, ibid.
17. Graf Waldersee, 'Von Deutschlands militaer-politischen Beziehungen zu Italien', *Berliner Monatshefte* (formerly *Kriegschuldfrage*) 7 (July 1929) pp. 642–3.
18. Ibid., p. 649.
19. Franz Conrad von Hoetzendorf, *Aus meiner Dienstzeit 1908–1918*, 5 vols (Vienna: Rikola Verlag, 1922-25) Vol. 3, pp. 86–8, 92, 153.
20. Waldersee, 'Von Deutschlands militaer-politischen Beziehungen zu Italien', p. 648.
21. Conrad, *Aus meiner Dienstzeit*, Vol. 3, pp. 89f, 91f.
22. Prince Liechtenstein to OK/MS, 6 February 1913, MKFF 41-25/1-7, 1913.
23. Unsigned, 10 February 1913, *Kriegsarchiv, Conrad Archiv F B3*.
24. Gianluco André, *L'Italia e il Mediterraneo alla Vigilia della Prima Guerra Mondiale, Tentativi di Intesa Mediterranea (1911–1914)* (Milan: A Giuffré, 1967) pp. 155–7.
25. 'Einsicht der OK/MS', 2 March 1913, OK/MS-999.
26. Montecuccoli to naval attachés in Rome and Berlin, 24 February 1913, OK/MS-2/GV, 1913. Also report by Colonel Bardolff, 15 February 1913, MKFF 41-25/3, 1913.
27. Unsigned, n.d., GS/OpB F89a.
28. Prince Liechtenstein to OK/MS, 6 April 1913, OK/MS-2/GV, 1913–15.
29. Szepticky's report, 9 April 1913, no. 112, Evb, no. 1819, Generalstab Evidenzbüro, FS539.

Also ibid., 29 March 1913, no. 6366, *OuA*, Vol. 5, p. 1100.
30. 'Marineabmachung mit Italien', 14 April 1913, OK/MS-I-1/7, 1913. Also OK/MS to Conrad, 13 April 1913, no. 6609, *OuA*, Vol. 6, p. 141.
31. Conrad, *Aus meiner Dienstzeit*, Vol. 3, p. 289; Horst Brettner-Messler, 'Die militaerischen Absprachen zwischen den Generalstaeben Oesterreich-Ungarn und Italien vom Dezember 1912 bis Juni 1914', *Mitteilungen des Oesterreichischen Staatsarchiv*, Vol. 23, 1971, p. 235.
32. Halpern, *The Mediterranean Naval Situation*, p. 244.
33. Colloredo-Mansfeld to OK/MS, 'Kooperation d. Dreibundflotte', 30 April 1913, no. 209, OK/MS-IX-9/3, 1913.
34. Waldersee, 'Von Deutschlands militaer-politischen Beziehungen zu Italien', pp. 650–1.
35. Halpern, *The Mediterranean Naval Situation*, pp. 244–5.
36. 'Conz ueber Marinekonvention', 6 May 1913, GS/OpB F89a.
37. Conrad, 'Ueber Neufassung der Marinekonvention, May 1913', GS/OpB F89a.
38. Conrad to Haus, 10 May 1913, OK/MS-6/GV, 1913-15.
39. Halpern, *The Mediterranean Naval Situation*, p. 246.
40. Haus to MKFF, 'Marineabkommen', 9 May 1913, MKFF 41-25/6, 1913.
41. Conrad to Francis Ferdinand, 'Ueber Marineabkommen', 10 May 1913, MKFF 41-25/6, 1913.
42. Bardolff's report, 'Hoechste Bemerkung Seiner Kaiserlichen Hohheit', 10 May 1913, MKFF 41-25/6, 1913.
43. Minute by Francis Ferdinand, 17 May 1913, MKFF 41-25/6, 1913.
44. Conrad, 'Ueber Neufassung der Marinekonvention', 24 May 1913, GS/OpB F89a.
45. 'Referat zur Revision und Ergaenzung des Marineuebereinkommen vom Jahre 1900', Beilage 20, n.d., no. 2452, 1913, MKFF 41/25/6, 1913.
46. 'Untertaenigste Referat ueber das demnaechst zur Verhandlung gelangende Marine-Uebereinkommen zwischen der Monarchie und Italien', n.d., no. 4196, 1913, ibid.
47. Gabriele Mariano, *Le Convenzione Navali della Triplece* (Rome: Ufficio Storico della Marina Militare, 1969) p. 380.
48. Unsigned, 30 June 1913, no. 5496, OK/MS-1/GV, 1913.
49. Di Revel to Kailer, 'Modifiche che si Propongono al Costo in Progetto della Convenzione Navale e del suo Allegato 15 Luglio 1913', 2 July 1913, OK/GV-1913-15, Sonderreihe.
50. Koehler to Cicoli, 'Marinekooperation im Dreibund', 11 July 1913, ibid.

8

The Balkan Wars and the Adriatic 1912–13

While the Turco-Italian War and the rapidly changing balance of power in the Mediterranean preoccupied European diplomats, there was a steady increase in tensions in the Balkans. Italy's humiliation of Turkey led to the establishment, with Russian support, of the Balkan League: an alliance of Serbia, Bulgaria, Greece and Montenegro.

After 1909 Serbia realized that she could not challenge the Austro-Hungarian hold on Bosnia. Therefore, she turned her attention to Macedonia where she faced a much weakened Turkey. To make the situation more complicated, Bulgaria had rather extensive claims in Macedonia. After protracted negotiations Serbia and Bulgaria concluded a treaty of alliance in March 1912 ostensibly directed against Turkey. However, the real purpose of the Serbian–Bulgarian alliance was revealed in the text of the military convention. The latter stipulated that the alliance would come into play in the event of an attack by Rumania or Turkey on either country, an attack by the Dual Monarchy on Serbia, or an invasion by Austria-Hungary of the Sanjak of Novibazar without Turkey's consent.[1]

The treaty was signed with the active encouragement of Russia. Foreign Minister Sazonov hoped that the Serbian–Bulgarian alliance would offset the Dual Monarchy's influence in the Balkans. Serbia and Bulgaria agreed to partition Macedonia and to have the Tsar draw the boundary line for a contested zone of that province. There was no mention in the treaty of Albania or the Turkish-held territory toward Salonika.

Athens believed that the liberation of Crete could best be accomplished by military action in Macedonia in concert with Serbia and Bulgaria. Additionally and because of Bulgaria's extensive claims in Macedonia, Greece wanted to be a party to such a partition. Hence, by May 1912, Greece and Bulgaria signed a separate treaty.

Vienna's policy toward the Balkans

After the Bosnian crisis, Vienna's policy toward Turkey was essentially

134

to let events take their course in case the expected dissolution of the Turkish Empire occurred. However, Count Aehrenthal believed the Dual Monarchy had to have some say in the ultimate disposition of the Turkish dominions. His successor Count Berchtold had scant idea of the anti-Austrian content of the agreements among the members of the Balkan League. However, he continued the policy of non-intervention because anything else would antagonize Bulgaria, on whom Vienna relied as a potential ally against Serbia. This policy was based on the (accurate) belief that the Balkan allies would sooner or later come to blows over the spoils.

By the summer of 1912, relations between Turkey and the small Balkan states had deteriorated to such an extent that Count Berchtold tried to stave off an impending explosion by urging the great European powers to persuade Turkey to avoid anything that might endanger peace in the Balkans.[2]

Montenegro was the last state to join the Balkan League, reaching an oral agreement with Bulgaria on 6 October 1912. The most difficult agreement to be reached was that between Serbia and Montenegro because of the prevailing hostility between their ruling houses. The Serbian–Montenegrin alliance of 24 October was directed against both Turkey and the Dual Monarchy and completed the Balkan League.

Outbreak of the First Balkan War

Before the last agreement among the small Balkan states was signed, Montenegro opened hostilities against Turkey on 8 October 1912. Within ten days all the other members of the Balkan League followed suit. It soon became obvious that Turkish troops were no match for their opponents. The Bulgarians inflicted a severe defeat upon the Turks, but failed to penetrate the Turkish defences at Chataldja, where they suffered heavy casualties. The Serbs won great victories over the Turks in Macedonia. The Montenegrins laid siege to Scutari and with the Serbs occupied the Sanjak of Novibazar (which Austria-Hungary had evacuated in 1909). However, their advance against Scutari was very slow and the city did not surrender as was widely expected.

The Greeks entered Salonika on 8 November. Two days later the Serbs reached Allesio on the Albanian coast, where nationalists in Valona proclaimed the independence of their country on 30 November. That very day Serbian troops seized the port of Durazzo and later occupied San Giovanni di Medua. By then the Turks were defeated on all fronts. The Balkan allies captured all the territory they laid claim to with the exception of the fortresses at Adrianople, Janina, and Scutari.

Special naval credit requested

Shortly before war broke out in the Balkans, Foreign Minister Berchtold convinced the common Ministerial Council on 14 September to give the Navy Commander another opportunity to present a revised budget for 1913. Admiral Montecuccoli presented on 3 October a programme calling for approval of a three-year supplementary special credit of 170 million crowns for the construction of two 24,500-ton dreadnoughts (to replace two *Monarch*-class battleships), six submarines, six high seas torpedo craft, two Danube monitors, two river patrol craft, one 40,000-ton floating dock, as well as supplementary funds for naval aviation.[3] Montecuccoli's request appeared excessive even to the Austrian members of the council, who had previously been in favour of his proposals. Therefore, the Austrian President Count Karl Stuergkh asked for more time to discuss the question with his colleagues.[4] The council hesitated to approve Montecuccoli's request because the Army (due to the tensions in the Balkans) had requested even larger supplementary expenditures than the Navy.

At a session of the Ministerial Council on 8 October, the Hungarian members strongly opposed Montecuccoli's plan for a supplementary credit. They wanted no large appropriations for the Navy at that time because of the government's past declarations and the chaotic financial situation in Hungary. The Hungarian ministers argued that the funds requested for dreadnoughts and a floating dock would be approved only after the four dreadnoughts under construction were paid for. Yet, they favoured the approval of the funds for the remaining part of Montecuccoli's programme.

The Austrian ministers in the council supported Montecuccoli's proposal but wanted a slight reduction in funds (but not in the number of ships) and a longer payment schedule. Although Count Berchtold strongly supported the Navy, the Hungarian ministers held firm to their position. Moreover, the members of the Hungarian Delegation passed a resolution aimed at prohibiting the Army and Navy from assuming even preliminary financial obligations without the prior consent of the Austrian and Hungarian governments.[5]

In the end, the common Ministerial Council approved a total of 205 million crowns in supplementary expenditures (*Ruestungkredit*) to modernize the Army and to build more ships for the Navy. In view of the situation in the Balkans, the Foreign Minister, the common Finance

Minister, and the Navy Commander assured the Delegations that these funds would not be regarded as a mobilization credit. The Austrian Finance Minister justified the *Ruestungkredit* by arguing that the Dual Monarchy had to be in a position to affect the final outcome of the hostilities in the Balkans.[6]

The Navy's share of the *Ruestungkredit* amounted to about 26 million crowns (to be spent in two annual instalments of 13 million crowns each starting in 1913), which was to be a supplement to the 312.4 million crowns special credit approved in 1911. These funds were intended for the construction of six submarines, six 250-ton high seas torpedo craft, two Danube monitors, two river patrol craft, one 40,000-ton floating dock, and for the establishment of naval aviation.[7]

The common Ministerial Council also decided that construction on the dreadnoughts funded in the 1911–15 programme should be speeded up. Therefore, the 54 million crowns appropriated for 1915 and 1916 could be made available in 1913 and 1914, and that was to make it possible to start construction on a second dreadnought squadron as early as 1915. Finance Minister Biliński assured the Navy Commander that approval of funds for 'construction of an additional four dreadnoughts in 1915' appeared secure. However, because of Hungarian opposition in the common Ministerial Council Montecuccoli failed to win approval of funds for timely replacement of the *Monarch*-class battleships. That in effect meant a delay of one to two years in the completion of the second dreadnought squadron. Montecuccoli realized that he alone could not move the common Ministerial Council to change its decision and therefore sought support from Archduke Francis Ferdinand.[8]

The Navy Commander also pressed anew the MKFF to approve his proposal to establish a large naval base in central Dalmatia. Montecuccoli argued that Sebenico was preferable to Spalato because of the impending establishment of a naval district command there in place of the existing coastal defence district, and noted that Sebenico already had many of the necessary naval facilities and that a part of the *Monarch*-class squadron was permanently deployed there. Spalato lacked the main prerequisites for a large naval base because its harbour was barely adequate for merchant ship traffic.[9] Moreover, political conditions in Spalato (where some protest demonstrations were held in the autumn of 1912) were no better than those in Sebenico. Consequently, Sebenico was selected as the site for a future main naval base in central Dalmatia.

Consideration was also given to a plan to build a new advanced naval base at Neum-Klek. General Conrad did not seriously consider the possibility of a large-scale Italian landing on the Austro-Hungarian coast. However, he thought Italy might carry out raids between the Narenta River estuary and Neum-Klek. Therefore, he wanted Neum and its small port to be fortified and fitted with a few coastal batteries. In addition, a number of coastal torpedo craft were to supplement the seafront defences in that part of the coast.

Although Admiral Montecuccoli essentially agreed with Conrad's proposal, he maintained that the employment of torpedo craft could be considered only if a sea-level canal was built at Stagno (at the boot of Sabbioncello Peninsula). The project to fortify Neum-Klek and build the Stagno Canal never got past the planning stage prior to the outbreak of war in 1914.[10]

The question of Serbia's access to the sea

The speedy approval of the *Ruestungkredit* was only one among many signs of the grave crisis in the Balkans that threatened to involve the Dual Monarchy in the hostilities. After the outbreak of the Balkan War, Vienna chose not to reoccupy the Sanjak of Novibazar thereby preventing Serbia and Montenegro from having a common border. Vienna at the same time was quite unwilling to tolerate the establishment of another power on the eastern shore of the Adriatic and Ionian Seas.[11] When Russian Foreign Minister Sazonov asked the Austro-Hungarian ambassador in St Petersburg on 3 October what was the view of his government on the question of a Serbian port in the Adriatic, Sazonov was told that the enlargement of the Serbian territory in itself would have no special importance but that the Dual Monarchy would not tolerate a threat to her access to Salonika and therefore could not accept Serbia's extension to the sea.[12]

By early November 1912, the question of Serbia's access to the sea became acute after Serbian troops threatened to reach the Albanian coast. Vienna proposed on 4 November to the powers that Albania be established as an independent state and that Serbia not be allowed to obtain access to the Adriatic. Thus Austria-Hungary raised two questions that were to preoccupy European diplomacy for many months to come.

Officially Vienna's objections to a Serbian port in Albania were that the Albanians wanted to be self-governing and there was no Serbian population living in Albania; that Serbia was incapable of governing Albania; she was entirely under Russia's influence; and that Serbia did not need a port on the Adriatic because she could find an outlet to the sea by way of Salonika or another Aegean port.[13] However, the most important reason for Vienna's refusal to make concessions on any issue to Belgrade was that the Dual Monarchy did not want any change in the balance of power in the Adriatic. The Viennese government feared that a Serbian port would develop into a Russian advance base that might enable Russia to encircle the Dual Monarchy from the south. Austria-Hungary also feared that Serbian access to the Adriatic would lead to close economic and military co-operation between Serbia and Italy. For example, Archduke Francis Ferdinand opposed a Serbian port in the Adriatic for just that reason.[14]

General Conrad, in a memorandum written on 16 November, stated that it was in the interest of the Dual Monarchy to exclude any other power from the Albanian coast as far south as Valona. He thought formal neutralization of that area would be an inadequate guarantee for the Austro-Hungarian strategic interests and therefore the Dual Monarchy had to obtain a foothold in Albania. Only Austro-Hungarian warships should have the right of permanent stay in Albanian ports, and policing duties in Albanian ports should be solely Austria-Hungary's responsibility. Conrad argued that the use of the port of Valona as a base for a foreign fleet would make the Adriatic a *'mare clausum'* ('closed sea') and thereby endanger the Austro-Hungarian Navy. However, as a base, Valona would safeguard the Austro-Hungarian fleet's freedom of action and greatly enhance the defence of the Adriatic. He considered it necessary to secure the Albanian ports and hinterland and to ensure the absolute exclusion of Italy from that area. However, Conrad urged that Austria-Hungary agree to allow a Serbian commercial port in the Adriatic, much as she had allowed the port of Antivari to be used by Montenegro.[15]

Italy for her part also opposed Serbian access to the Adriatic because of her concern that if Serbs occupied part of Albania's coast the Russian fleet might soon appear and use a Serbian port in the Adriatic. Therefore Italy wanted an autonomous Albania to constitute a counterweight to the possible spread of Slav influence. Rome also feared that if Serbia obtained a strip of Albanian territory to acquire an outlet to the sea, the Dual Monarchy might some day gain another part of Albania to the detriment of Italy's interests there.[16]

Russia tried to modify Vienna's policy, arguing that its opposition to Serbian aspirations would only increase Serbian hatred of Austria-Hungary. The Belgrade government protested in November 1912 to Berlin regarding Vienna's opposition to a Serbian port in the Adriatic.

There was much nervousness in European capitals at that time as to whether the Dual Monarchy would take military measures to force the Serbs to withdraw their troops from the Adriatic coast.

Like Serbia, Greece also had territorial designs on Albania. Greek naval vessels appeared off the Bay of Valona on 1 and 14 December and occupied the island of Saseno (Sazan) guarding the Bay. The Greek government then laid claim to Saseno as belonging to the Greek-held Ionian Islands. Greek troops entered the port of Santi Quaranta south of Valona on 8 December and Greek warships patrolling the Albanian coast harassed Austro-Hungarian merchant vessels.

Austria-Hungary orders mobilization

By the end of November, the question of Serbian access to the sea was overshadowed by the so-called 'consular affair' concerning the alleged mistreatment of the Austro-Hungarian consul in Prisrena by Serbian troops. The situation was further complicated by the mobilization of troops in two Russian military border districts. The Dual Monarchy ordered mobilization on 13 November of its Army corps in Sarajevo, Ragusa, Agram, and Timişoara, a total of about 300,000 men. Moreover, both the fleet and the Danube flotilla were fully mobilized.

The major part of the *Active Eskadre* was in the Aegean when war broke out in the Balkans. The Navy Section immediately ordered the armoured cruiser *K.u.K. Maria Theresia* to sail into the northern Aegean and await further orders. However, General Conrad disagreed with Admiral Montecuccoli's deployment of the *Active Eskadre*. He tried to convince Montecuccoli on 22 November of the need to recall the *Active Eskadre* but only succeeded in persuading the Navy Commander to order the *Active Eskadre* to concentrate. Thereafter the Navy Section ordered the scout-cruisers *Aspern* and *Admiral Spaun* at Constantinople to join the fleet. They were to be replaced by the torpedo depot ship *Gaea*. Simultaneously, the Emperor ordered a mobilization of the Third and Fourth Battle Squadron and other ships then not in commission were made ready for active service. This meant that these ships were to embark with all fuel, food, and ammunition and 25 per cent of their crews. The Emperor also ordered the call-up of some reservists from the class of 1907.[17]

By the end of November, the Austro-Hungarian Navy had in combat readiness seven battleships, six cruisers, eight destroyers, 28 torpedo craft, and six submarines. An additional six battleships, two cruisers, ten destroyers, and 31 torpedo craft were being readied for active service.

The *Active Eskadre* was recalled from the Aegean to the Adriatic. To replace the cruisers *Admiral Spaun* and *Aspern*, which joined the fleet, the Austrian Lloyd steamer *Bukovina* was dispatched to Constantinople instead of the *Gaea*, while another steamer from the same company, the *Salzburg*, was sent to Salonika with 180 soldiers on board.[18]

By 30 November the Emperor ordered an additional call-up of naval reservists of 1905 and 1906 classes. A total of 10,000 reservists were called up during this crisis.[19]

Naval budget of 1913

Because of the tensions in the Balkans, the Delegations promptly approved in December 1912 130 million crowns for naval expenditures in 1913. This amount included 53.6 million crowns in the regular naval budget, 49.4 million crowns as the third instalment of the 312.4 million crown special credit, and 26 million crowns of the *Ruestungkredit*.[20] Besides the ships already built or on order, the budget provided funds to start construction on one 1,000-ton fast minelayer, nine new class 250-ton high seas torpedo craft, and two 7,000-ton colliers. The last two vessels were officially designated 'squadron accompanying ships' (*Geschwaderbegleitschiffe*). However, their size clearly indicated that they would be used to support the battle fleet beyond the Adriatic. Another 484,000 crowns (four times as much as in 1912) was allocated for naval aviation. This included 122,800 crowns of the ordinary budget and the rest from the Navy *Ruestungkredit*.[21] Finally the budget for 1913 provided funds for an increase of naval personnel by about 1,540 officers and men. Hence, the peacetime strength of the Austro-Hungarian Navy in 1913 would be about 16,300, 80 per cent of whom would be on sea duty. Navy personnel strength in 1913 was to be 619 line officers, 192 line officer apprentices, 156 naval architects, 91 physicians, 1,100 petty officer cadets, and 15,909 petty officers and seamen.[22]

The implementation of the 1911–15 naval construction programme proceeded at a rapid pace in the last half of 1912. The first Austro-Hungarian dreadnought, *Viribus Unitis*, was commissioned on 26 September 1912 while the second, *Tegetthoff*, was then nearing completion; and the third, *Prinz Eugen*, was laid down in November. However, construction of the fourth dreadnought, *Szent István*, at the Danubius shipyard progressed slowly, because of the inexperienced labour force and great technical difficulties. Between October and November 1912 two 3,500-ton scout-cruisers (*Saida, Helgoland*) and three 870-ton *Tatra*-class destroyers were laid down at the Danubius shipyard in Porto Re.

Because of rapid progress in dreadnought construction at the Stabilimento Tecnico, Montecuccoli pressed the common government to approve funds for the second dreadnought division. The Chief of the MKFF, Colonel Bardolff, advised the admiral on 3 November to prepare a new proposal for the Emperor. He emphasized that it was impossible to further delay the construction of the new dreadnoughts in 1913. Archduke Francis Ferdinand urged Montecuccoli on 6 December to present his programme at the earliest opportunity to the common Ministerial Council rather than to wait until the next session of the Delegations. He was concerned that the issue of naval credits in the Delegations would pass without any decision being reached and that might leave the large slipways at the Stabilimento Tecnico shipyard idle after completion of the dreadnoughts then under construction and cause the dismissal of large numbers of skilled workers.[23]

Critique by the Austrian navalists

The growing strength of the Navy led to a lively debate in the Dual Monarchy on the value of sea power in safeguarding the country's national interests. Supporters of a faster and larger naval build-up were critical of the progress achieved by 1912. For example, a retired Rear-Admiral, Franz Mirth, in a pamphlet *Unsere Flotte Sinkt* (Our Fleet Sinks), criticized the inadequacy of the Navy budget and urged that annual expenditures for modernizing the fleet be increased to 80 million crowns. He advocated a battle fleet of 16 dreadnoughts with a corresponding number of cruisers, destroyers, and other smaller combatants. But, some critical voices were also heard. In a pamphlet entitled *Die Probleme der oesterreichische Flottenpolitik* (The Problems of Austrian Naval Policy), an anonymous author argued against building dreadnoughts, because they were useless for defending the Dual Monarchy's coast. He asserted that there was no reason to fear Italian control of the sea and that in any case a naval victory would not bring Austria-Hungary any great advantage. Instead, the author advocated the build-up of a coastal defence navy composed of inexpensive cruisers and torpedo craft.

Warming of relations between Vienna and Rome

By the autumn of 1912 the apparent similarity if not identity of views in Vienna and Rome on the Balkan crisis and the concentration of the French fleet in the Mediterranean led to the greatly improved relations between these two Triple Alliance partners. This political climate augured well for the talks between Foreign Ministers Berchtold and San Giuliano held in Pisa and Florence late in October. San Giuliano assured Berchtold of Italy's favourable attitude toward the Dual Monarchy and asserted that the Triple Alliance had never been as popular in Italy as it was then.[24] He also raised the question of renewing the Triple Alliance. San Giuliano wanted to insert a protocol to the then existing articles of the alliance recognizing Italy's position in Libya. He also insisted that two separate agreements already concluded between Italy and Austria-Hungary in respect of Albania and Italy's right to compensation if Austria-Hungary occupied the Sanjak of Novibazar become part of the Triple Alliance Treaty.

However, Berchtold felt that Italy was being unreasonable and that San Giuliano was trying to obtain advantages to the detriment of the Dual Monarchy. As early as January 1910 Kiderlen-Waechter and von Aehrenthal had decided that renewing the agreement, which was to expire in 1914, had to come about on Italy's initiative. Rome did not take any step in that direction until July 1911, when she made the renewal conditional on a special agreement with Austria-Hungary on Italy's position in Tripoli and Cyrenaica. However, Vienna did not accede to Rome's request and the outbreak of the Turco-Italian War suspended further talks.[25]

During Berchtold's visit the *Neue Freie Presse* cited a statement by the Italian deputy Pirmeni (who was close to Prime Minister Giolitti) that 'cordial relations between Italy and Austria-Hungary signified the renewal of the Triple Alliance Treaty'. Pirmeni argued that Italy's expanded position in the Mediterranean made it necessary to extend the Triple Alliance to the Mediterranean so as to protect the interests of Germany, the Dual Monarchy, and Italy by land and sea. Hence, the Italian and Austro-Hungarian fleets should be jointly employed in the Mediterranean to prevent it from becoming a 'French lake'. Pirmeni also wrote in *La Stampa* that because of the danger of the Mediterranean becoming a monopoly of the Triple Entente, it was absolutely necessary to reach an agreement on Austro-Italian naval co-operation.[26]

The German ambassador in Rome, Gottlieb von Jagow, falsely claimed to Bethmann Hollweg on 27 October that Italian public opinion was convinced that Italy's position in the Mediterranean could best be protected by co-operation between the Austro-Hungarian and Italian navies. An article in the December issue of *Die Flagge* asserted that in case of war the British Navy could inflict great economic misery on the Dual Monarchy simply by closing the Strait of Otranto. Therefore, the only solution for the Dual Monarchy was a defensive naval alliance with Italy.[27]

Renewal of the Triple Alliance Treaty

The Triple Alliance Treaty was renewed for the fourth and last time on 5 December 1912 in Vienna. The terms were the same as before, with two exceptions. The status quo in regard to the territories Italy acquired during the Turco-Italian War was defined, and Italy's wishes concerning her agreements with the Dual Monarchy in respect of the Balkans were noted.

There was little enthusiasm in Italy for renewing the Triple Alliance. While some large newspapers favoured it, many leading Italian politicians criticized the government for its action. In Austria-Hungary and Germany, in contrast, the press almost without exception welcomed the renewal of the Triple Alliance.

Despite its renewal, the Triple Alliance remained a diplomatic arrangement more likely to work in peacetime than war. The essential contradiction in Italian policies remained. Although irredentism remained hidden, it had not disappeared. The war party in Vienna continued to flourish. More ominously for Italy, General Conrad was recalled on 12 December to the post of Chief of the General Staff. Although Conrad's war-mongering was at the moment primarily directed against Serbia and Montenegro, he remained an implacable enemy of Italy.

The ambassadors' conference in London

In the meantime, Foreign Minister Kiderlen-Waechter urged the great European powers on 18 November to convene a conference to settle the conflict between Turkey and the Balkan League. It was agreed that the powers and the belligerents would meet at a conference in London. By 3 December, all the Balkan allies, with the exception of Greece, which objected to Turkey's refusal to surrender to Greek troops the fortress of Janina, signed an armistice with Turkey.

The armistice opened the way for the conference of ambassadors in London which started on 16 December. Subsequent discussions focused on the question of Serbia's access to the sea and the future status of Albania. Berchtold reiterated Vienna's position that Serbia should give up any idea of acquiring more Albanian territory and should instead recognize the new state of Albania. Berchtold contended that because Albania deserved the opportunity to develop into a self-sufficient state, her borders should be liberally drawn. Vienna insisted that Serbia develop closer economic ties and peaceful relations with Austria-Hungary. Because the Austro-Hungarian commercial and political interests should not suffer as a result of the war in the Balkans, a railroad link with Salonika should be arranged for the Dual Monarchy regardless of any territorial changes that might take place in the Balkans.[28]

The first ambassadorial conference in London lasted two months and ended in failure. Nevertheless, the problem of a Serbian port was settled on 20 December. The formula then adopted provided a commercial outlet for Serbia in a free and neutral Albanian port to be served by a railway under international control and under the protection of a special international force. Serbia was to have freedom of transit for all merchandise, including munitions of war.[29] However, no decision was reached on the Albanian boundaries.

By the end of 1912 the situation in the Balkans, despite the armistice and continuing efforts by the great European powers to end the war, remained tense. The Dual Monarchy's troops on the borders of Serbia and Montenegro, the Danube flotilla, and the fleet all remained fully mobilized and in the highest state of combat readiness. Both London and Paris urged Vienna to demobilize so that Russia could do the same. However, Austria-Hungary did not want to demobilize until Serbia withdrew her troops from Albania. Vienna also feared that demobilization would increase the demands of the Balkan states at the London conference of ambassadors.[30]

When the conference of ambassadors resumed work on 2 January 1913, it had to resolve two problems: the question of Albania's borders and the fate of the Aegean Islands. Albania was undoubtedly the more difficult problem because of the diametrically opposed interests of the main parties involved and the direct involvement of the great powers. Serbian delegates at the London conference were instructed to insist that the northern border of Albania run along the Mat River or at most no further north than along the Drin River whereby the town of Scutari would be given to Montenegro (whose delegates operated under similar instructions). In contrast, Vienna proposed that Albania's northern border include the towns of Scutari, Ipek, Djakovica, and Prisrena. Austria-Hungary wanted the eastern Albanian border to run from Prisrena southward between Lake Ochrida and Lake Prespa but was ready to make concessions on this point if Scutari went to Albania.

Italy initially supported Montenegro's claims to Scutari but changed her mind after hearing rumours (subsequently proved to be true) that Montenegro proposed to conclude a customs union with the Dual Monarchy and to exchange Mount Lovcen for Scutari.[31] San Giuliano argued (implausibly) on 30 December 1912 that possession of Mount Lovcen (which dominated the Gulf of Cattaro and the land route to the Montenegrin capital of Cetigne) would improve the Austro-Hungarian strategic position in the Balkans. However, Italy could not allow that to happen because good relations between Vienna and Rome depended upon maintaining the *status quo* in the Adriatic. The Italian press reacted to rumours of an Austro-Montenegrin agreement in even stronger terms.

Italian public opinion was generally opposed to the Dual Monarchy having another strongly fortified, secure base in the Bay of Cattaro that would threaten Italy's weakly defended southern Adriatic coast. But the strongest opposition came from Russia, which on 4 January 1913 informed King Nicholas I of Montenegro that Russia would never allow the cession of Mount Lovcen to the Dual Monarchy. Two days later, Foreign Minister Berchtold publicly denied that any agreement on the Scutari question between Vienna and Cetigne was contemplated. This statement, coupled with his private assurances to Ambassador Avarna that Austria-Hungary was to adhere to Article 7 of the Triple Alliance, led to a change in Italy's attitude toward Montenegrin wishes in regard to Scutari. San Giuliano promised that Italy would support Austria-Hungary on the Scutari question and would seek to influence Russian policy on that issue.[32] Nevertheless, the wide differences between the Dual Monarchy and Russia on the Scutari problem were not resolved during the discussions held in London in January 1913.

The Scutari crisis

The great powers dispatched a note on 17 January urging the Porte to surrender Adrianople and the Aegean Islands; Turkey agreed five days later. But before the Turkish government could act, the 'Young Turks' engineered a *coup d'état* on 23 January. The new government at Constantinople was ready to give up part of Adrianople but not the Aegean Islands. This led the Balkan allies to renounce the armistice and renew hostilities against Turkey on 3 February. The Bulgarians attacked Adrianople and the Greeks resumed their advance in Epirus to capture the fortress of Janina and reach the Ionian Sea. The Greek Navy (which had been mostly active in the Aegean in the first phase of the war) blockaded the Albanian coast from the south to the port of Durazzo.

The Montenegrins and Serbs attacked the fortress of Scutari on 7–9 February but suffered great losses. King Nicholas I of Montenegro requested fire support from the Serbs on 15 February; Montenegrin public opinion wanted both Serbian troops and artillery to be sent. By order of King Peter I Karadjordjevic on 21 February, 30,000 men of the *Primorski Korpus* (Littoral Corps) were to be transported on board 65 Greek ships (chartered by Serbia) from Salonika to San Giovanni di Medua. At Serbia's request the Greek government agreed to protect these troop transports with warships.[33] However, because the Greeks were redeploying their troops from Macedonia to Epirus, preparations for the transport of Serbian troops to Albania went slowly.

In the meantime, the Austro-Hungarian General Staff received a report on Serbia's plans to ship troops to Albania in order to hasten the fall of Scutari. General Conrad told Berchtold on 28 February that the Serbian transports had to be turned back by the Austro-Hungarian warships, and, if necessary, sunk. He proposed that the fleet sail to the Straits of Otranto to stop the Serbian transports, but the Emperor believed such an action would violate the neutrality and therefore he rejected it.[34]

Naval developments

Before the end of his tour as Navy Commander, Admiral Montecuccoli was criticized in the Austrian Delegation for awarding some naval orders to German firms. At issue was an order for five 790-ton *Germania*-class submarines given to the Krupp shipyard. This order was not given to the Whitehead Co. shipyard because it wanted to charge seven per cent more than Krupp. Likewise a contract for a 40,000-ton floating dock was given to the Blohm & Voss shipyard in Hamburg because the Cantiere Navale Tecnico shipyard would have charged the Navy 485,000 crowns more than the German firm.[35]

Admiral Montecuccoli requested the common Ministerial Council in January 1913 to start the new naval construction programme in 1914 and not in 1915 as had been previously envisaged. He made this request to avoid the perennial problem of idle slipways and the consequent need to lay off workers at the Stabilimento Tecnico. However the council refused to approve his proposal and suggested that the Navy raise the issue during the forthcoming debate on the budget of 1914.[36] That was the last opportunity for Montecuccoli to urge approval of a new construction programme before his retirement on 21 February after nearly 54 years of active service in the Navy.

Admiral Montecuccoli was regarded as a sailor-statesman of the first order, trusted by the Emperor and highly respected in both parts of the Monarchy. Although there was some discontent with Montecuccoli within the naval officer corps, he had been highly successful in defending the Navy's interests in the common Ministerial Council and the Delegations.

The new Commander of the Austro-Hungarian Navy was 62-year-old Vice-Admiral Haus. In addition to his post of Fleet Inspector, he assumed all the posts held by Montecuccoli. Although the provisional statute remained formally in force, the post of Fleet Inspector was not filled by another flag officer. In effect, Montecuccoli skilfully outmanoeuvred Archduke Francis Ferdinand and retained the principle of unity of command in the Navy. Admiral Haus was committed to the same goals.[37]

Admiral Haus was regarded as more proficient in the technical aspects of the naval profession than his predecessor. He was also a highly gifted linguist. However, some navalists justifiably feared that he lacked Montecuccoli's political skill. Haus was also less bold than Montecuccoli in circumventing legal obstacles to funding ship construction.

Crisis in the Adriatic

While these naval developments were taking place the war in the Balkans entered its final phase. The Greeks entered Janina on 5 March and then captured Santi Quaranta on the Epirate coast; the Bulgarians with some aid from Serbia captured Adrianople on 26 March. Montenegrin and Serbian troops resumed their attacks on Scutari, but again failed to take the fortress because of exceptionally strong Turkish resistance. The Serbian forces of the *Primorski Korpus* were shipped on board Greek transports to San Giovanni di Medua beginning on 1 March. However, this action was poorly organized and badly conducted. That allowed the Turkish cruiser *Hamidie* on 17 March to bombard the unprotected Greek transports, sinking two and lightly damaging three others. The Serbs suffered 130 casualties in dead and wounded. An Austro-Hungarian merchant vessel, the *Skodre*, anchored in San Giovanni di Medua during the attack and rescued some Serbian soldiers from a sinking Greek ship. However, the ship's captain refused to continue rescue efforts for fear of incurring damage to his ship. The Montenegrin commander of the port forced the captain to resume these efforts. That action later prompted Vienna to demand an apology from Montenegro.[38] Despite this incident, the transport of Serbian troops continued during March under the protection of Greek warships. When the Serbian government ordered the end of this operation on 7 April, only 17,000 men instead of the planned 30,500 were shipped across the sea to San Giovanni di Medua.[39]

By 10 March General Conrad repeated his earlier proposal to Berchtold that the Austro-Hungarian fleet sail to the Strait of Otranto and if necessary use force to prevent the transport of Serbian troops to Albania. Two days later Vienna informed Rome that the Dual Monarchy would not view with equanimity the shipment of Serbian troops to Albania and suggested that if the London conference did not achieve any result then both countries should conduct a naval demonstration off the Albanian coast. However, Rome's response to Vienna's proposal was ambiguous.[40]

The great powers, after receiving Turkish agreement to start peace talks, urged the Balkan states to cease hostilities. The Balkan allies responded on 14 March by demanding that Turkey surrender all disputed territories, including the fortress of Scutari. A day later the powers threatened to withdraw all financial aid to the Balkan allies if they did not stop military actions.

Scutari became the most intractable problem to resolve because Montenegro apparently wanted to seize the fortress despite opposition from the powers. The Dual Monarchy was determined not to allow Scutari to fall into Montenegrin hands before hostilities with Turkey ended. Montenegro's mistreatment of Albanian Catholics and her continued bombardment of Scutari's unprotected civilian population led Vienna to demand on 18 March that Cetigne stop shelling the town until the civilian population was evacuated. Berchtold and Conrad met with the Emperor on the same day and asked him to approve the deployment of a battle squadron to the Bay of Cattaro, whence it could reach the Montenegrin coast in a short time.

The Emperor approved the request and Conrad ordered Admiral Haus on 19 March to send three battleships, one armoured and one light cruiser, and a torpedo flotilla to the Bay of Cattaro. This move was designed to lend credence to the Austro-Hungarian warnings against Montenegro.[41] The Dual Monarchy also intended to close her common border with Montenegro. If all these measures failed to have the desired effect, the Army and the Navy would then be readied for eventual military action against Montenegro and her ally Serbia.

International naval demonstration

The great powers unanimously urged Montenegro and Serbia on 22 March to end the siege of Scutari, evacuate all their troops from Albania, and cease hostilities with Turkey. Because both Cetigne and Belgrade refused this appeal, the powers were alarmed at the possibility of unilateral military action by the Dual Monarchy to resolve the crisis over Scutari and quickly agreed on 31 March to initiate a naval demonstration against Montenegro unless she ceased military activity against Scutari.

Although the ambassadorial conference in London approved an international naval demonstration against Montenegro, there was disagreement as to which powers would participate. By 2 April, the Austro-Hungarian, Italian, and German governments had ordered warships to be sent to Antivari. Although Russia excused herself on the grounds that she did not have any warship in the Mediterranean, Foreign Minister Sazonov agreed that a naval demonstration against Montenegro should take place. France's ambiguous and vacillating attitude made Grey hesitate as he did not want to order British ships to proceed to Antivari until he learned that the French government had done likewise. Grey pointed out to Ambassador Cambon that if the naval demonstration did not materialize or failed in its purpose, the only alternative was to give a mandate to the Dual Monarchy and Italy to deal with Montenegro alone.[42]

Berchtold asked Ambassador Cartwright on 2 April whether the British government was to take part in the proposed naval demonstration. He considered the matter urgent because Montenegro was expected to renew the bombardment of Scutari on the following day. Berchtold informed Cartwright that his government wanted to extend the blockade of the coast as far south as Durazzo to prevent the further transport of Serbian troops to Albania. However, Grey did not want to send British ships unless France and Russia sent theirs because otherwise it might appear that Great Britain was a partner of the Triple Alliance. At the same time he thought the only honourable course for the British government was to make the naval action work.[43]

The delay in executing the naval demonstration placed the Viennese government in a difficult position. Any time lost would allow more Serbian reinforcements to arrive and make the fall of Scutari more imminent. If the fortress fell, Serbia, Montenegro, and their protectors could argue that military action by the Dual Monarchy was no longer justified. Vienna would then have the option of either backing down or blockading Montenegro and risking the very war she hoped to avoid.[44]

Finally, five great powers instructed their ships to proceed to Antivari. British Vice-Admiral Cecil Burney, who had been appointed commander of the international fleet, sailed from Corfu aboard his flagship accompanied by one French warship. Taking part in the fleet demonstration were the British battleship *King Edward VII*, the French armoured cruiser *Edgar Quinet*, the Italian battleship *Ammiraglio di Saint Bon* and armoured cruiser *Francesco Ferrucio*, and the German cruiser *Breslau*.[45] The Austro-Hungarian squadron of three battleships (*Erzherzog Franz Ferdinand, Zrinyi, Radetzky*), one scout-cruiser (*Aspern*), and a torpedo flotilla commanded by Vice-Admiral Maximilian Njegovan joined the ships of the other powers at Antivari.

Berchtold instructed Ambassador Cartwright on 7 April that the purpose of the naval demonstration was to prevent Serbian troop reinforcements from taking part in the siege of Scutari. In case the demonstration failed Berchtold wanted the naval vessels of the powers to proceed to Albanian and Montenegrin harbours and land a sufficient number of troops to secure the coastal towns. He admitted this would require large forces that could only come from Italy and the Dual Monarchy. Berchtold praised Italy's behaviour during the Scutari crisis but was highly critical of France. He complained bitterly about Serbia's policies and was convinced that Belgrade and Athens wanted to carry on the war for some time to secure a greater part of Albania.[46]

Vice-Admiral Burney received instructions from his government on 7 April to blockade the coast between the mouth of the Drin River and Antivari after obtaining the consent of the other naval commanders. He was ordered to warn any transports carrying troops or war matériel to keep out of the blockaded zone; if this warning was disregarded, the naval vessels were to indicate they would prevent a landing. Only if the ships of the powers were attacked first were they to open fire. There was a delay in blockading the Montenegrin and Albanian coasts as the French naval commander on the scene opposed the extension of the blockade as far south as Durazzo to inconvenience the Serbian and Greek troops deployed there. Vienna persuaded the other powers on 7 April to send one British cruiser (*Dartmouth*) and Austro-Hungarian cruiser (*Aspern*) each to Durazzo to reconnoitre the Serbian troops there.[47]

Naval blockade

After the Montenegrin government rejected the appeal of the great powers to cease siege of Scutari, the international fleet instituted a close blockade of the Montenegrin and Albanian coasts from the mouth of the Boyana River to the Drin River on 10 April. No vessels were permitted to enter the blockaded zone and those already in it were ordered to leave within 48 hours. The Austro-Hungarian Navy was the first navy to use airplanes for military purposes in late April 1913. Three French-built Donnet-Leveque seaplanes were attached to the Austro-Hungarian Second Battle Squadron. Initially, the airplanes were accommodated on board the *Radetzky*-class battleships, but when this proved to be an unsatisfactory arrangement (because of lack of deck space and hoisting gear), a temporary air station was established at the subsidiary of the Navy Yard in Teodo. These seaplanes played a valuable role in visual observation, photographic reconnaissance, and message delivery along the Montenegrin coast.[48] One of the first results of the naval demonstration off the Montenegrin coast was that Serbia disembarked her troops from the Greek ships at Salonika that were about to sail to San Giovanni di Medua.

Under pressure from the powers, Belgrade withdrew Serbian troops from Scutari, making the siege a purely Montenegrin affair. Montenegrin troops resumed the bombardment of Scutari on 18 April but four days later the second ambassadorial conference in London agreed in principle to offer financial assistance to Montenegro in return for an end of the siege. Vienna withdrew its proposal to land detachments from the international fleet in order to force Montenegro to halt the siege of Scutari after she failed to win unanimous acceptance.[49]

Fall of Scutari

The fortress of Scutari surrendered on 22 April and two days later Montenegrin troops entered the city. Afterwards, the powers had some difficulties in persuading King Nicholas I of Montenegro to withdraw from Scutari without losing face. As a result, the blockade was to include Durazzo on 23 April. A day later the council of the international squadron decided to dispatch a landing party of 1,000 men (300 Austro-Hungarian, 300 British, 200 Italian, 100 German, and 100 French sailors) to seize Scutari in the name of the powers. However, the final decision was left up to their governments.[50]

At the ambassadorial conference in London on 25 April, Austria-Hungary, supported by her two Triple Alliance partners, requested that the troops should land to compel King Nicholas I to obey the wishes of the great powers, but France and Russia opposed it. After complicated proposals and counter-proposals led nowhere, Vienna decided that decisive action was necessary to force Montenegro to retreat. At the common Ministerial Council session held on 2 May the Hungarian ministers strongly opposed any action that might lead to war with Montenegro and Serbia as this would only bring more Slavs into the Dual Monarchy. The Hungarians favoured more limited measures to force Montenegro to evacuate Scutari. Therefore, the council decided to call into service all non-active reservists in Bosnia, Herzegovina, and Dalmatia and to authorize five million crowns for strengthening defences in the Bay of Cattaro.[51] A majority of the council also urged Francis Joseph I to issue an ultimatum to Montenegro unless she withdrew her troops from Scutari. However, on the Emperor's order Berchtold only issued a warning to the government in Cetigne. This had the desired effect because King Nicholas I decided on 4 May to withdraw his troops from Scutari.

After the fall of Scutari Italy proposed that the powers occupy Antivari. However, she later refused to take any military action with Austria-Hungary against Montenegro unless Great Britain participated. San Giuliano lectured Berchtold that Article 7 of the Triple Alliance did not allow the Dual Monarchy to act without Italy's consent. If Vienna took unilateral action against Montenegro it appeared certain that Italy would take Valona.[52] On 14 May a detachment from the international blockading fleet landed in Scutari and the city passed under the control of the powers. Thus, the Scutari crisis, which had kept Europe in suspense for many months, was over.

The final peace agreement ending the First Balkan War was reached only after Foreign Secretary Grey warned the Balkan allies that they had to accept the terms of the powers or go home empty-handed. This had a salutary effect, and on 30 May the peace preliminaries were signed. The powers reserved for themselves the right to delineate the Turkish frontier in Europe, to define Albania's boundaries, and to dispose of the Aegean Islands. The Balkan allies were authorized to divide the remaining Turkish possessions in Europe.

Demobilization of the fleet

The Fleet remained mobilized until 28 May, while the Danube flotilla did not demobilize until September 1913. The two Army corps in Ragusa and Sarajevo did not return to peacetime status until mid-August 1913. As in the Bosnian crisis of 1908–9, the Navy's mobilization was executed quickly and without great difficulties. It was also the first time in 47 years that the Navy was fully mobilized. The additional cost of maintaining the Navy on a war footing amounted to 40 million crowns, a substantial sum at that time. By comparison, Army expenditures were about 317 million crowns.[53]

Naval budget for 1914

Shortly after Admiral Haus assumed the post of the Navy Commander he presented the naval budget for 1914. The 76 million crowns eventually approved by the Delegations on 15 March included funds for continued construction of 16 new 250-ton high seas torpedo craft, one 1,000-ton minelayer, five 790-ton submarines, two 7,000-ton colliers, and one 40,000-ton floating dock. This sum did not include the 68 million crown fourth instalment of the 1911–15 construction programme and the second 13 million crown instalment of the Navy's *Ruestungkredit*. Also, the cost of the Navy's mobilization for the war in the Balkans was not included in the budget.[54]

By the spring of 1913 the construction of ships funded in the 1911–15 programme (with the exception of those built at the Danubius shipyard in Fiume and the 3,500-ton cruiser at the Cantiere Navale Tecnico at Monfalcone) was proceeding extremely well. This was especially the case with the remaining two dreadnoughts at the Stabilimento Tecnico.

In the midst of the Scutari crisis the Stabilimento Tecnico proposed to join with the Skoda and Vitkovice Works to start construction of a new 24,500-ton dreadnought at their own risk but according to Navy specifications and plans. It was agreed to regard this proposal as provisional until the Delegations approved it and Archduke Francis Ferdinand advised Admiral Haus on 18 April not to inform the government of the proposal.[55] However, the Navy Commander replied that construction of a new dreadnought could not begin without public knowledge and noted that he had already promised to inform the government of any action of that nature.

The Austrian government was favourably disposed toward Admiral Haus's proposal presented in May 1913. However, the Hungarian government opposed any new naval construction programme. Moreover, Francis Joseph I and Berchtold both failed to change the minds of the Hungarian Prime Minister and Finance Minister on that issue. At a session of the council held on 14 May, Admiral Haus, Berchtold, and Finance Minister Biliński were unable to budge the

Hungarian ministers. The Hungarians regarded the Stabilimento Tecnico's proposal as a new financial commitment that they simply could not defend in their Parliament. They warned that if the Navy Section presented any plans for a new class of dreadnoughts to the Stabilimento Tecnico shipyard, it would suffer the consequences. In other words, the Hungarian government would provoke a crisis by submitting its resignation.[56]

Admiral Haus, with the support of the MKSM, made a final effort to secure the Emperor's support for a new construction programme. But the Emperor did nothing more than vaguely indicate that his efforts to move the Hungarians might prove unsuccessful. Nevertheless, the Navy's consistent pressure apparently convinced the Austrian and Hungarian governments of the need to replace the old *Monarch*-class with a new class of dreadnoughts.

Admiral Haus decided to force the issue by ordering the Navy Section to prepare plans for a new 24,500-ton superdreadnought that would carry 14-inch guns instead of the 12-inchers mounted on the *Viribus Unitis*. By June 1913 the Skoda Works agreed after confidential talks with Admiral Haus to start preliminary work on 14-inch guns at its own risk. In the summer of 1913, the Navy also sent preliminary specifications for the new dreadnought class to all three firms that were to participate in the programme.

NOTES

1. Ernst Helmreich, *The Diplomacy of the Balkan Wars 1912–1913* (Cambridge MA: Harvard University Press, 1938; reprinted New York: Russell & Russell, 1969), p. 110.
2. Glen St J. Barclay, *The Rise and Fall of the New Roman Empire. Italy's Bid for World Power 1890–1943* (New York: St Martin's Press, 1973), p. 56.
3. 'Protokoll des Ministerrates fuer gemeinsamen Angelegenheiten', 3 October 1912, p. 552, Haus-Hof und Staatsarchiv, Politische Archiv-XL-310 (hereafter HHSA) .
4. 'Protokoll des Ministerrates fuer gemeinsamen Angelegenheiten fuer 9 August 1912', 8 October 1912, p. 588, ibid.
5. K. K. Hof und Staatsdruckerei, 'Resolution der gemeinsamen Delegation des ungarischen Reichstag', 11 October 1912, Protokoll, Punkt 6.
6. 'Rundschau in allen Marinen', *Marine Rundschau* 11 (November 1912), p. 1544.
7. Ibid., p. 1544.
8. Biliński's letter, 10 October 1912, no. 4556, Kriegsarchiv, Praesidial Kanzlei, Marinesektion-XV-7/8, 1912 (hereafter PK/MS); Montecuccoli to MKFF, 30 October 1912, PK/MS-XV-7/8, 1912.
9. 'Basa Sebenico', undated, no. 766, Kriegsarchiv Militaer Kanzlei des Erzherzog Franz Ferdinand 41-14, 1913 (hereafter MKFF).
10. Eduard Ritter von Steinitz, 'Die Reichsbefestigung Oesterreich-Ungarn zur Zeit Conrads von Hoetzendorf', *Militaerwissenschaftlichen Mitteilungen* 12 (December 1936), pp. 923-39, at pp. 928–9.
11. Helmreich, *Diplomacy of the Balkan Wars*, p. 189.
12. R. Giesche, *Der Serbische Zugang zum Meer und die Europaeische Krise 1912* (Stuttgart, 1932), p. 18.

13. Ralph Paget to Grey, 11 November 1912, no. 176, *British Documents on the Origins of the War 1898–1914*, ed. G. P. Gooch and Harold Temperley, 11 vols (London: HMSO, 1926–38) (hereafter *BD*) Vol. 9(2), pp. 133–5.
14. Giesche, *Der Serbische Zugang*, p. 18; Leopold Chlumecky, *Franz Ferdinand. Wirken und Wollen* (Berlin: Verlag fuer Kulturpolitik, 1929) pp. 124, 130–1, 134, 160.
15. Franz Conrad von Hoetzendorf, *Aus meiner Dienstzeit 1908–1918*, 5 vols (Vienna: Rikola Verlag, 1922–25) Vol. 2, pp. 332–3.
16. R. Rodd to Grey, 9 November 1912, no. 172, *BD*, Vol. 9(2), p. 128.
17. Unsigned, 23 November 1912, MKFF, F203, 1912; W. Deutschmann, 'Die militaerischen Massnahmen in Oesterreich-Ungarn waehrend der Balkankrise 1912-1913' (University of Vienna, unpublished Ph.D. dissertation, 1965) pp. 69–70.
18. Ibid., pp. 70–1, 74.
19. 'Die fremden Kriegsmarinen', *Nauticus* (1914) p. 173.
20. 'Die fremden Kriegsmarinen', *Nauticus* (1913) p. 157; 'Informazioni e Notizie. Marina Militare', *Rivista Marittima* 1 (January 1913) pp. 79-81; 'Rundschau in allen Marinen', *Marine Rundschau* 12 (December 1912) p. 1683.
21. 'Die fremden Kriegsmarinen', *Nauticus* (1913) p. 160.
22. Ibid., p. 161; Luigi Barberis, 'Statistiche del Personale Militare. Di Alcuni Marine Estere', printed as supplement to *Rivista Marittima* 4 (April 1913) pp. 23, 31, 48.
23. Bardolff to Montecuccoli, 3 November 1912, MKFF, Mm/100, 1912; Bardolff to Montecuccoli, 6 December 1912, PK/MS-XV-7/8, 1912.
24. Berchtold's report on talks with San Giuliano, 22–23 October 1912, no. 4181, *Oesterreich-Ungarns Aussenpolitik von der Bosnischen Krise 1908 bis zum Kriegsausbruch 1914. Diplomatische Aktenstuecke des Oesterreichisch-Ungarischen Ministeriums des Aeussern*, ed. Ludwig Bittner, Alfred Francis Pribram, Heinrich Srbik, and Hans Uebersberger, 9 vols (Vienna: Oesterreichischer Bundesverlag fuer Unterricht, Wissenschaft und Kunst, 1930) (hereafter *OuA*) Vol. 4, p. 713.
25. Berchtold to S. Biegelbein, 1 November 1912, no. 4220, ibid., pp. 738–40.
26. 'Rundschau in allen Marinen', *Marine Rundschau* 10 (October 1912), p. 1386.
27. Jagow to Bethmann Hollweg, 27 October 1912, *Die Grosse Politik der Europaeischen Kabinette 1871–1914*, ed. Johannes Lepsius, Albrecht M. Bartholdy, Friedrich Thimme, 40 vols (Berlin: Deutsche Verlagsgesellschaft fuer Politik und Geschichte, 1927) (hereafter *GP*) Vol. 30(1), pp. 558-9; 'Maritime Verschiebungen im Mittelmeer', *Die Flagge* 12 (December 1912), p. 7.
28. Berchtold to Szögyèny, 28 November 1911, no. 4673, *OuA*, vol. 4, pp. 1048–54.
29. Helmreich, *The Diplomacy of the Balkan Wars*, p. 251.
30. Ibid., p. 258.
31. Mihajlo Vojvodic', *Skadarska Kriza, 1913 Godine* (Belgrade: Zavod za Izdavanje Udzbenika Socijalisticke Republike Srbije, 1970) p. 44.
32. Ibid., pp. 44–6.
33. Ibid., p. 63; *Prvi Balkanski Rat 1912-13 (Operacije Crnogorske Vojske)* (Belgrade: Istoriski Institut Jugoslovenske Narodne Armije, 1960), pp. 331–2.
34. Deutschmann, 'Die Militaerischen Massnahmen', pp. 158, 162–3.
35. 'Die fremden Kriegsmarinen', *Nauticus* (1913, p. 158; 'Rundschau in allen Marinen', *Marine Rundschau* 3 (March 1913), pp. 381–2.
36. 'Protokoll des Ministerrates fuer gemeinsame Angelegenheiten', 4 January 1913, p. 837, HHSA-XL-311.
37. 'Nachtrag zum Statut fuer die Flotteninspektor', 16 July 1912, MKFF Mm/67, 1912.
38. *Prvi Balkanski Rat*, p. 336; Conrad, *Aus meiner Dienstzeit*, Vol. 3, pp. 171–6.
39. *Prvi Balkanski Rat*, p. 339.
40. Vojvodic', *Skadarska Kriza*, p. 84.
41. Deutschmann, 'Die militaerischen Massnahmen', p. 166.
42. Grey to F. Bertie, 2 April 1913, no. 795, *BD*, Vol. 9(2), pp. 645–6; Grey to Cartwright, 1 April 1913, no. 781, ibid., p. 635; Grey to F. Bertie, 1 April 1913, no. 782, ibid., pp. 635–6.
43. Cartwright to Grey, 2 April 1913, no. 792, ibid., p. 642; Grey to F. Bertie, 2 April 1913, no. 795, ibid., pp. 645–6.
44. Grey to G. Buchanan, 3 April 1913, no. 794, ibid., pp. 646–7.
45. Vojvodic', *Skadarska Kriza*, pp. 102–3.
46. Cartwright to Grey, 7 April 1913, no. 812, *BD*, Vol. 10(2), p. 658.

47. Ibid., enclosures no. 1 and 2, 7 April 1913, no. 817, ibid., p. 662; Cartwright to A. Nicolson, 11 April 1913, no. 837, ibid., p. 679; Vojvodic', *Skadarska Kriza*, p. 106.
48. R. D. Layman, *To Ascend from a Floating Base. Shipboard Aeronautics and Aviation 1783–1914* (London: Associated Universities Press, 1979) pp. 195–6.
49. Grey to F. Bertie, 21 April 1913, no. 869, *BD*, Vol. 10(2), p. 707.
50. Vojvodic', *Skadarska Kriza*, p. 143.
51. Ibid., p. 171.
52. William C. Askew, 'Austro-Italian Antagonism, 1896-1914', in Lilian Parker Wallace and William C. Askew, *Power, Public Opinion and Diplomacy. Essays in Honor of Eber Malcolm Carroll by his Students* (Durham, NC: Duke University Press, 1959), p. 208.
53. Unsigned, 20 January 1914, no. 184, PK/MS-XII-7/3, 1914.
54. 'Die fremden Kriegsmarinen', *Nauticus* (1913) p. 158; 'Rundschau in allen Marinen', *Marine Rundschau* 3 (March 1913), p. 381.
55. Unsigned, 18 April 1913, MKFF-41-2.4-8, 1913; Bardolff to Haus, 18 April 1913, MKFF-41-2/4-3, 1913.
56. 'Protokoll des Ministerrates fuer gemeinsamen Angelegenheiten', 14 May 1913, pp. 1116–17, 1120–25, 1128, HHSA-XL-311.

9

The road to war

[handwritten marginalia: Italy + AH could get sg. when it was to oppose SN. But it would work w/ Fr + GB too]

After the end of the Balkan Wars tension remained high throughout the area because of the unresolved problem of Albania's borders, hostility between Bulgaria and her erstwhile allies, and the growing hostility between Austria-Hungary and Serbia. Relations between Vienna and Rome were characterized both by co-operation and competition for influence in Albania. Italy sought to win the Dual Monarchy's support for her policy of checking French predominance in the Mediterranean. At the same time Rome tried to reach an accommodation with France and Great Britain.

The Albanian problem

The powers decided that Albania would become an independent, neutral state ruled by Prince Wilhelm von Wied. There was much discussion as to the extent of Albania's territory. Although the Dual Monarchy and Italy succeeded in denying Serbia access to the Adriatic, they were faced with Greece's aspirations, supported by France, concerning the southern part of Albania and including the coast facing the Corfú Channel. Greece specifically demanded the entire Ionian coast of Albania, including Valona and the island of Saseno. After the powers decided to make Valona the principal port of the new state, Greece proposed that the southern border of Albania run along the line drawn from a point midway between Valona and Chimarra then north of Argyrokastro and Tepelena to Lake Ochrida. Austria-Hungary and Italy wanted Albania to be as large as possible, and hence both powers strongly opposed the Greek proposal. The Austro-Hungarian General Staff was alarmed by the possibility that Greece might establish herself along the entire Epirate coast opposite to Corfú. In that case the Greek Navy would control one shore of the strategically important Strait of Otranto. Italy had identical fears and wanted Albania's southern border to run as far as the mouth of the Kalamas River.[1]

The question of the southern Albanian border was finally settled on

11 August 1913, when the London ambassadorial conference decided that the coastal region to the Bay of Phtelia (including the island of Saseno) and to Cape Stylos and the Kaza of Koritza with the west and south shore of Lake Ochrida was to belong to Albania. An international boundary commission was established to begin work on 1 September and it ended its work in the week of 30 November. Greek troops were obliged to evacuate the territories given to Albania by the end of December 1913.[2]

The work of the southern Albanian boundary commission was beset by difficulties because of the Greek efforts to incite the local population to oppose incorporation into the new Albanian state. This prompted Vienna and Rome to warn Greece on 31 October that their representatives had instructions to regard all villages where opposition existed as Albanian. They also insisted that Greek troops leave the territories already assigned to Albania.[3]

Austro-Italian rivalry in Asia Minor

Despite co-operation between Vienna and Rome in regard to Greece, both countries continued to engage in efforts to extend their influence in Asia Minor. Vienna's attention turned toward Asia Minor in the spring of 1913 when a secret mission that had been sent there reported favourable commercial and colonial prospects in southern Anatolia. By August 1913 Vienna informed Rome that it planned to open a consulate in Adalia.

Italy and Austria-Hungary also became interested in a railway project in Asia Minor. Although San Giuliano knew that Great Britain would oppose any unilateral advantage by Italy in Asia Minor, he nevertheless devised a scheme to reach an agreement with Vienna on spheres of influence in that area. He calculated that Great Britain would not strongly oppose this when faced with the presence of two great powers supported by Germany. San Giuliano also thought the Dual Monarchy's attention could be diverted from the Adriatic by offering her some territory in Asia Minor marked for Italian expansion. Although Italy was to reserve the best territory there, Austria-Hungary would be possibly brought into conflict with the Triple Entente.[4] Thus the Dual Monarchy would have a common interest with Italy in preventing France from obtaining a dominant position in the Mediterranean.

Curiously, the Italian King thought that as soon as Italy concluded an agreement over Asia Minor with her two partners she should try to reach an accord with France and Great Britain. The main reason for the

King's attitude was the so-called 'Hohenlohe Decrees' that led to a temporary deterioration of relations between Rome and Vienna. The governor of Trieste, Prince Conrad von Hohenlohe, a close friend of Archduke Francis Ferdinand, issued an order on 24 August that effectively barred Italian nationals from public service jobs in the city. There was an immediate uproar in Italy where irredentists started a new campaign against the Dual Monarchy. San Giuliano instructed Avarna on 31 August to suspend ongoing negotiations with Berchtold on division of spheres of influence in Asia Minor. He also asserted that the 'Hohenlohe Decrees' threatened grave consequences between the two allied nations.[5] San Giuliano demanded that the decrees be rescinded, but to no avail. On 19 September he complained to Berlin that Vienna's attitude made genuine friendship between Italy and Austria-Hungary impossible.

After Berlin did nothing to influence Vienna, San Giuliano instructed the Italian chargé d'affaires in Paris to sound out France on the possibility of reaching a Mediterranean agreement. He subsequently used the talks on a possible accord with France as a lever to persuade Germany to influence Vienna's policies toward Italy. Rumours of Franco-Italian talks reportedly caused the 'most painful impression' in Berlin.[6]

Disputes over Albania continue

Meanwhile, a dispute arose in the Admiral's Commission at Scutari on 19 September 1913 over alleged preferential treatment by the Commission President, Admiral Burney, in assigning a contract to construct a bridge over the Drin River to an Italian firm. The Austro-Hungarian representative in the Admiral's Commission, Rear-Admiral Barry, refused to cast a vote without further instructions from his government. He was later on directed not to attend commission meetings. The Italian admiral also left Scutari temporarily, but returned on 27 September. Ambassador Cartwright informed Berchtold on 9 October that his government considered the action of Admiral Burney entirely justified.[7]

Because of further difficulties between the Austro-Hungarian and Italian admirals, the British government thought that it would be impossible to continue the Admiral's Commission's work unless a majority vote of the members could be accepted; otherwise a single member might obstruct any action proposed. Rear-Admiral Barry did not attend any meetings of the commission after 15 September, and the

German member (a Navy captain) did not sign minutes of the meetings held after 1 October. The Admiral's Commission was dissolved officially on 16 October and its duties were taken over by the then newly created Control Commission in Scutari.

In the midst of the above-described controversy Italian Ambassador Avarna was authorized to warn Berchtold that if Vienna embarked on a policy of antagonizing Rome in Albania, Italy could count on the support of the Triple Entente while Austria-Hungary could only be sure of German support. The Italian ambassador in Berlin informed the German government that Italy preferred that Albania go to Serbia than come under the influence of the Dual Monarchy.[8]

A new crisis between Vienna and Belgrade erupted in the autumn of 1913 over Albania. In skirmishes along the eastern Albanian border between Serbian and Albanian troops, the Serbs suffered some heavy casualties that led to a partial mobilization of their Army. Afterwards, Serbian troops moved into Albania for the avowed purpose of 'restoring order'. The Serbian press clamoured for revision of the Albanian frontiers. However, Belgrade informed Vienna that its troops would be withdrawn after order was restored. Vienna did not believe Belgrade's assurances, and General Conrad again urged his government to crush Serbia and thereby put an end to the incessant controversies between the two countries.

The threat of unilateral Austro-Hungarian military action against Serbia came soon after Serbian troops had crossed into Albanian territory on 14 October. After the London conference refused Vienna's request for joint action against Serbia, Vienna formally asked Belgrade to recall its troops. The Serbian reply was evasive. This prompted Vienna, after consulting Berlin, to send an ultimatum to Belgrade threatening to take proper measures if Serbian troops were not withdrawn within eight days. Germany, although fearful of escalating the conflict, reluctantly endorsed the Dual Monarchy's move. Russia, however, realized that Vienna meant business and strongly urged Serbia to leave Albania.[9] Although the crisis then ended, it further worsened relations between Vienna and Belgrade.

The new fleet expansion programme

In a political atmosphere filled with tensions in the Balkans, Admiral Haus presented to the common Ministerial Council a new five-year (1915-19) fleet expansion programme on 5 October 1913. Totalling 427 million crowns, the programme was to provide funds for the construction of four 24,500-ton superdreadnoughts, three 4,800-ton scout-cruisers, six 800-ton destroyers, two 520-ton Danube monitors, and one 450-ton supply ship. The proposed programme also included funds for the build-up of the naval base in Sebenico (5.4 million crowns), the expansion of the Navy Yard, construction of an ammunition dump, coaling station and radio station in Pola (16.2 million crowns), and the expansion of naval aviation (4.0 million crowns).[10] Admiral Haus reiterated his support for Montecuccoli's plan to expand the Navy to 16 battleships, 12 cruisers, 24 destroyers, 72 high seas torpedo craft, 12 submarines, and eight Danube monitors.

By the autumn of 1913, despite almost eight years of uninterrupted fleet expansion and modernization, the Austro-Hungarian fleet consisted of only three old *Monarch*- and three somewhat newer *Habsburg*-class battleships, four old armoured cruisers, three older 20-knot *Zenta*-class light cruisers, and 15 obsolescent torpedo craft. However, the Austro-Hungarian Navy required the construction of six battleships, three cruisers, six destroyers, 12 torpedo craft, and four submarines.[11]

The Navy's commissioning programme for 1919 envisaged that the *Active Eskadre* was to consist of: four new superdreadnoughts (*Schlachtschiff VIII-XI*), four *Tegetthoff*-class dreadnoughts, five cruisers (*Sankt Georg*, two *Admiral Spaun*-class, and two new 4,800-ton class), six Tatra destroyers, 24 250-ton high seas torpedo craft, one torpedo depot ship (*Gaea*), and six minesweepers. Also in active service would be two *Franz Joseph I*-class armoured cruisers (one deployed in East Asia and one serving as a training ship) and two *Zenta*-class protected cruisers (one in the Levant and one serving as a training ship). The *Reserve Eskadre* was to consist of three *Radetzky*- and three *Erzherzog*-class battleships, two *Admiral Spaun*- and one new 4,800-ton class cruiser, six *Huszar*-class destroyers, and 12 *Kaiman*-class high seas torpedo craft. The Danube flotilla would comprise four monitors and five patrol craft.[12]

In defending his proposal Admiral Haus argued that three old *Monarch*-class battleships had to be replaced by superdreadnoughts and noted that 'the entire world cannot understand why we wait for this'. The Navy Commander asserted that the Balkan Wars of 1912–13 would have had another outcome if Turkey had had two dreadnoughts.[13] Haus also assured the ministers that in view of the past declaration of the Hungarian government and the Emperor's order, he took a 'wait-and-see' attitude toward the plan of the Stabilimento Tecnico shipyard to build a superdreadnought at its own risk. Nevertheless, he let it be known that the Stabilimento Tecnico and the Skoda Works received plans for the proposed superdreadnoughts so that they would be in a position to begin construction a month and a half after orders were given and be able to complete the ships within 36 months.

The Hungarian Finance Minister, Dr Teleszki, opposed the proposed fleet expansion programme on the grounds that after mid-1917 the construction schedule would cause the governmental debt to rise to about 180 million crowns. However, the Austrian Finance Minister, Wenzel Ritter von Zalesky, strongly favoured the proposed fleet expansion programme. He reminded his colleagues that the Delegations in the autumn of 1912 had declared that timely credits for replacement of *Monarch*-class ships would be approved after the expiration of the previous 312.4 million crown special credit. Nonetheless, Dr Teleszki's objections were accepted by the Ministerial Council.[14]

The common Ministerial Council approved in principle the new 427 million crown special credit for naval construction to be presented to the Delegations. However, it stipulated that the first instalment of the new credit (about 45 million crowns) would not be available to the Navy until 1 January 1915. Subsequent instalments through the fiscal year 1918–19 were not to exceed 100 million crowns each.[15]

Naval budget for 1914 approved

The common Ministerial Council also discussed anew the naval budget for 1914 that had been approved in March 1913. It did so because an impending change in the fiscal year in the Dual Monarchy made it necessary to decide naval expenditures for the first half of 1914.[16] The Navy Commander proposed to the council that the funds for ship replacement and new construction in Title VII of the regular budget be increased from 24 million crowns to about 100 million crowns to avoid having recourse to a special credit. The Austrian press reported in the summer of 1913 that Admiral Haus urged approval of the Navy Act in order to obtain an increase of Title VII to 100 million crowns starting in fiscal year 1914–15.[17] Haus repeated his predecessor's complaints about the small increase in the regular Navy budget, that amounted to only 1.5 million crowns a year as opposed to the 6.5 million he requested, and noted that such small increases were not only inadequate for maintaining in active service large modern ships but had led to the cancellation of summer fleet manoeuvres and gunnery firing exercises in 1913.[18]

The naval budget for the first six months of 1914 amounted to about

38 million crowns. It provided funds for continued construction of a 1,000-ton fast minelayer, nine 250-ton high seas torpedo craft, and two 7,000-ton colliers. Almost three million crowns were allocated for the expansion of naval aviation. The budget also included a small sum for preliminary work on the build-up of Sebenico into a large naval base in central Dalmatia.

Total naval expenditures for January–June 1914 were in fact much larger if the various special credits for the Navy are included. The latter included a sum of 134 million crowns intended for construction of six 250-ton high seas torpedo craft, two submarines, two Danube monitors, two river patrol craft, and one 40,000-ton floating dock. Also, besides 37.8 million crowns in the regular budget, the Navy expenditure included 47.8 million crowns as a share of the fourth instalment of the 312.4 million crown special credit, 1.5 million crowns for the build-up of facilities in Pola's fortress area, 7.2 million crowns as a one-time credit for special Navy expenditures, and 40.4 million crowns as the Navy's share of the special credit during the Balkan crisis, 1912–13.[19] The extraordinary size of naval expenditures for the first half of 1914 and their prompt approval by the Delegations undoubtedly reflected the impact of the Balkan Wars and general European tensions.

The details of financing the proposed 1915–19 fleet expansion programme were worked out by the common Ministerial Council in Vienna on 14 December 1913. Three days later, Admiral Haus met with representatives of the Austrian and Hungarian Finance Ministries and the common Finance Ministry and agreed that no annual instalment of the 427 million crown programme could exceed 100 million crowns. It was also stipulated that annual expenditures had to agree with annual appropriation. This meant a very slow building rate, for if all four planned superdreadnoughts were laid down simultaneously, or if construction was started in pairs, they could not enter service until the first half of 1919.[20]

The common Ministerial Council tentatively decided to delete from the programme the construction of two colliers, thus reducing Title VII of the budget. This, combined with only a 1.5 million crown annual increase in the Navy's regular budget to meet greater ship maintenance costs and an increase in personnel, led in Admiral Haus's opinion to 'a decisive weakening of the budget'. Moreover, the Finance Minister avoided giving the Admiral any assurance of future increases in the regular Navy budget. That prompted Haus to inform General Bolfras that he could defend the regular budget in the Delegations only at 'the explicit order of His Majesty'. After expressing gratitude for the

Emperor's understanding and support, Haus stated that with the aforesaid constraints on the Navy budget 'it is not only impossible to replace older ships in a timely manner by modern units, but also to maintain the fleet qualitatively at the required level'.[21]

An attempt by the Austrian Navy League to increase funds for Title VII met with strong opposition in government circles. The common Ministerial Council had consistently (and deliberately) reduced this item of the budget over the years because it had instead approved large ship construction credits. Although at the same time funds for other items of the budget were increased, that made no significant change in annual naval expenditures. Haus stated that in future he would not propose any special credit but would try to increase Title VII to an annual sum of 66 to 72 million crowns. The common Finance Minister opposed Haus's proposal on financial and technical grounds.[22]

Naval progress

The second dreadnought *Tegetthoff* entered service in July 1913. The first 890-ton, 32-knot *Tatra*-class destroyers were completed in the autumn of that year. They were the first Austro-Hungarian destroyers powered by steam turbines and designed for employment in the Mediterranean. Three of the seven new 250-ton high seas torpedo craft laid down at the Stabilimento Tecnico were launched by December 1913, and at the Danubius shipyard work on three more 250-ton high seas torpedo craft commenced. Ten 78-ton *Schichau*-class torpedo craft were converted into minesweepers by 1913. Also three 790-ton *Germania*-class submarines built at Kiel were laid down. The 1,100-ton, turbine-powered 21-knot minelayer *Chamaeleon* was launched at the Navy Yard in Pola and the first of two *Pola*-class 3,200-ton colliers (carrying 7,000 tons of coal) was laid down at the Stabilimento Tecnico.[23]

By the autumn of 1913 the Balkan crisis of 1912–13 resulted in the establishment of the new naval district command in Sebenico.[24] This command, which replaced the then existing coastal defence district (*Kuesten Verteidigungsbezirk*), was to be headed by a Rear-Admiral. The area of responsibility of naval district Sebenico extended from the Istrian–Dalmatian border in the north to the Bay of Spizza in the south; the command encompassed all shore facilities and ships for local defence of the coast. In the administrative chain of command the ships and naval installations in the Bay of Cattaro were subordinated to the Rear-Admiral in Sebenico.

The establishment of a naval district in Sebenico was only the first step in strengthening the defences in central Dalmatia. The base itself was still undeveloped and weakly defended and the situation along the rest of the Dalmatian coast was not much better. The defences in the Bay of Cattaro were especially inadequate. The Army Inspector in Sarajevo, General Oskar von Potiorek, who in July 1913 conducted the last inspection tour of the Bay of Cattaro before the outbreak of the First World War, thought the state of the landfront defences would only be adequate in the event of war with Montenegro alone. He thought that the Bay of Cattaro would be indefensible if the Montenegrins attacked by land and their allies forced their way into the gulf by sea. He requested that two new forts be built at the entrance to the Bay of Cattaro; and additionally, that three fortifications in the Bay of Castelnuovo be reinforced. The build-up in the defences of the Bay of Cattaro could be completed within three years.[25] However, General Potiorek's recommendations were not put into effect because of the outbreak of the First World War.

Implementation of naval convention

Co-operation among the Triple Alliance fleets after the signing of the new naval convention in June 1913 went smoothly. However, the Italians and Germans were more enthusiastic about it than the Austro-Hungarians. Despite the somewhat strained relations between Vienna and Rome in the early autumn of 1913, Italian Admiral di Revel planned to meet Admiral Haus to discuss in detail arrangements for joint action as envisaged in the supplementary agreement of the naval convention.[26] He proposed on 20 October that the meeting take place in Switzerland, Germany, or a large Italian town such as Milan or Turin. Haus responded on 17 November and suggested that di Revel select a place in Switzerland; both admirals were to be accompanied by only one officer.[27]

The meeting between the Italian and Austro-Hungarian Navy Commanders took place around 20 December in Zurich. There were no records on the Austro-Hungarian side about either the exact date or the conversations held and the only record of the meeting is an unsigned memorandum by di Revel. Because the meeting was held at a time of heightened tension over the border issue in southern Albania, that was one of the topics discussed. More important, Haus and di Revel agreed on the division of zones in the event of a naval blockade of Greece. The Austro-Hungarian fleet was to be responsible for that part of the Greek coast from Corfú to Cape Mallas. Italian Foreign Minister San Giuliano urged Prime Minister Giolitti on 8 November to prepare a naval action against Greece if she did not withdraw her forces from northern Epirus by 31 December 1913. However, the contemplated action proved to be unnecessary because Athens, faced with a firm joint stand by Vienna and Rome, agreed to withdraw her troops from the disputed territories by 31 March 1914.[28]

The problem of the southern Albanian border was resolved on 20 December when the international boundary commission announced that it accepted the British plan. This decision, known as the 'Protocol of Florence', stated that the borderline was to run from Phtelia Bay on the coast to south-west of Mount Kazan and thence across the Sarandoporos River (north of Koritza). Thus the disputed towns of Argyrocastro, Santi Quaranta, Tepeleni, Koritza, and Cape Stylos were included in Albania. In exchange the powers agreed to give Greece all the Aegean Islands then in dispute with Turkey.[29]

Haus and di Revel discussed in great detail various scenarios for joint action against the French fleet in the western Mediterranean. The technical aspects of the naval agreement, including logistical support for the Austro-Hungarian fleet, signalling, and formations and evolutions of the combined squadrons were also discussed. Significantly, both Navy commanders agreed to hold joint naval manoeuvres in the autumn of 1914 in the western Mediterranean.

Another question considered by Haus and di Revel was the most effective use of the excellent German battle-cruiser *Goeben*. The new commander of the *Mittelmeerdivision*, Rear-Admiral Wilhelm von Souchon, in October 1913 met with Admiral Haus to discuss these matters. He held talks with the Italian Fleet Commander, Vice-Admiral Duke of Abruzzi in December. Both admirals agreed that she had to be employed at the beginning of a war against French troop convoys and only afterwards to join the Austro-Italian fleet. Di Revel and Haus also decided to request German Chief of the Admiralty Staff von Pohl to deploy two large German destroyers as escorts for the *Goeben*.[30] The German admiral in his response to Haus on 5 January 1914 agreed to the proposed employment of the *Goeben*, but regretted that no destroyers and high seas torpedo craft could be deployed in the Mediterranean at that time. He asked instead if these ships could come from either the Italian or the Austro-Hungarian Navy.[31]

Austro-Italian rivalry in Albania

While the implementation of the clauses of the naval convention of 1913 proceeded apace, relations between the Dual Monarchy and Italy worsened because of their conflicting aims in the Adriatic and Albania. Moreover, tensions between Vienna and Belgrade remained high. Under these circumstances it seemed almost certain that the Delegations would approve Admiral Haus's proposed five-year ship construction programme.

Vienna and Rome collaborated in opposing Greek territorial ambitions in Albania, but they remained wary of each other's activities in that country. From the beginning of 1914 Austro-Italian rivalry in Albania was increased by a controversy over how to strengthen the position of the Prince of Wied. The sore point between Vienna and Rome was Italy's intensified economic penetration of southern Albania and Montenegro. Berchtold and San Giuliano at their 14–18 April meeting in Abbazia reached a general agreement on future policies in Albania. However, the ministers traded accusations about the activities of their respective diplomatic and commercial representatives there.

Between April and August 1914 tensions between Vienna and Rome over Albania grew steadily. The Prince of Wied's rule was increasingly challenged by the native tribes who, instigated by Italian agents, were in a state of open rebellion. However, Italy failed to prevent the strengthening of the Austro-Hungarian political influence in the country. This was why San Giuliano wanted to internationalize the Albanian problem. By early June he sought British support for Italy's policies in Albania. Moreover, he suggested sending British and Italian troops to Durazzo. However, Foreign Secretary Grey believed British public opinion would not favour such action because it would mean a military occupation of Albania. In Grey's view the Prince of Wied could be better protected by sending warships to the port of Durazzo. Great Britain was ready to participate in such an undertaking if each of the other Mediterranean powers sent one naval vessel and even if Russia abstained from such an action.

However Italy was not then ready to send troops to Albania if the Dual Monarchy did the same because Italian public opinion would not support it. Another reason was Serbia's threat to take action of her own in Albania if the Austro-Hungarian troops were sent to Albania.[32]

In the end, the powers agreed to send warships off Durazzo to demonstrate their support for the Prince of Wied. The three Triple Alliance partners sent one warship each as did Great Britain. By 15 June, during the siege of Durazzo by insurgents, the Prince of Wied asked British Rear-Admiral E.C.T. Troubridge to bombard the city. Troubridge turned down this request because of the lack of instructions from his superiors. An armistice came into effect in Durazzo on 20 June and ten days later the Prince requested the British Admiral to blockade the coast to prevent the insurgents from getting arms. But Admiral Troubridge also refused this request.[33]

London attributed much of the responsibility for the unrest in Albania to Italy, whose agents were instructed to turn the Albanian Moslems against the pro-Austrian Catholic Albanian party. The Moslems were also vehemently opposed to the Prince of Wied's rule.[34]

The Durazzo affair led to a violent campaign against Italy in the Austro-Hungarian press spearheaded by the *Neue Freie Presse*. Some newspapers went as far as to advocate that the incompatibility of interests between the Dual Monarchy and Italy in the Adriatic be openly acknowledged and that it was useless to pursue a chimerical policy of reconciliation. Tensions between Vienna and Rome became so bad that Berchtold threatened on 24 June that Vienna would follow a separate course. He even suggested that a union of Albania with Greece might be desirable.[35]

The British ambassador in Rome, Rodd, observed that Italy's position was weak because of her chaotic financial situation. On the one hand, she was in no position to counter the Austro-Hungarian influence in the eastern Adriatic lest her weakness be revealed; yet on the other hand, Italy's public opinion would be adverse to any government action in concert with Vienna's. However, events in Albania and the possibility of a further worsening of relations between Vienna and Rome led the Italian Foreign Ministry (Consulta) to believe that the best way to prevent this from happening was to replace the Prince of Wied with another ruler so that Rome and Vienna could make a new start in Albania. By the end of June 1914 the crisis over Albania reached a critical point when, with Rome's knowledge and encouragement, 'volunteers' for Albania began to be recruited in Italy.[36]

The growing opposition to the Prince of Wied's rule by the Albanian populace also prompted Serbia and Greece to push their claims against that country. The Serbian ambassador in Vienna told the British ambassador there on 26 June that because both the Dual Monarchy and Italy were at loggerheads in Albania the best solution would be for Serbia to take over northern and southern Albania. Thereby Serbia would acquire access to the sea and would not cast her eyes beyond the Dual Monarchy's frontier. The ambassador suggested that Serbian and

Greek Adriatic ports could be neutralized by an international treaty to remove any fear by Austria-Hungary and Italy that Russia would use these ports as naval bases. If that happened Serbia would be willing to satisfy Bulgaria with a slice of Macedonia. Hence, the Balkan states would live peacefully side by side.[37]

By early July 1914 Austro-Italian tensions over Albania decreased somewhat, but opposition to the Prince of Wied's rule continued to grow. While Rome thought the prince's position was untenable, Vienna's policy was to support him at any price. The Greeks on their part supported Epirote rebels who threatened in mid-July to capture Valona. There were also press reports that Italian troops intended to occupy Valona. Therefore, Chancellor von Bethmann Hollweg said that such an action by Italy without notifying Vienna in advance would be undesirable for Germany because sooner or later it would cause friction between Italy and Austria-Hungary. Berchtold requested the German government to advise Italy that in case of Epirote capture of Valona an international fleet demonstration and occupation of that port by a small landing detachment should be carried out.[38]

Tensions between Vienna and Rome over the Albanian question continued until the outbreak of the First World War and beyond. Moreover, it seems that this issue partly influenced Italy's attitude toward the belligerents in the initial phase of the ensuing world conflict.[39]

The Triple Alliance's naval co-operation intensifies

Despite growing difficulties between Vienna and Rome, there were still strong proponents of co-operation between the two countries in the Mediterranean. Among them was the Hungarian President, Count Stephen Tisza. He stated in January 1914 that the Austro-Hungarian fleet was valuable because it increased the strength of 'our alliance with Italy, a nation which in respect to the balance of power in the Mediterranean has great value for us'. Tisza categorically denied that the Dual Monarchy was strengthening her fleet against Italy, insisting that 'we are strengthening the fleet to provide valuable service to Italy'.[40]

The Germans and the Italians led the efforts to intensify co-operation among the Triple Alliance fleets in the Mediterranean. Admirals di Revel and Souchon held talks in Rome in January 1914 on joint action in the Mediterranean. Afterwards, Souchon and Haus agreed that the first task of the Triple Alliance fleets was to hamper the movement of French troop transports from North Africa.

Admiral von Pohl in January 1914 designated Commander Arnim (who had succeeded Koehler in the Admiralty Staff) to act as his personal representative, to ensure that other provisions of the naval convention were put into effect. Arnim conducted a special mission to Vienna in April 1914 to standardize norms for the requisition and utilization of German merchant vessels in the Mediterranean by the Austro-Hungarian and Italian fleets in case of war. Although the Italians showed great interest in this matter, the Austrians were apparently cool.[41]

Co-operation among the three Triple Alliance fleets on other matters stipulated by the naval convention progressed reasonably well in the winter and spring of 1914. The Germans prepared a common signal book printed in German just before the outbreak of the First World War; about 400 copies were delivered to the Austro-Hungarians. An Italian version was also to be printed in Berlin because of the alleged lack of adequate secrecy in Rome. Manoeuvring data for various classes of naval vessels were also exchanged and the Italians prepared stocks of coal in Augusta for use by the Austro-Hungarian fleet. Intelligence information, mostly on the French and British navies, was exchanged regularly among the commands of all three navies for a full year preceding the outbreak of the war.[42]

Naval construction progress

By the spring of 1914 almost all the dreadnoughts, cruisers, and destroyers approved in the 1911–15 construction programme were either in service or nearing completion. The third and last dreadnought, Prinz Eugen, built at the Stabilimento Tecnico, was completed in March 1914 and was expected to be commissioned four months later. The rapid construction of dreadnoughts at Trieste impressed the British who noted that this had not been achieved at the cost of poor workmanship. The British professional journal *Naval and Military Record* wrote 'there is no doubt that given the financial means the Austro-Hungarian Navy could be developed at a rate that would quickly give it a commanding position in the Mediterranean'.[43]

By the spring of 1914 the fourth dreadnought, *Szent Istvan*, was about 70 per cent complete. However, she was not expected to enter service before the beginning of 1915. A similar situation existed with the construction of two 3,500-ton cruisers at the Danubius shipyard. The first of these cruisers (*Helgoland*) was not commissioned until August 1914 and the second (*Novara*) until January 1915. The building of the third cruiser (*Saida*) at the Cantiere Navale also proceeded slowly because of great technical difficulties, and she was not completed until August 1914. The construction of *Tatra*-class destroyers at Porto Re was behind schedule and the last three ships did not enter service until July 1914.

The construction of twelve 250-ton high seas torpedo craft proceeded with great difficulty in both Porto Ré and Monfalcone. Only one 74T-class torpedo craft built at the Stabilimento Tecnico was finished by the beginning of 1914, while three others of the same class were expected to enter service in July 1914.

By the spring of 1914, for lack of additional orders, there was a slowdown in the work of the Austrian shipyards. A particularly difficult situation developed at the Stabilimento Tecnico, when about 1,000 workers were laid off after the completion of the *Prinz Eugen* in March because the keel of a new dreadnought was not laid down as expected.[44]

The delay in the approval of the new five-year ship construction programme by the Delegations was the principal reason for the difficulties encountered by the Stabilimento Tecnico. This prompted the Austrian Navy League to petition the Delegations in January 1914 to replace ships which had reached the age limit. The League argued that this 'should be an automatic procedure provided in the regular Navy budget'. It also urged that funds be authorized to build a number of foreign service cruisers to make possible a 'dignified representation' of the Dual Monarchy abroad without weakening the *Active Eskadre* at home.[45]

The ship construction programme, 1915–19, is submitted

By mid-April 1914 Admiral Haus presented the long-awaited new fleet expansion programme (1915–19) to the Delegations. By then the Navy's case had made many converts in the Delegations, even among Hungarian deputies. Count Tisza spoke for many of his colleagues when he asserted that 'a great power cannot adopt an Army and Navy organization according to momentary political requirements'. Moreover, he added, the Austro-Hungarian Navy had to be strengthened to make the alliance with Italy worthwhile.[46] The Hungarian Delegation approved the Navy's proposal after less than half an hour of discussion. In the Navy Commission of the Hungarian Delegation, debate focused on securing Hungary's share (36.4 per cent) of naval orders for her industry. Hungarian Deputy Prince Windischgraetz complained of delay in the approval of the fleet expansion programme and advocated an increase in the Navy budget to avoid the use of a special credit: a view the Navy had urged for a long time.

Discussion in the Austrian Delegation was also favourable to the Navy's request. This led Admiral Haus to claim that no other Austro-Hungarian Navy Commander had had an easier time in securing approval for his programme of fleet expansion.[47] Of interest are the discussions of some deputies that throw light on why the new 1915–19 ship construction programme was expeditiously approved by the Delegations. Count Luetzow, the former Austro-Hungarian ambassador in Rome and deputy, argued that the Mediterranean was in the forefront of the interests of the great powers. He asserted that Russia's goal was to open the Straits and hoped British public opinion would not attach less importance to the question than before.

The influential Viennese newspaper *Neue Freie Presse* wrote that Luetzow's words expressed the views of many deputies in the Austrian Delegation who were concerned that Russia's Black Sea dreadnought squadron might one day operate in the Mediterranean. The paper claimed that such fast approval of the naval expansion programme had a deeper meaning because it showed that the Dual Monarchy was determined to protect her position on the seas at any price. Count Luetzow also repeated von Aehrenthal's prediction that Austria-Hungary would have Italy as an ally as long as she remained strong. Therefore, strengthening the Austro-Hungarian fleet was necessary to safeguard 'our possessions, freedom of sea routes, and alliance with Italy'.[48]

It seems safe to say that the Delegations approved the 1915–19 fleet expansion programme because of their concern over the possible employment of the Russian fleet in the Mediterranean in conjunction with the French and British fleets. Italy was still viewed as an ally with which the Dual Monarchy would co-operate to maintain a favourable balance of power in the Mediterranean.

The 1915–19 ship construction programme was approved by the Delegations on 28 April 1914 and was to come into force on 1 July. Of the 427 million crown special credit, all but 26 million were to be spent on ship construction. Orders for the construction of four new 24,500-ton *Ersatz Monarch*-class superdreadnoughts were evenly shared between Austrian and Hungarian shipyards; the three 4,800-ton scout cruisers, two Danube monitors, and one supply ship also went to Austrian industries; and the six 800-ton destroyers were allocated for construction at the Hungarian shipyards. Naval orders were shared according to the existing quota agreement between the two parts of the Monarchy. Austrian industry's share was 269.6 million crowns and

Hungary's 154.3 million crowns, while orders from abroad amounted only to three million crowns.[49]

The first of the projected superdreadnoughts (*Schlachtschiff-VIII*) was to be laid down in July 1914 (later changed to September) and others were to follow in 1915 and 1916, so that all of them would be completed by May 1919 (see Figure 8). The *Ersatz Monarchs* were the first Austro-Hungarian battleships that instead of a flushdeck had a lengthened forecastle deck, often found on British ships. They were in fact the first Austro-Hungarian ships designed to operate on the open oceans.

Admiral Haus explained to the Delegations in April 1914 that the *Ersatz Monarch* was armed with 14-inch guns instead of 15-inch guns because the latter would mean an increase of displacement to 30,000 tons, with each ship costing 72 million crowns. However, Admiral Haus's statement was in error because the new *Ersatz Monarch* was to cost 81.6 million crowns.[50] Like the *Tegetthoff* class, her superstructure was kept to a minimum and the secondary battery was concentrated at two levels abreast of the funnels and bridge. Although the *Ersatz Monarch* retained the same layout, she was better designed than the *Tegetthoff* class with smaller list in heavy seas and more reserve stability. The *Ersatz Monarch*, unlike her predecessors, was to have oil-burning instead of mixed combustion boilers and turbine propulsion of 31,000 SHP output capable of attaining a maximum speed of 21 knots. In that respect the *Ersatz Monarch* would have been clearly inferior to their counterparts in other navies.

FIGURE 8
SCHEDULE OF SHIP CONSTRUCTION PROGRAMME, 1915–19

Ship type	No.	Tonnage	Price (millions of crowns)	Laid down	Completed	Building time (months)
Battleships						
Schlachtschiff VIII	4	24,500	83.55	1 July 1914	30 June 1917	36
Schlachtschiff IX	4	24,500	81.55	1 Jan. 1915	31 Dec. 1917	36
Schlachtschiff X	4	24,500	81.55	1 June 1916	31 May 1919	36
Schlachtschiff XI	4	24,500	81.55	1 June 1916	31 May 1919	36
Cruisers						
Kreuzer K	3	4,800	15.45	1 July 1914	31 Dec. 1916	30
Kreuzer L	3	4,800	15.45	1 July 1915	31 Dec. 1917	30
Kreuzer M	3	4,800	15.45	1 July 1915	31 Dec. 1917	30
Destroyers	6	800	20.15	1 July 1915	30 June 1918	36
Danube monitors	2	520	4.89	1 July 1916	30 June 1919	36
Supply ships	1	450	0.33	1 July 1915	30 June 1915	12
Total	16	118,690	399.92			

Source: Haus's letter, 19 March 1914, no. 1035, *Kriegsarchiv, Praesidial Kanzlei, Marinesektion-XV-7/7, 1914*

The naval budget of 1914–15 is approved

The Delegations also approved in April 1914 naval expenditures for the fiscal year 1914–15 amounting to about 176 million crowns. The ordinary budget included funds for one 870-ton Laurenti-class submarine to be built at the Italian Fiat shipyard in San Giorgio and another under licence at the Cantiere Navale. The naval expenditures for 1914–15 also included funds to start construction of three superdreadnoughts, one cruiser, and one supply ship, envisaged under the 1915-19 fleet expansion programme. The first regular instalment of the funds, about 200,000 crowns to start the expansion of Sebenico into a large naval base, was also allocated. The Delegations were informed that Sebenico's expansion was necessary because of the large number of ships coming into service and the need to relieve congestion in the Navy's only large base in Pola.[51]

Naval expenditures for 1914–15 totalled 76.2 million crowns in the regular budget (for continuing the construction of the 1,000-ton minelayer *Chamaeleon*, nine 250-ton high seas torpedo craft, one 870-ton submarine, and two 7,000-ton colliers) and 47.5 million crowns as the last instalment of the 1911–15 special credit (for construction of 12 250-ton high sea torpedo craft and three submarines), a 7.2 million crowns one-time special credit (for the construction of six 250-ton high seas torpedo craft, two submarines, two Danube monitors, two river patrol craft, one 40,000-ton floating dock, and the expansion of naval aviation), and 45.3 million crowns as the first instalment of the 1915–19 special credit. Austro-Hungarian naval aviation, which at the beginning of 1914 comprised only 15 airplanes, was to acquire 80 airplanes by 1919.[52]

The Navy also announced plans to increase its personnel in the 1914–15 fiscal year by 1,800 men to a total of 22,900 officers and men. This increase was necessary because of the Navy plans to keep three *Habsburg*-class battleships and one armoured cruiser in active service during the winter beginning in fiscal year 1914-15. These ships were to absorb about half the naval recruiting contingent each year and would have the same role as the Third Battle Squadron in the German High Seas fleet.[53]

The navy's composition

By mid-1914 the Austro-Hungarian Navy consisted of 114 ships with 238,000 tons. In terms of tonnage, the Navy occupied sixth place among the European navies and eighth among world navies: the same rank it had held in 1904. In comparison with the Italian Navy, the Austro-Hungarian fleet had roughly equal numbers of battleships, small cruisers, and coastal torpedo craft (see Figure 9). It had in service three dreadnoughts plus five built or planned. The corresponding figures for the Italian Navy were four and six. In this category, both navies lagged far behind the British and German fleets which in May 1914 had in service 29 and 17 dreadnoughts respectively. However, both Austria-Hungary and Italy were ahead of the Russian Navy, which then occupied sixth place in the world in terms of tonnage. Russia had only one dreadnought in service, but an additional 12 were under construction or planned in 1914.[54]

Naval balance in the Mediterranean

By May 1914 the Austro-Hungarian Navy in comparison to the Italian Navy had in service three times as many armoured cruisers and submarines and almost twice the number of destroyers and coastal torpedo craft. However, Italian superiority over the Austro-Hungarian fleet was in fact far less imperative than the number of ships and total tonnages indicated. This was because the Italian Navy had to protect three coasts as well as colonial possessions in Africa and the Aegean Sea. It also lacked the Austro-Hungarian fleet's ability to concentrate its entire strength in the Adriatic. The Austro-Hungarian naval policy makers in fact were successful at accomplishing their goal of having a fleet roughly equal, if not superior, to the Italian fleet in the Adriatic.

The intensified naval race among the great European powers and the redistribution of the British and French fleets brought about significant changes in the Mediterranean power balance from mid-1912 onwards. France's decision to concentrate almost her entire fleet in the Mediterranean signified the end of her policy of maintaining equality with the German Navy. Instead, she chose to obtain a dominant position in the western Mediterranean over the combined Italian and Austro-Hungarian fleets. The redistribution of the French fleet was practically completed following the transfer of the Third Battle Squadron in early 1913 from the Atlantic to Bizerte, Tunisia. Two other battle squadrons of the first battle fleet were based at Toulon. By the summer of 1914 the French fleet in the Mediterranean consisted of 17 battleships, while the combined battleship strength of the Triple Alliance fleets there stood at 23. However, the French fleet had only three dreadnoughts as opposed to six for the combined Italian and Austro-Hungarian fleets. Also, excluding dreadnoughts, only five of the French battleships had been

FIGURE 9

COMPARATIVE NAVAL STRENGTH OF ITALY AND AUSTRIA-HUNGARY, MAY 1914

| | Italy | | Austria-Hungary | | Italy/Austria-Hungary |
	No.	Tonnage	No.	Tonnage	Tonnage ratio
Dreadnoughts	3	67,676	3	60,042	1.1:1.0
Other battleships	8*	98,564	12	114,840	0.9:1.0
Armoured cruisers	11	86,602	3	18,800	4.6:1.0
Torpedo cruisers	6	5,030	2	3,060	1.6:1.0
Protected cruisers	10	31,374	5	15,050	2.1:1.0
Scout-cruisers	5	13,047	2	7,080	1.8:1.0
Destroyers	31	121,514	18	10,860	1.2:1.0
High seas torpedo craft	29	6,221	25	4,000	1.6:1.0
Coastal torpedo craft	41	5,009	29	2,920	1.7:1.0
Submarines	20	4,427	6	1,412	3.1:1.0
Total	173	330,464	105	238,064	1.4:1.0

Note: *Exclusive of six obsolescent battleships with 76,166 tons.
Source: Aldo Fraccaroli, *Italian Warships of World War I* (London: Ian Allen, 1970);
René Greger, *Austro-Hungarian Warships of World War I* (London: Ian Allen, 1976).

built after 1900. The French Navy also had serious problems connected with its ammunition. So-called 'B-powder' then used in the French Navy was highly unstable and it caused the explosion on the battleships *Iena* in 1907 and *Liberté* in 1911. As a result of the *Liberté* disaster, which left 210 men dead and 136 badly injured, Navy Minister Théophile Delcassé ordered the replacement of all ammunition manufactured before 1907, thereby for all practical purposes disarming the French fleet. The 'powder crisis' was not resolved until after 1913.

Besides battleships, the first battle fleet in the summer of 1914 comprised two cruiser divisions with nine cruisers, six destroyer flotillas with 37 destroyers, and two submarine flotillas (four destroyers and 16 submarines). In the north only three cruisers, 23 destroyers and 18 submarines were deployed.[55]

From mid-1912 until the outbreak of the First World War there were no significant changes in the disposition of the British fleet in the Mediterranean. During the winter of 1912–13 a six-ship battle squadron from home waters was temporarily deployed in the Mediterranean. However, by the end of 1915 the British planned to deploy eight battleships instead of four battle-cruisers at Malta. The fleet in the Mediterranean was to have the same number of destroyers after the redistribution plan of July 1912 was put in force.[56]

The Russian Black Sea fleet in the summer of 1914 consisted of eight mostly very old battleships and only one dreadnought. An additional three dreadnoughts were then under construction or on order. The rest of the fleet comprised only two large and three small cruisers, 22 destroyers, more than 100 torpedo craft, and eight submarines.

The comparative strength of the Triple Alliance and the Triple Entente in July 1914 showed that both sides had almost equal strength in battleships, cruisers, and submarines. The Triple Alliance fleets then had six dreadnoughts to four for the French and Russian fleets combined. They also enjoyed a comfortable superiority in destroyers and a huge lead in torpedo-craft (see Figure 10). However, the strength of the Austro-Hungarian fleet was substantially less than indicated because of a very inadequate number of cruisers. Nevertheless, the naval balance in the Mediterranean just before the outbreak of the war apparently favoured the Triple Alliance.

FIGURE 10
NAVAL BALANCE IN THE MEDITERRANEAN: TRIPLE ENTENTE v. TRIPLE ALLIANCE, MAY 1914

Type	France	Britain	Russia	Total	Italy	Austria-Hungary	Germany	Total
Dreadnoughts	3	-	1	4	3	3	-	6
Semi-dreadnoughts	6	-	2	8	2	3	-	5
Pre-dreadnoughts	8	-	5	13	8	9	-	17
Battle-cruisers	-	4	-	4	-	-	1	1
Cruisers	9	8	5	22	26	12	1	39
Destroyers	41	12	22	75	31	18	-	49
Torpedo craft	3	-	13	16	70	54	-	124
Submarines	16	-	8	24	20	6	-	26
Total	86	24	56	166	160	105	2	267

Source: 'Staerkevergleich der acht groessten Seemaechte', *Nauticus* (1914) pp. 634–9; Aldo Fraccaroli, *Italian Warships of World War I* (London: Ian Allen, 1970); René Greger, *Austro-Hungarian Warships of World War I* (London: Ian Allen, 1976)

NOTES

1. R. Rodd to Grey, 15 April 1913, no. 851, *British Documents on the Origins of the War 1898–1914*, ed. G. P. Gooch and Harold Temperley, 11 vols (London: HMSO, 1926–38) (hereafter *BD*) Vol. 10(2), p. 69; Ernst Helmreich, *The Diplomacy of the Balkan Wars 1912–1913* (Cambridge, MA: Harvard University Press, 1938; reprinted New York: Russell & Russell, 1969) p. 335.
2. Edith Pierpont Stickney, *Southern Albania or Northern Epirus in European International Affairs 1912–1923* (Stanford, CA: Stanford University Press, 1926) p. 34.
3. Ibid., p. 37; R. J. B. Bosworth, *Italy, the Least of the Great Powers. Italian Foreign Policy Before the First World War* (London/New York: Cambridge University Press, 1979) p. 321.
4. Bosworth, *Italy, the Least of the Great Powers*, pp. 284, 384.
5. Gianluco André, *L'Italia e il Mediterraneo alla Vigilia della Prima Guerra Mondiale, Tentativi*

di Intesa Mediterranea (1911–1914) (Milan: A Giuffré, 1967) p. 175.

6. Ibid., pp. 210–13.
7. Editor's note following Lord Granville to Grey, 26 September 1913, no. 21, *BD*, Vol. 10(1), pp. 17–18.
8. William C. Askew, 'Austro-Italian antagonism, 1896–1914', in Lilian Parker Wallace and William C. Askew, *Power, Public Opinion and Diplomacy. Essays in Honor of Eber Malcolm Carroll by his Students* (Durham NC: Duke University Press, 1959) p. 209.
9. Arthur J. May, The Habsburg Monarchy 1867–1914 (Cambridge, MA: Harvard University Press, 1951) pp. 467–8.
10. Ibid.
11. 'Informazioni e Notizie. Marina Militare', *Rivista Marittima* 1 (January 1914) p. 81.
12. 'Foreign navies', *Navy League Annual* (1914) pp. 45–6. Unsigned, n.d., no. 1199, Kriegsarchiv, Praesidial Kanzlei, Marinesektion-SV-7, 1913 (hereafter PK/MS).
13. Franz Conrad von Hoetzendorf, Aus meiner Dienstzeit 1908–1918, 5 vols (Vienna: Rikola Verlag, 1922–25) Vol. 3, p. 744.
14. Ibid.
15. Ibid., p. 745.
16. The fiscal year which until 1914 coincided with the calendar year was subsequently to start on 1 July and end on 30 June.
17. Von Hoetzendorf, *Aus meiner Dienstzeit 1908–1918*, p. 744; 'Informazioni e Notizie. Marina Militare', *Rivista Marittima* 11 (November 1913) pp. 399–401. 'Rundschau in allen Marinen', *Marine Rundschau* 9 (September 1913) p. 1118.
18. Conrad, *Aus meiner Dienstzeit*, Vol. 3, p. 743.
19. 'Budget der K.u.K. Kriegsmarine (fuer die ersten sechs Monate 1914)', *Mitteilungen aus dem Gebiete des Seewesens* 1 (January 1914) pp. 606–61; ibid., pp. 51–64; 'Foreign navies', Navy League Annual (1914) p. 46.
20. Haus to Bolfras, 13 January 1914, Kriegsarchiv, Militaer Kanzlei Seiner Majestaet 51-1/3-1, 1914 (hereafter MKSM); Haus to Bolfras, 3 January 1914, MKFF and Bardolff to Haus, 23 January 1914, ibid.
21. Haus to Bardolff, 13 January 1914, MKSM 51-1/3, 1914.
22. 'Die fremden Kriegsmarinen', *Nauticus* (1914), p. 166.
23. René Greger, *Austro-Hungarian Warships of World War I* (London: Ian Allan, 1976) p. 113.
24. The statute for naval district Sebenico was issued by the Emperor on 17 April 1913. For details see supplement to *Marine-Normalverordnungsblatt*, Vol. 21, no. 1688, 17 April 1913, PK/MS (Vienna: Aus der K.K. Hof- und Staatsdruckerei, 1913).
25. Potiorek to Conrad, 'Ueber die militaerische Ausgestaltung d. Bocche de Cattaro', 15 April 1914, no. 1509, Kriegsarchiv Operations Kanzlei, Marinesektion-VI-1/1, 1914 (hereafter OK/MS); Eduard Ritter von Steinitz, 'Die Reichsbefestigung Oesterreich-Ungarn zur Zeit Conrads von Hoetzendorf', *Militaerwissenschaftlichen Mitteilungen* 12 (December 1936), pp. 923–39.
26. Emperor Francis Joseph I was the last to sign the Triple Alliance naval convention on 12 October. It went into effect on 1 November 1913.
27. Di Revel to Haus, October 1913, OK/MS-25/GV, 1913; Haus to de Revel, 17 November 1913, ibid.
28. R. J. B. Bosworth, *Italy, the Least of the Great Powers: Italian Foreign Policy before the First World War* (London/New York: Cambridge University Press, 1979) p. 321.
29. Stickney, *Southern Albania*, pp. 40-1.
30. Paul G. Halpern, *The Mediterranean Naval Situation (1908–1914)* (Cambridge, MA: Harvard University Press, 1970), pp. 257–8.
31. Pohl to Haus, 5 January 1914, OK/MS-GV, 1913-15, Sonderreihe.
32. Grey to R. Rodd, 4 June 1914, no. 136, *BD*, Vol. 10(1), pp. 118–20.
33. Editor's note following E. Goschen to E. Grey, 5 June 1914, no. 137, ibid., pp. 120–1.
34. Minutes by Edgar Grey, Eyre Crowe and Arthur Nicolson, 1 July 1914, ibid., pp. 125–7.
35. W. Askew, 'Austro-Italian antagonism', p. 210.
36. R. Rodd to Grey, 23 June 1914, no. 447, *BD*, Vol. 10(1), pp. 122–3; Flotow to Betthmann Hollweg, 20 June 1914, no. 14507, *Die Grosse Politik der Europaeischen Kabinette 1871–1914*, ed. Johannes Lepsius, Albrecht M. Bartholdy, Friedrich Thimme, 40 vols (Berlin: Deutsche Verlagsgesellschaft fuer Politik und Geschichte, 1927) (hereafter *GP*) Vol. 36(2), pp. 707–8.

37. Maurice de Bunsen to Grey, 26 June 1914, no. 140, *BD*, Vol. 10(1), pp. 124–5.
38. Tschirschky to Bethmann Hollweg, 14 July 1914, no. 14537, *GP*, Vol. 36(2), pp. 734–5; Bethmann Hollweg minute, 18 July 1914, ibid., p. 737.
39. W. Askew, 'Austro-Italian antagonism', p. 210.
40. 'Informazioni e Notizie. Marina Militare', *Rivista Marittima* 2 (February 1914) pp. 274–5.
41. 'Protokoll ueber die Frage der Ueberlassung und Benuetzung deutscher Handelschiffe durch Oesterreich-Ungarn', 20 April 1914, OK/MS-11/GV, 1913.
42. Various worksheets, OK/MS-GV, 1913-15; Halpern, *The Mediterranean Naval Situation*, p. 261.
43. *Viribus Unitis* was built in 26 months, *Tegetthoff* in 31 months, and *Prinz Eugen* in 27 months. 'Professional notes', *USNI Proceedings* 3 (May–June 1914) p. 827.
44. 'Die fremden Kriegsmarinen', *Nauticus* (1914) p. 164.
45. 'Professional notes', *USNI Proceedings* 2 (March–April 1914) pp. 491–92; 'Informazioni e Notizie. Marina Militare', *Rivista Marittima* 2 (February 1914) p. 275.
46. 'Die fremden Kriegsmarinen', *Nauticus* (1914) p. 164.
47. 'Rundschau in allen Marinen', *Marine Rundschau* 6 (June 1914) p. 964.
48. Ibid., pp. 964–5.
49. Haus letter, 19 March 1914, no. 1035, PK/MS-XV-7/7, 1914; *Die Flagge* 5 (May 1914) p. 150. Unsigned, 19 February 1914, no. 1035, PK/MS-XV-7/7, 1914.
50. 'Rundschau in allen Marinen', *Marine Rundschau* 6 (June 1914) p. 964.
51. 'Budget der K.u.K. Kriegsmarine fuer das Jahr 1914–15', *Mitteilungen aus dem Gebiete des Seewesens* 8 (August 1914) p. 832; 'Die fremden Kriegsmarinen', *Nauticus* (1914) p. 170.
52. 'Die fremden Kriegsmarinen', *Nauticus* (1914) p. 1712; 'Rundschau in allen Marinen', *Marine Rundschau* 6 (June 1914) p. 830.
53. 'Rundschau in allen Marinen', *Marine Rundschau* 6 (June 1914) p. 963; 'Professional notes', *USNI Proceedings* 1 (January–February 1914) p. 190.
54. 'Staerkevergleich der acht groessten Seemaechte', *Nauticus* (1914) pp. 634–9; 'Die fremden Kriegsmarinen', ibid., p. 141.
55. 'Die fremden Kriegsmarinen', *Nauticus* (1914) p. 118.
56. 'Comparative strength', *Navy League Annual* (1914) p. 70; 'Liste der Kriegschiffe der groesseren Seemaechte', *Nauticus* (1914) pp. 592–600.

10

Summary and conclusions

The Dual Monarchy occupied a commanding geostrategic position in the Adriatic and the Balkans. She possessed a well-indented coast with numerous offshore islands offering many natural harbours and protected anchorages. Her position in the Balkans offered her an opportunity to advance through Macedonia to the Aegean Sea or through Albania to the Ionian Sea. If either of these goals had been achieved, Austria-Hungary would have become a true Mediterranean power. Her seaboard faced the Adriatic Sea, and thus was too far from the main sea routes of the Mediterranean. Both shores of the entrance to the Adriatic were in the hands of other, potentially hostile powers.

By 1904 the Dual Monarchy possessed the solid industrial base needed for the maintenance of a strong Navy and merchant marine. Six years later Austria-Hungary became almost entirely self-sufficient in the construction of naval vessels and armaments.

By then only a small part of the Navy's weapons and equipment had to be acquired from abroad. Austria-Hungary also had a relatively large, skilled and experienced seafaring population in the littoral necessary for the growth of sea power in all its aspects. However, there was a distinctive lack of interest among almost all strata of the population in maritime affairs. Moreover, the proponents of an active policy to promote the sea interests of Austria-Hungary then had little influence. The constitutional arrangement between the two parts of the Monarchy, coupled with perennially weak finances, was another great obstacle to an active and sustained policy in the pursuit of sea interests.

While the supporters of a larger and stronger fleet were neither very numerous nor influential in 1904, a few years later they had emerged as an important factor in the making of Austro-Hungarian naval policy. The heir to the throne, Archduke Francis Ferdinand, was a staunch and consistent supporter of the efforts of Admirals Montecuccoli and Haus to expand and modernize the Austro-Hungarian Navy. The Archduke's growing influence, especially in the last few years before his tragic death at the hands of a Serbian assassin in Sarajevo, proved to be highly effective and ultimately beneficial for the Navy.

Although Admiral Montecuccoli's political skills in handling the Emperor and the Delegations were widely recognized, he would not have been successful in obtaining approval for his proposals without the presence of officials at the highest level. Both Montecuccoli and Haus were, unlike their predecessors, fortunate in having Archduke Francis Ferdinand on the Navy's side in any conflict with the Army on budgetary matters or questions of prerogatives.

Archduke Francis Ferdinand also strongly supported the development of the Austro-Hungarian merchant marine and maritime industries in general. For example, he was a patron of the widely acclaimed exhibition of Austro-Hungarian shipping companies and maritime industries (Adria-Ausstellung) held in the summer of 1913 in Vienna. It was the aim of the heir to the throne to make the Dual Monarchy a strong sea power with a respected place among maritime nations.[1]

Not surprisingly, the Austrian industrial and financial institutions were among the most important supporters of a larger and stronger Navy. The construction of dreadnoughts proved to be a bonanza for Austrian shipbuilding and naval armament industries. The profits of firms such as the Stabilimento Tecnico, the Skoda Works and the Vitkovice Works rose steadily after 1904 as ships became more complex and correspondingly more expensive. Within a decade, the price of building a battleship more than tripled. For example, while the *Habsburg* (built in 1902) cost 17.3 million crowns, the *Viribus Unitis* (built in 1911) cost 60.6 million crowns. The cruiser *Aspern* was built in 1900 for 4.6 million crowns, while the *Saida* built 14 years later cost twice as much.[2]

The participation of industry in the construction of the dreadnought *Viribus Unitis* explains why heavy industry and many other industrial branches had a vested interest in the continued expansion of the Austro-Hungarian Navy. This 20,000-ton dreadnought required the employment of some 5,500 labourers working 75 million man-hours over a 26-month period. In addition to the Stabilimento Tecnico shipyard and the Skoda and Vitkovice Works, about 150 other firms participated in the dreadnought's construction.[3]

The expansion of the Austro-Hungarian Navy and the merchant marine was welcome for the population of the Austrian littoral, which otherwise did not enjoy many opportunities for employment. For example, by 1913 about 50,000 civilians earned their living directly, and another 50,000 indirectly, from the sea. An additional 10,000 civilians worked in the shipbuilding industries.[4]

The important role of the Austrian Navy League in bringing about the strengthening of the fleet must be emphasized. From its humble beginnings in 1904 the Navy League grew by mid-1914 into an association with 201 local chapters with over 43,000 members.[5] By then it was established among all strata of the Austrian population. The League made great efforts to popularize the navalists' cause, especially in the aftermath of the Austro-Hungarian annexation of Bosnia. It conducted a campaign to collect money for the purchase of two seaplanes for the Navy and one training ship for the merchant marine. The League also provided sustained support for the maintenance of the Shipping Technical Testing Establishment in Vienna.[6] However, the real extent of the League's support among high state officials and the military is difficult to gauge. Nevertheless there was no doubt that the League was very successful in awakening the interest for large sectors of public opinion in the Navy's expansion.

The main opponent of a large, rapid fleet expansion in the Dual Monarchy were the Hungarians. However, their opposition to larger fleet expansion progressively declined after 1904 because of the increasing participation of Hungarian industries in the ship construction programme. This was especially the case after 1911 when dreadnought construction began (see Figure 11). Also the impact of the Turco-Italian War and the Balkan crises in 1912–13 convinced even the Hungarians of the need to build a modern Navy. Nevertheless, securing approval of the naval budget before 1914 was always a difficult task because the Hungarian ministers in the common Ministerial Council and the Hungarian Delegation demanded various political concessions from the Austrians in return for their support of naval expenditures. Also, large increases in the Navy's budget were often rejected because of the bad financial situation in Hungary.

Another source of opposition to steady increases in Navy appropriation was the common Army, as represented by the War Minister and the Chief of the General Staff. Their views had strong support from Emperor Francis Joseph I, who regarded the Army as much more important than the Navy. Echoed by many others, General Conrad thought that although the Dual Monarchy required a strong Navy, she had a far greater need for a strong Army. He believed (correctly) that in a war, no matter what the fleet might achieve, the final outcome would be decided on land.

In the end, the Navy did succeed in drawing away a significant amount of funds sorely needed for the strengthening and modernization of the common Army. The Army's opposition to Navy plans failed, no doubt, largely because of Archduke Francis Ferdinand's great influence in both military and political matters in the Dual Monarchy.

The level of naval expenditures by the Dual Monarchy was determined by the outcome of the struggle between proponents and opponents of fleet expansion and by purely financial considerations. In general the perennially bad state of Austro-Hungarian finances after 1900 imposed severe restraints upon the size of the Army and Navy budgets. Hence, even by 1914 Austria-Hungary spent less on defence in absolute terms than any other great European power with the exception of Italy. With only 11.6 crowns per capita devoted to defence, the Dual Monarchy was outspent by every other great power with the exception of Russia. Despite the steady increase of the defence budget between 1904 and 1913 from some 515 million crowns to 717 million crowns, its share of state expenditures actually declined from 58 to 44 per cent.[7]

Between 1904 to 1913 the Navy's regular budget rose steadily from about 50 million crowns to 76 million crowns. However, if various special credits are included, then naval expenditures actually increased in the same period from 72 to about 175 million crowns, an impressive growth rate indeed (see Figure 12). At the same time expenditures for the common Army were increased only from 445 million crowns to 584 million crowns. In other words, the Navy expenditures rose at almost twice the rate of the Army's. By 1913 they comprised some 19 per cent of the total defence budget as opposed to 13.6 per cent ten years earlier.

In comparison with the other great naval powers of the day, Austria-Hungary between 1904 and 1914 was consistently in last place in regard to expenditures (see Figure 13). Italy, her neighbour and her main potential opponent, increased her naval expenditures in the same period from about 109 to 210 million crowns. The ratio between Italian and Austro-Hungarian naval expenditures in 1904 was 1.3 to 1.0. By 1910 this ratio peaked at 1.9 to 1.0. Afterwards the Italian naval budget declined, although in 1913 it still was 1.6 times as large as that of Austria-Hungary.

There were some critical differences in the structure of Italian and Austro-Hungarian naval budgets. Although Italian naval expenditures were listed as those of the Navy Ministry, they in fact included subsidies for the merchant marine and lighthouse service. The Italian Navy also had to bear some of the cost of harbour defence and coastal fortifications. For example, subsidies for the Italian merchant marine made up about 10–11 per cent of the total Navy annual budget in the period 1906–14.

In contrast the Dual Monarchy naval expenditures were exclusively

Summary and conclusions

FIGURE 11
NAVAL ORDERS, 1908-19 (IN MILLIONS OF CROWNS)

Year	Austrian industry	Hungarian industry	abroad	Total
1908	32.48	17.21	9.38	59.07
1909	48.41	10.48	8.07	66.96
1910	46.10	22.17	3.10	71.37
1911	42.61	24.39	–	67.00
1911–15	196.67	113.37	2.02	312.06
1915–19*	269.57	154.28	3.00	426.85

Note: *The entire programme was cancelled after the outbreak of the First World War
Source: *Die Flagge* (Vienna) 1 (January 1912), p.5; Haus to Bolfras, 13 January 1914, *Kriegsarchiv, Militaer Kanzlei Seiner Majestaet-51-1/3-1, 1914;* Unsigned, n.d. 1911, *Kriegsarchiv, Praesidial Kanzlei, Marinesektion-XV-7/5, 1911;* Haus letter, 9 March 1914, no. 1035, Ibid., *XV-7/7, 1914.*

devoted to the Navy whereas the Army was forced to spend from its budget rather substantial sums for the construction and maintenance of coastal fortifications. Likewise, the Austrian and Hungarian Trade Ministries shared subsidies for their respective merchant marines and other expenditures associated with maritime activities.

The 1.2 billion crowns Austria-Hungary expended on fleet expansion

FIGURE 12
NAVAL EXPENDITURES OF AUSTRIA-HUNGARY, 1904-14
(IN MILLIONS OF CROWNS)

Year	Regular naval expenditure	Special credit	Total naval expenditure	Common Government expenditure	Naval expenditure as percentage of state budget	Population (in millions)	Naval expenditure per head in crowns
1901	43.5	–	43.5	NA	–	45.8	0.9
1904	50.0	22.1	72.1	879.5	8.2	47.0	1.5
1905	28.9	52.9	81.8	915.0	8.9	47.9	1.7
1906	31.3	26.3	57.6	931.0	6.2	47.8	1.2
1907	45.4	19.6	65.0	1,141.9	5.7	49.2	1.3
1908	56.9	3.4	60.3	1,187.0	5.1	49.8	1.2
1909	58.4	32.6	91.0	1,441.8	6.3	51.0	1.8
1910	67.0	18.0	85.0	1,450.7	5.9	51.5	1.7
1911	68.0	55.0	123.0	1,502.0	8.2	52.0	2.4
1912	34.0	67.0	101.0	1,592.2	6.3	52.3	1.9
1913	53.6	62.4	116.0	1,730.5	6.7	52.7	2.2
1914	37.8	95.4	133.2	NA	NA	53.3	2.5
1914–15	76.2	100.0		176.2	NA	NA	NA

Source: *Mitteilungen aus dem Gebiet des Seewesens, 1901–1914:* Alois Brusatti, ed., *Die Habsburger Monarchie 1848–1918, Vol.1 Die Wirtschaftliche Entwicklung* (Vienna: Verlag der oesterreichische Akademie der Wissenschaften, 1973), p.94; 'Zusammenstellung der Ausgaben der Grossmaechte fuer die Landesverteidigung in den letzten zehn Jahren', *Nauticus* (1914), p.534.

and modernization after 1904 produced impressive results. By 1914 about 80 combatant vessels totalling some 180,000 tons were completed. Italy in the same period built 122 combatants with 248,000 tons. Despite this great progress, the Austro-Hungarian Navy by mid-1914 had still not reached the goal that Admiral Montecuccoli had announced in 1905. Also in terms of tonnage the Austro-Hungarian Navy was far behind most of the major navies of the day.

Like other major navies of the day, the Austro-Hungarian Navy considered battleships the backbone of its strength. This was one of the reasons that about 34 per cent of the funds for ship construction between 1904 and 1914 were spent on battleship construction. Yet, by mid-1914 the Austro-Hungarian Navy lagged behind other major navies in the number and tonnage of battleships and dreadnoughts.

By 1904 the aims of the two principal players in the Adriatic question, Austria-Hungary and Italy, were clearly defined. Austria-Hungary was not willing to compromise on the question of Italian *irredenta* which could only weaken her hitherto secure position in the Adriatic and encourage other nationalities to break away from Vienna. Her goal was to strengthen and if possible extend her control over the eastern Adriatic shore.

Vienna considered Albania a bridge to exercise her influence in the western Balkan peninsula and sought to unite Albanian Moslems and Catholics to build a bloc against Orthodox Slavs. Although Austro-

FIGURE 13

NAVAL EXPENDITURES OF GREAT POWERS, 1905–13 (IN MILLIONS OF CROWNS)

	1905	1910	1913
Total naval expenditure			
Great Britain	795.7	970.1	1,111.4
Germany	271.2	500.3	553.0
Italy	121.0	200.2	246.5
France	304.0	360.6	500.4
Russia	297.4	233.4	609.4
Austria-Hungary	92.1	85.1	143.7
United States	586.7	668.4	694.1
Naval construction			
Great Britain	271.0	359.0	386.5
Germany	113.3	273.4	268.2
Italy	41.2	71.5	67.2
France	112.9	119.5	213.4
Russia	109.8	34.2	262.9
Austria-Hungary	56.9	38.0	78.7
United States	208.4	165.3	203.0

Source: Navy League Annual (1914), p.183

Hungarian policy toward Albania was to maintain the *status quo*, she also tried to expand her influence there to the detriment of Italy and all other foreign powers. However, if the *status quo* could not be maintained, Vienna wanted Albania to be established as an independent state, with close political, economic, and cultural ties with the Dual Monarchy so as to keep Albania from coming under Italian domination or from being allied with Montenegro and Serbia against the Dual Monarchy. Austria-Hungary was not uninterested in the size of an eventually autonomous Albania, because she wanted the northern part of Albania in order to block Slavic access to the Adriatic. Vienna also desired Valona and Durazzo so that she could enjoy freedom in the Adriatic. The very existence of Austria-Hungary, it was believed, depended on the continued control of the eastern coast of the Adriatic. Any hostile control of that coast would mean the end of the Monarchy as a sea power.

Italy's ultimate goal was to make the Adriatic *'mare nostrum'* (our sea) and therefore firm control of Albania was a prerequisite. Her interests focused on controlling Valona and the island of Saseno. Italy also supported the establishment of an autonomous Albania should the Turkish Empire collapse. Whether such a state would be small or large was not important to her. Control of Valona by a hostile power was intolerable to Italy. Rome also agreed with Vienna, although for different reasons, that Serbia's outlet on the Adriatic was unacceptable in any circumstances. Although both Italy and Austria-Hungary agreed that an autonomous but weak Albania should be eventually established, their diametrically opposed interests in the Adriatic were bound to increase their rivalries after 1904.

Prior to 1904, Vienna's policy in the Mediterranean focused on the protection of her extensive political and economic interests in the Levant. The Dual Monarchy was vitally interested in the fate of Turkey, and especially the Straits. In Vienna's view, the Turkish Straits could not come under Russian control as it would increase Russia's influence in the Balkans and encircle Austria-Hungary from the south. Vienna's policy was to treat the Straits Question as one affecting the vital interests of the other great Mediterranean powers. Austria-Hungary was also opposed to any Italian action against Tripoli, because of her concern that such a move was bound to reopen the Eastern Question with all its unpredictable consequences for the Habsburg position in the Balkans.

The Austro-Hungarian interests in the western Mediterranean before 1904 were negligible. However, as one of the partners of the Triple Alliance, Austro-Hungary became embroiled in those problems of the

187

western and central Mediterranean that concerned Italy and Germany. The growing polarization and conflict of interests between the opposing alliance systems in the decade prior to 1914 were the principal factors that made any crisis over Morocco, Tripoli, and the Straits a matter of concern to all the great European powers, including the Dual Monarchy. Another factor that contributed to Vienna's growing involvement in Mediterranean problems was that after 1909 the Austro-Hungarian Navy gradually emerged as a significant factor affecting the naval balance in the area.

In retrospect, 1904 represents the turning point in the development of Austro-Hungarian naval policy between 1867 and the outbreak of the First World War because the Delegations approved the first multi-year ship construction programme. This turn of events was initiated by Italy's decision in 1904 to strengthen her defences in the Adriatic. It came at an opportune time for those in the Dual Monarchy who advocated a larger and stronger Navy. Although Italy's naval expansion in 1904 after many years of stagnation gave a much needed impetus to Austrian navalists, Austria still had to give Hungarian industry a share of naval orders to secure approval by the Hungarian Delegation of the programme to modernize and expand the fleet. In the long run this compromise proved to be highly beneficial for the Navy as it gave the Hungarians a direct stake in continued expansion of the Navy. The approval of the first special credit by the Delegations made it much easier for Austrian navalists to obtain ever-increasing funds for ship construction in subsequent years.

The approval by the Delegations in December 1905 of the first four-year special credit for ship construction was crucial for the successful development of Austro-Hungarian sea power. That event was also the first notable victory for Austrian navalists and their supporters in the Dual Monarchy. However, the approval of the special credit was accomplished at the rather large cost of awarding Hungary a share of naval orders. That was in turn bound to delay the implementation of the naval construction programmes as Hungarian shipyards had to be expanded and modernized first before they could build modern warships. Nevertheless, the agreement between Austria and Hungary on sharing naval orders was necessary to secure approval of the fleet expansion programme. Giving the Hungarians a stake in the fleet's expansion made it more likely that they would support increased naval expenditures in the future. Under the Dual Monarchy's constitutional arrangement, no increase in these expenditures was possible if the Hungarian Delegation opposed it.

The special credit of 1905 enabled the Austro-Hungarian Navy to start the long-overdue modernization of its torpedo force and the development of its submarine arm. More important was the then announced intention to build three 14,500-ton battleships – a significant departure in naval policy. These ships were the first large Austro-Hungarian warships capable of being employed in combat in the Mediterranean.

Another factor which contributed to the success of those in Austria-Hungary who agitated for a larger and stronger Navy was the growing influence after 1906 of the heir apparent, Archduke Francis Ferdinand, whose strong interest and enthusiasm for the Navy was of immeasurable value in marshalling support and softening opposition among high government officials and the Army for naval expansion and modernization.

But for all the strength and influence of the navalists, the large fleet expansion programme would not have been possible without a major international crisis, the annexation of Bosnia. The Bosnian crisis represented a watershed in the conduct of Austro-Hungarian naval policy between 1904 and 1914. The Navy drew up a multi-year fleet expansion programme designed to continue the build-up of its torpedo force and to strengthen the battle fleet by constructing the first dreadnought squadron. This decision had some important repercussions beyond Austro-Hungarian borders. Great Britain for the first time began to take a serious view of the Dual Monarchy's naval build-up. The Austro-Hungarian naval build-up caused even deeper concern in Italy. Rome was now faced with the choice of either matching the naval expansion of her rival in the Adriatic or continuing with a slowdown of her own ship construction programme. Not surprisingly, Italy passed a new Navy Act aimed at increasing the margin of her naval superiority over the Dual Monarchy.

The annexation of Bosnia also led to the increased popular support for the efforts of Austrian navalists to create a larger and stronger Navy. This proved to be a crucial factor in obtaining approval for larger Navy expenditures in the future.

Between 1909 and 1911 the single most important event for the Austro-Hungarian Navy was the approval by the Delegations of the 312.4 million crown special credit for ship construction. This marked the first time that both the Austrian and Hungarian Delegations agreed to grant funds for a naval construction programme lasting more than three years and on such a large scale. However, the fleet expansion programme of 1911–15 was not a Navy Act like those of Germany and

Italy. Rapid technological changes would require frequent revisions in a Navy Act that had to be approved by the Delegations. The constitutional arrangement between the two parts of the Monarchy was so complex that even if the Navy Act was enacted, lengthy discussions in the common Ministerial Council and the Delegations on Navy expenditures would lead to many delays and prolong the implementation of the Navy Act. Therefore, the five-year special credit for ship construction was perhaps the best solution under the circumstances. Eventual approval of the ship construction programme for 1911–15 was due in large part to the strong and relentless pressure of the country's navalists as well as Austrian industrial and financial interests. Admiral Montecuccoli also deserves a large share of the credit for his skilful manipulation of the Emperor, the common ministers, and the Hungarian Delegation. The strong and consistent support of Archduke Francis Ferdinand proved to be indispensable to Montecuccoli's efforts to obtain a large increase in funds for ship construction.

Despite the repeated denials by Admiral Montecuccoli and other naval and government high officials, there was little doubt that the 20,000-ton dreadnoughts were suitable for employment in the Mediterranean. Hence, the fears of Italy and other Mediterranean powers were not groundless. Italy's position in respect to the Dual Monarchy, despite her intensified naval build-up in the Adriatic, was much weaker in the summer of 1911 than in 1909. More importantly, the trends in the naval balance in the Adriatic clearly favoured Austria-Hungary. But unknown to the participants at the time, the Austro-Italian naval race was about to be transformed by other events in the Mediterranean.

The Turco-Italian War was the first major conflict which took place in the Levant between 1900 and 1911. Vienna's policies at that time were designed to prevent Italy from obtaining a foothold in Albania or strengthening her influence there; to support Turkey against Italy's territorial pretensions in the Aegean or the Levant; and to prevent the opening of the Straits to Russian warships. The principal tool of the Dual Monarchy's policy was diplomacy. Vienna was more successful in dealing with Italy's action against Turkey in the Adriatic and the Ionian Seas because Rome was aware that she could not violate with impunity the Austro-Hungarian vital interests there. In the Adriatic, Vienna was always able to back up her diplomacy by threatening to use her fleet. However, to protect her interests in the Levant or the Straits, Austria-Hungary had to rely on diplomacy in concert with the other great European powers. The Dual Monarchy played a crucial role in Turkey's refusal to submit to Russia's wishes concerning the opening of the Straits. However, Austria-Hungary and the other powers were unable to prevent the Italian occupation of the Dodecanese Islands.

The Turco-Italian War had a profound impact upon the conduct of Austro-Hungarian naval policy, although this was not apparent in the spring of 1912. While both Austria-Hungary and Italy had made great efforts after 1904 to obtain a commanding position in the Adriatic, eight years later they began to co-operate more closely in the Mediterranean. To be sure, Austro-Italian rivalry in the Adriatic and the Balkans continued until the outbreak of the First World War and both powers intensified their naval build-up. However, the thrust of their naval policies after the summer of 1912 was to prevent the Triple Entente, and especially France, from obtaining dominance in the Mediterranean. Undoubtedly Italy had a greater interest than the Monarchy in seeing that France did not become the mistress of the Mediterranean.

The ultimate beneficiary of Austro-Italian naval rivalry was Germany. France was forced to redeploy her battle fleet to the Mediterranean, thereby weakening the Triple Entente's position in the North Sea. At the same time the continued build-up of the Austro-Hungarian and Italian fleets appeared destined to give the Triple Alliance a dominant position in the Mediterranean. As long as the underlying animosities between the Dual Monarchy and Italy persisted, both countries needed Germany's friendship and active support to protect their national interests and their status as great powers. Thus, both Austria-Hungary and Italy co-operated with each other and with Germany, as the strongest Triple Alliance partner.

The two Balkan Wars changed the political map of the peninsula beyond recognition. Turkey and the Dual Monarchy were the real losers in these conflicts. The success of the small Balkan states in the war with Turkey weakened Austro-Hungarian influence and prestige throughout the area. By the summer of 1913 her bitter enemies, Serbia and Montenegro, emerged enlarged and strengthened. Vienna acquiesced in Serbian control of Macedonia, thereby making it possible for Belgrade to interfere in Albanian affairs. Ironically, this allowed Serbia to threaten both Vienna's and Rome's interests there. However, Vienna succeeded in barring Serbia from access to the Adriatic Sea, although at the price that Montenegro and Serbia divided the Sanjak of Novibazar and thereby came to share a common border. Hence, Vienna's dream of reaching Salonika was in tatters. Moreover, the international position of Serbia and Montenegro in the aftermath of the Balkan Wars was such that the Dual Monarchy could not impose her will on them without risking a wider European conflict. In retrospect, the violent changes of the status quo in the Balkans that began with the annexation of Bosnia and ended with the Balkan Wars were cataclysmic events that led to a rapid erosion in Austro-Hungary's hitherto secure position in the Adriatic and permanently barred her way to the Aegean.

Vienna's apparent willingness to use force to stop Montenegro's action against Scutari was the single most important factor in bringing about joint action by the powers. The Austro-Hungarian Navy was effectively used to support the country's diplomacy during the Scutari crisis. If it had not been for the Emperor's opposition, the fleet would have been employed against Serbia's troop transports, and that probably would have widened the war in the Balkans. Subsequently, Austria-Hungary provided the largest number of ships for the international naval demonstration off the Montenegrin and Albanian coasts. This was also the first time that warships of all three Triple Alliance partners participated together in support of their countries' diplomatic action.

By the spring of 1913 co-operation among the Triple Alliance fleets in the Mediterranean was much wider in scope than was publicly known. Secret conversations were already underway to bring about an arrangement on joint action by the Austrian, German and Italian fleets in the Mediterranean in case of war with the Triple Entente.

The high state of tension among the Dual Monarchy, Serbia, and Montenegro during the Balkan crisis of 1912–13 convinced even the Hungarians of the need to strengthen the Army and the Navy, as indicated by the relatively easy and rapid approval of a large *Ruestungkredit* in the autumn of 1912. Both the Army and Navy subsequently played a significant role in supporting Vienna's policy.

The making of the naval convention of 1913 provides an interesting insight into the workings of the Triple Alliance. Because Italy most needed the co-operation of the other two Triple Alliance partners to protect her interests in the Mediterranean, it was only natural that she persistently sought to conclude a naval arrangement with the Dual Monarchy. However, the underlying animosity and intense rivalry between these two countries in the Adriatic and the Balkans were almost insurmountable obstacles to the genuine naval co-operation in the Mediterranean.

Germany had two main reasons to encourage Italy and the Dual Monarchy to reach a satisfactory agreement on co-operation between their fleets. The first was to force the British Navy to disperse its strength; the second was to prevent the arrival in France of large reinforcements from North Africa. This explains why the German

General Staff raised the question of reviving the naval convention of 1900 and acted with dispatch in handling the preliminary naval talks between Rome and Vienna. In fact, without Germany's active role no revision of the naval convention of 1900 would have been possible.

The greatest potential sacrifice under the terms of the naval convention of 1913 was clearly borne by Austria-Hungary. While she was to employ her fleet in the western Mediterranean to defend Italy's and Germany's interests, the only benefit she would receive was a German promise to send additional reinforcements to the eastern front, one that was conditional on the success of Germany's campaign in the west. Hence, Vienna's lack of enthusiasm for closer co-operation with Italy in the Mediterranean was at least understandable.

The success of supporters of the Austro-Hungarian Navy to bring about within only a decade a significant strengthening of the fleet was the result of several factors. The crises and wars which erupted with increasing frequency after 1900, and especially in the aftermath of the annexation of Bosnia, lent force to the arguments of those in Austria-Hungary who urged a larger and faster increase in naval expenditures. The steady expansion of the Italian Navy provided both an example to be imitated and a justification for Austro-Hungarian proponents of rapid fleet expansion. Without the presence of these external factors a larger and faster naval build-up would have been more difficult. Of course naval advocates were also helped by the support of high government officials.

The question can be posed whether Austria-Hungary conducted a sound naval policy between 1904 and 1914. Without a doubt, there was a constancy and clarity of purpose by those who urged the maintenance and steady expansion of the fleet. Nevertheless, the opponents of naval expansion were equally determined to prevent this from happening. They had an ally (though an unwitting one) in the press in both parts of the Dual Monarchy. The media was by and large slow in awakening the public to the need for a stronger Navy. The end result of this interplay was that the course of action followed fell short of the expectations of Navy enthusiasts. This should not come as a surprise when one realizes that Austria-Hungary was a typical continental power. Moreover, one should hardly expect constancy in the conduct of naval policy by a multinational state whose component parts operated on different levels of economic and political development.

In contrast, the Italian Navy always enjoyed great support both in Parliament and among the public. This meant a relatively easy approval of naval appropriations. The reasons for this are obvious. Italy's peninsular position, coupled with a scarcity of natural resources, reinforced the urge of the populace to pursue maritime interests. Additional factors that increased support for a strong Navy were Italy's heavy dependence on imports from overseas of many vital raw materials and food and her possession of colonies in North and East Africa. As a result, Italy conducted a more consistent naval policy than the Dual Monarchy.

However, Italy's ambitions to become a stronger sea power were constantly frustrated by the generally weak state of her finances and the industrial base. Although the Dual Monarchy had similar financial difficulties, her industry was more self-sufficient, better organized and more efficient than Italy's. In contrast, the Austro-Hungarian naval construction programmes, with the exception of large ships built in Hungarian shipyards, did not experience the significant delays that were so characteristic of their Italian counterparts.

A crucial question to be answered is whether the Austro-Hungarian naval build-up was necessary, or, as many critics argued, a waste of the country's sorely needed resources. Clearly, the Dual Monarchy needed to expand and modernize her fleet after 1904 to protect her interests in the Adriatic. But the question was whether she should have built a large number of destroyers, torpedo craft, and submarines instead of strengthening the battle fleet. For purely defensive purposes, a strong coastal defence fleet would have been more than adequate to protect the Austro-Hungarian interests in the Adriatic. Why, then, were battleships and dreadnoughts built? Because modern battleships were then considered the backbone of the fleet of any country claiming the status of a great naval power. The dreadnought, particularly, became not only the very core of naval might, the ultimate 'capital ship' of the day, but also a symbol and a fashion to be emulated. Therefore, Austria-Hungary, if she intended to become a power factor in the Mediterranean, had to possess a strong battle fleet with a corresponding number of smaller combatants and auxiliaries. Navalists believed that if the Dual Monarchy did not build dreadnoughts she would cease to be a great sea power.

Prior to the outbreak of the First World War, it was not clear that submarines would make battleships and armoured cruisers of little use in a narrow sea such as the Adriatic. Surely it would have been more sensible and valuable for Austria-Hungary to spend her limited funds on building smaller surface combatants and submarines than on semi-dreadnoughts and dreadnoughts. The cost of building one *Tegetthoff*-class dreadnought, for instance, would have been adequate for construction of six scout-cruisers, 20 destroyers, and 35 submarines.

Between 1904 and 1914 the naval policies of both Austria-Hungary and Italy passed through three distinctive phases. First, from 1904 to 1909 each country began to direct her naval build-up against the other. During that time the first large special credits for naval construction were proposed and approved. The second phase, from the Bosnian crisis of 1908 to the end of the Turco-Italian War, was characterized by an intensified naval race between the Dual Monarchy and Italy in which each sought to check the other's pretensions in the Adriatic. During that period both the Austro-Hungarian and Italian navies began dreadnought construction. This represented a new qualitative change in the direction of their naval build-up and an enormous increase in ship construction expenditures. The third phase started in 1912, when the naval race in the Adriatic for all practical purposes had ended, although both the Dual Monarchy and Italy continued their naval expansion until the outbreak of the First World War. This change came about as a result of the Turco-Italian War of 1911-12 and the growing polarization between the two opposing alliance systems in Europe. Although still engaged in rivalry in the Adriatic, after 1912 Austria-Hungary and Italy entered into a period of co-operation within the Triple Alliance. Mediterranean problems were in fact one aspect of Austro-Italian relations where a great similarity if not identity of interests existed between the two countries. This was the case even when they were engaged in a bitter rivalry for dominance in the Adriatic. Nevertheless, had it not been for Germany, the suspicions and underlying hostility between the Dual Monarchy and Italy would have been too strong to bring about co-operation among the Triple Alliance fleets in the Mediterranean. Foreign observers who watched Austro-Hungarian naval progress before 1914 were essentially correct in perceiving that the Austro-Italian naval race would ultimately work to the advantage of Germany. However, the Austro-Hungarian urge to become a strong sea power as quickly as possible did not require Germany's encouragement or support because it was based on the interplay of her needs to acquire the status of a great sea power in both the Adriatic and the Mediterranean.

NOTES

1. Theodor von Sosnosky, *Franz Ferdinand. Der Erzherzog-Thronfolger. Ein Lebensbild* (Munich/Berlin: Verlag R. Oldenbourg, 1929) p. 114.
2. *Jahresberichte der K.u.K. Kriegsmarine fuer das Jahr 1911*, pp. 110–15.
3. Franz Mirtl, *Unsere Flotte Sinkt* (Vienna: 1912) pp. 38–9.
4. Ibid., pp. 15, 70; 'Fremde Handelsmarinen im Jahre 1908', *Nauticus* (1909) p. 351.

5. Leo Reiter, 'Die Entwicklung der K.u.K. Flotte und die Delegation des Reichsrates' (Vienna University, unpublished Ph.D. dissertation, 1949) p. 168.
6. Friedrich Wallisch, *Die Flagge Rot-Weiss-Rot. Maenner und Taten der Oesterreichen Marine in Vier Jahrhunderten* (Graz: Verlag Styria, 1956) p. 216.
7. 'Zusammenstellung der Ausgaben der Grossmaechte fuer die Landesverteidigung in den letzten zehn Jahren', *Nauticus* (1914) p. 535; Alois Brusatti, ed., *Die Habsburger Monarchie 1848-1918 Vol. 1: Die Wirtschaftliche Entwicklung* (Vienna: Verlag der Oesterreichischen Akademie der Wissenschaften, 1973) p. 93; 'Zusammenstellung der Ausgaben der Grossmaechte fuer die Landesverteidigung in den letzten zehn Jahren', *Nauticus* (1914) p. 534.

Appendices

APPENDIX 1
AUSTRO-HUNGARIAN SEABORNE TRADE, 1904–13 (IN 000 METRIC TONNES)

Region	1904				1913			
	Import	Export	Total	%	Import	Export	Total	%
Total	5,885.10	4,606.20	10,491.30	100.00	14,112.20	6,287.20	20,399.40	100.00
Black Sea	110.20	16.00	126.20	1.20	83.20	29.60	112.80	0.60
Mediterranean	1,681.90	1,607.80	3,289.70	31.60	2,713.80	2,659.80	5,373.60	26.30
West Europe and Scandinavia	3,542.10	2,664.70	6,207.80	59.20	10,552.40	3,140.00	13,692.40	67.10
North America	82.80	58.30	141.10	1.30	134.00	144.30	278.30	1.40
South America	129.70	116.30	246.00	2.30	171.30	77.00	248.30	1.20
Central America and Caribbean	2.40	0.02	2.40	0.02	19.40	0.40	19.80	0.10
Africa	3.20	6.20	9.40	0.10	2.40	2.50	4.90	0.02
South Asia	314.20	128.60	442.80	4.20	383.40	208.10	591.50	2.90
South-east Asia	2.70	0.06	2.80	-	27.30	2.00	29.30	0.10
Far East	14.80	7.70	22.50	0.20	8.70	20.30	29.00	0.10
Australia	0.05	0.50	0.60	-	16.30	3.20	19.50	0.10

Source: Statistical Department of the Imperial-Royal Trade Ministry, *Statistik des Auswaertigen Handels des Oesterreich-Ungarische Zollgebiete in Jahre 1904* (Vienna: K. K. Hof- und Staatsdruckerei, 1905) pp. 485–507; ibid, 1913 (Vienna, 1913), pp. 538–43

APPENDIX 2
AUSTRO-HUNGARIAN SEABORNE TRADE WITH THE BLACK SEA COUNTRIES, 1904–13 (IN 000 METRIC TONNES)

Country	1904			1913		
	Import	Export	Total	Import	Export	Total
Bulgaria	2.30	6.40	8.70	4.40	13.60	18.00
Rumania	76.10	25.00	101.10	37.60	8.80	46.40
Serbia	0.20	0.03	0.20	0.03	0.04	0.10
Russia	31.70	7.10	38.80	41.20	7.20	48.40
Total	110.30	38.50	148.80	83.20	29.60	112.90
% of total seaborne trade	6.60	1.00	3.80	3.10	1.10	2.10

Source: As for Appendix 1.

APPENDIX 3
AUSTRO-HUNGARIAN SEABORNE TRADE WITH THE MEDITERRANEAN COUNTRIES, 1904–13 (IN 000 METRIC TONNES)

| Country | 1904 | | | 1913 | | | % |
	Import	Export	Total	Import	Export	Total	
France	10.20	114.50	124.70	18.20	61.60	79.80	2.10
Italy	380.40	578.90	959.30	352.10	1,106.90	145.90	37.90
Spain	13.60	20.80	34.40	94.20	27.10	121.30	3.20
Turkey	94.50	155.90	250.40	51.40	295.60	346.60	9.00
Greece	86.50	61.80	148.30	102.80	97.60	200.40	5.20
British possessions	0.60	8.70	9.30	2.30	4.60	6.90	0.20
Egypt	23.90	1,034.10	1,058.00	33.60	1,401.00	1,434.60	37.20
Algeria	13.60	10.30	23.90	112.40	25.50	137.90	3.60
Tunisia	1.40	7.10	8.50	41.20	10.40	51.60	1.30
Morocco	0.10	0.70	0.80	0.20	11.90	12.00	0.30
Tripoli	-	-	-	0.02	0.30	0.30	-
Total	624.80	1,992.80	2,617.60	808.00	3,042.50	3,042.50	100
% of total seaborne trade	10.60	43.30	25.00	5.70	48.40	18.90	

Source: As for Appendix 1.

APPENDIX 4
AUSTRO-HUNGARIAN FOREIGN TRADE, 1900–12 (IN MILLIONS OF CROWNS)

| Country | Imports | | | | Exports | | | |
	1900	1905	1908	1912	1900	1905	1908	1912
Germany	635.0	803.6	993.9	1,440.6	1,015.6	1,103.4	1,045.4	1,243.4
United States	152.7	203.5	221.5	349.2	146.8	161.3	228.2	248.3
England	148.8	156.9	215.4	255.7	212.3	199.4	230.8	266.6
British India	83.9	124.7	136.1	223.6	43.1	81.7	92.8	144.8
Russia	89.1	137.8	127.1	227.4	68.5	89.8	91.9	176.6
Italy	114.2	106.6	117.7	163.2	63.6	94.5	83.0	105.0

Source: As for Appendix 1.

APPENDIX 5
EMIGRATION FROM AUSTRIA-HUNGARY, 1906–13

	Total	1906	1907	1908	1909	1910	1911	1912	1913
Austria-Hungary	73,334	10,908	10,868	3,271	8,101	7,948	8,701	9,556	13,981
Germany	656,011	89,196	113,279	35,720	86,285	87,895	47,763	73,038	121,961
Belgium	200,281	22,005	36,721	12,408	23,012	25,115	20,013	28,653	32,354
Netherlands	70,241	4,797	8,083	2,584	6,463	9,994	9,295	11,669	17,354
France	42,890	5,669	5,932	2,335	3,844	5,567	4,984	6,495	8,065
Italy	14,959	3,779	2,471	1,416	2,103	2,396	1,113	916	765
Total	1,057,722	136,354	177,354	57,734	129,808	138,915	91,868	131,227	194,462

Source: Hans Chmelar, *Hoehepunkte der Oesterreichischen Auswanderung. Die Auswanderung aus dem in Reichsrat vertretenen Koenigreichen und Laendern in den Jahren 1905–1914* (Vienna: Verlag der Oesterreichischen Akademie der Wissenschaft, 1974), p. 71

Appendices

APPENDIX 6
EMIGRATION THROUGH AUSTRO-HUNGARIAN PORTS, 1906–13

	United States	South America	Canada	Total
1906	17,687	-	-	17,687
1907	20,097	-	-	20,097
1908	5,470	4,744	-	10,214
1909	16,020	5,445	-	21,465
1910	14,932	6,218	-	21,150
1911	10,993	11,636	-	22,629
1912	14,014	12,650	-	26,664
1913 (Jan.–June)	14,205	2,582	7,376	24,163
Total	113,418	43,275	7,376	164,069
% of total	69.1	26.4	4.5	100

Source: As for Appendix 5.

APPENDIX 7
STRUCTURE OF THE AUSTRIAN MERCHANT MARINE, 1904

	Oceangoing		Large coastal		Small coastal		Total	
	No.	Tonnage	No.	Tonnage	No.	Tonnage	No.	Tonnage
Sailing vessels								
Trieste	2	2,125	2	330	27	674	31	3,129
Gorizia	-	-	-	-	80	718	80	718
Gradisca	-	-	-	-	-	-	-	-
Istria	1	573	-	-	319	4,632	320	5,205
Quarnero	6	6,273	1	182	277	4,006	188	6,550
Dalmatia	1	1,353	4	253	758	7,246	763	8,852
Total	10	10,324	7	765	1,461	17,276	1,478	28,365
Steamers								
Trieste	99	196,834	5	1,883	48	7,481	152	206,198
Gorizia	-	-	-	-	-	-	-	-
Gradisca	-	-	-	-	3	49	3	49
Istria	-	-	-	-	-	-	-	-
Quarniero	14	29,192	1	220	3	86	17	29,498
Dalmatia	16	22,416	11	324	33	1,568	60	24,308
Total	129	248,442	17	4,457	97	9,459	243	262,358
Grand total	139	258,766	24	5,192	1,558	26,735	1,721	290,693

Source: Statistik der Seeschiffahrt und des Seehandels in dem Oesterreichische Reich im Jahre 1904 (Trieste)

APPENDIX 8
STRUCTURE OF THE AUSTRIAN MERCHANT MARINE, 1912

	Oceangoing		Large coastal		Small coastal		Total	
	No.	Tonnage	No.	Tonnage	No.	Tonnage	No.	Tonnage
Sailing vessels								
Trieste	-	-	2	257	20	340	22	597
Gorizia	-	-	-	-	87	956	87	956
Gradisca	-	-	-	-	13	330	13	330
Istria	-	-	-	-	398	5,786	398	5,786
Quarnero	-	-	1	228	258	5,325	259	5,553
Dalmatia	-	-	2	129	730	7,196	732	7,325
Total	-	-	5	614	1,443	19,603	1,448	20,217
Steamers								
Trieste	123	308,151	14	5,235	70	10,877	207	324,470
Gorizia	-	-	-	-	-	-	-	-
Gradisca	-	-	-	-	-	-	-	-
Istria	-	-	-	-	18	476	18	476
Quarniero	18	41,522	1	137	6	329	25	41,988
Dalmatia	24	49,228	7	2,129	53	3,813	84	55,170
Total	165	398,901	22	7,501	160	15,825	347	422,227
Grand total	165	398,901	27	8,115	1,603	35,428	1,795	442,444

Source: As for Appendix 7.

APPENDIX 9
AUSTRIAN MERCHANT MARINE, MARCH 1914 (OCEANGOING VESSELS)

Shipping company	No.	Brutto Register Tons (BRT)	Average age of ships
Austrian Lloyd	61	231,384	12.6 yrs
Austro-Americana	36	156,351	12.1
Tripcovich & Co.	18	64,443	13.2
Gerolimich & Co.	10	40,645	10.4
17 small carriers	68	220,727	-
Total	193	713,550	

Source: Almanach d. K.u.K. Kriegsmarine 1915.

APPENDIX 10
HUNGARIAN MERCHANT MARINE, MARCH 1914

Shipping company	No.	Brutto Register Tons (BRT)	Average age of ships
Adria (Fiume)	34	75,442	18.4 yrs
Ungaro-Croata (Fiume)	47	17,424	12.2
Ungaro-Croata Tramp Service (Fiume)	6	22,666	10.7
Levante (Fiume)	12	42,156	7.1
Oriente (Fiume)	6	26,405	10.7
Atlantica (Budapest) and 3 small carriers	5	3,725	19.0
Total	121	231,653	

Source: As for Appendix 9.

Appendices

APPENDIX 11
AUSTRO-HUNGARIAN MILITARY EXPENDITURES, 1904–14 (IN MILLIONS OF CROWNS)

Year	Population (million)	State expenditures	Defence budget	Defence budget as % of state expenditures	Defence budget per head (crowns)	Army budget	Navy budget
1904	47.0	879.5	514.8	58.5	11.0	444.6	70.2
1905	47.4	915.0	574.9	66.3	12.8	493.1	81.8
1906	47.8	931.2	519.3	55.7	10.9	461.7	57.6
1907	48.2	1,141.9	521.0	45.6	10.8	456.0	65.0
1908	48.8	1,187.0	624.1	54.4	13.2	563.8	60.3
1909	51.0	1,441.8	741.5	52.1	14.7	650.5	91.0
1910	51.5	1,450.7	627.6	44.2	12.4	542.6	85.0
1911	52.0	1,502.0	646.3	43.0	12.4	523.3	123.0
1912	52.3	1,592.2	637.2	42.5	12.9	536.2	101.0
1913	52.7	1,730.5	717.0	44.3	14.5	583.8	133.2
1914	53.3	NA	853.8		16.0	677.6	176.2

Source: 'Zusammenstellung der Ausgaben der Grossmaechte fuer die Landesverteidigung in den letzten zehn Jahren', *Nauticus* (1914), p. 534; ibid (1913), p. 450; Alois Brusatti, ed., *Die Habsburger Monarchie 1848–1918, Vol. 1 Die Wirtschaftliche Entwicklung* (Vienna: Verlag der Oesterreichische Akademie der Wissenschaften, 1973), p. 93.

APPENDIX 12
NAVAL BUDGETS OF AUSTRIA-HUNGARY AND ITALY, 1905–14
(IN MILLIONS OF GERMAN MARKS)

Year	Austria-Hungary			Italy			Italy/Austria-Hungary Ratio
	Population	Per head	Budget	Population	Per head	Budget	
1905	47.7	2.0	96.65	33.3	3.2	105.50	1.1:1.0
1906	47.8	1.0	48.62	33.6	3.7	125.95	2.6:1.0
1907	48.2	1.1	55.15	33.8	3.5	118.80	2.2:1.0
1908	48.8	1.4	69.93	34.0	3.9	132.80	1.9:1.0
1909	51.0	1.7	85.31	34.3	3.7	127.21	1.5:1.0
1910	51.5	1.6	83.60	34.5	5.6	191.59	2.3:1.0
1911	52.0	2.0	104.77	34.7	7.1	247.87	2.4:1.0
1912	52.3	2.3	118.80	34.9	5.0	173.51	1.5:1.0
1913	52.7	2.9	155.26	35.1	7.5	263.60	1.7:1.0
1914	53.3	2.8	150.68	35.3	7.4	260.23	1.7:1.0

Source: Nauticus (1914), pp. 534–5.

APPENDIX 13
EXPANSION OF THE AUSTRIAN NAVY LEAGUE, 1904–14

Year end	Local chapters*	Members
1904§	1	39
1905	NA	195
1906	NA	NA
1907	4	1,252
1908	13	1,835
1909	25	3,036
1910	31	4,539
1911	72	12,636
1912	147	26,836
1913	184	36,395
1914†	201	43,260

Notes: *September 1904; § June of respective year; † June 1914.
Source: Leo Reiter, 'Die Entwicklung der K.u.K. Flotte und die Delegation des Reichsrates' (University of Vienna, Ph.D. dissertation, 1949), p. 168

Sources and selected bibliography

Unpublished sources

This book is primarily based on research at the War Archives (Kriegsarchiv) in Vienna. Most of the original material dealing with the Austro-Hungarian Navy is contained in the Neue Marine Archiv covering the period 1864–1918. However, that section is incomplete because much valuable material was lost after the break-up of the Dual Monarchy and during the Second World War. The entire documentation for the Navy Technical Committee, Intelligence Bureau and Sea Transport Command, for example, has been destroyed. Nevertheless, the Neue Marine Archiv is still rich in material dealing with the Austro-Hungarian Navy in the period before 1914.

The majority of the files consulted belong to the Operations Chancellery (OK/MS) and the Presidial Chancellery (PK/MS) of the Navy Section. The OK/MS files are classified under subsections: -I (Kriegschiffe); -II (Eskadre); -III (Schiffsbewegungen); – VI (Verteidigungswesen); -VIII (Kriegsfaelle); -IX (Mobilisierung); -X (Fremde Maechte); and -XII (Signalstationen). The subsections for the PK/MS are: -I (Kriegsfaelle); -II (Mobilisierung); -VIII (Personel); -X (Bauten, Befestigungen); -XI (Kriegswaffen); -XII (Fremde Maechte); and -XV (Verschiedene). In addition, a special collection (Sonderreihe) of the OK/MS and the PK/MS for the years 1913–15 were also used.

Another valuable source of material for the Austro-Hungarian Navy in Vienna is the files of the Military Chancellery of Archduke Francis Ferdinand (MKFF) and (of somewhat less importance) of the Military Chancellery of the Emperor (MKSM). Also useful were the files of the Operations Bureau of the General Staff and Conrad's Archive. The Haus-Hof und Staatsarchiv contained many valuable documents dealing with the maritime aspects of the Austro-Hungarian diplomacy as well as strictly naval matters.

The most important material for my purposes was contained in the Protocols of the Ministerial Council for Common Affairs (Protokolle Ministerrates fuer gemeinsame Angelegenheiten) for the period 1908–14. Another source used for this study was Record Group 38 (Office of Naval Intelligence) at the Old Army and Navy Branch, National Archives and Records Service, Washington, DC. This record group contains reports from US naval attachés in Rome dealing with the Austro-Hungarian Navy in the period before 1914. Because the United States did not have a naval attaché in Vienna until September 1914 the attaché in Rome collected information on the Austro-Hungarian Navy. The majority of the documents in these files are clippings from Austro-Hungarian or other foreign newspapers regarding technical aspects of the Austro-Hungarian Navy. The most valuable material in RG-38 is the periodic correspondence between the US naval attaché in Rome and the Navy Section in Vienna. It contains mostly information on Austro-Hungarian naval training.

The description of the diplomatic aspects of Austro-Hungarian naval policy between 1904 and 1914 has been drawn primarily from published documents of the Austro-Hungarian, German and British foreign ministries. The Austro-Hungarian diplomatic documents contain a mass of valuable information concerning some strictly naval matters, such as the negotiations and the text of the Triple Alliance naval convention of 1913. The British documents include naval aspects of the situation in the Mediterranean and British views on the Austro-Hungarian naval build-up in the period between 1909 and 1914.

A large number of memoirs and biographies written by leading Austro-Hungarian political and military leaders after 1918 are also a valuable source in understanding motives behind Austro-Hungarian naval policy. The most important are the memoirs of General Franz Conrad von Hoetzendorf, the Chief of the Austro-Hungarian General Staff in 1906–11 and 1912–17. They are rich in detail on the Austro-Hungarian military plans, developments in the common armed forces, and Conrad's views on the politico-military problems of the day. Another group consists of several biographies written by close advisors or friends of the heir apparent, Archduke Francis Ferdinand, that explain his views regarding the development and importance of sea power for Austria-Hungary.

Published sources

Oesterreich-Ungarns Aussenpolitik von der Bosnischen Krise 1908 bis zum Kriegsausbruch 1914. Diplomatische Aktenstuecke des Oesterreichisch-Ungarischen Ministeriums des Aeussern, ed. Ludwig Bittner, Alfred Francis Pribram, Heinrich Srbik and Hans Uebersberger, 9 vols (Vienna: Oesterreichischer Bundesverlag fuer Unterricht, Wissenschaft und Kunst, 1930).

British Documents on the Origins of the War 1898–1914, ed. G. P. Gooch and Harold Temperley, 11 vols (London: HMSO, 1926–38).

Die Grosse Politik der Europaeischen Kabinette 1871–1914, ed. Johannes Lepsius, Albrecht Mendelsohn-Bartholdy and Friedrich Thimme, 40 vols (Berlin: Deutsche Verlagsgesellschaft fuer Politik und Geschichte, 1922–27).

Italy's Foreign and Colonial Policy: A Selection from the Speeches Delivered in the Italian Parliament by Senator Tommaso Tittoni During His Six Years in Office 1903–1909 (London: Smith, Elder, Co., 1914).

Policy and Operations in the Mediterranean, 1912–1914, ed. E. W. R. Lumby (London: William Clowes & Sons, 1970).

The Secret Treaties of Austria-Hungary 1879–1914, ed. Alfred Francis Pribram, trans. Archibald Cary Coolidge, 2 vols (Cambridge, MA: Harvard University Press, 1920–21).

Memoirs, diaries and biographies

Bardolff, Carl Freiherr von, *Soldat im Alten Oesterreich. Erinnerungen aus meinem Leben* (Jena: Eugen Diedrichs Verlag, 1938).
Bayer von Bayersburg, Heinrich, *Oesterreichs Admirale,* 2 vols (Vienna: Bergland Verlag, 1960).
Churchill, Winston S., *The World Crisis,* 6 vols (London: Thornton, Butterworth, 1923–31).
Hoetzendorf, Franz Conrad von, *Aus meiner Dienstzeit 1908–1918,* 5 vols (Vienna: Rikola Verlag, 1922-25).

Sources and selected bibliography

Kiszling, Rudolf, *Erzherzog Franz Ferdinand von Oesterreich-Este. Leben, Plaene und Wirken am Schicksalweg der Donaumonarchie* (Graz/Koeln: Verlag Bohlau, 1953).
Sosnosky, Theodor von, *Franz Ferdinand. Der Erzherzog-Thronfolger. Ein Lebensbild* (Munich/Berlin: Verlag R. Oldenbourg, 1929).

Monographs, articles and general studies

André, Ganluco, *L'Italia e il Mediterraneo alla Vigilia della Prima Guerra Mondiale. I tentativi de Intesa Mediterraneo 1911–1914* (Milan: A. Giuffré, 1967).
Askew, William C., *Europe and Italy's Acquisition of Libya 1911–1912* (Durham, NC: Duke University Press, 1942).
Barclay, Thomas, *The Turco-Italian War and its Problems* (London: Constable and Company, 1912).
Bauer, Ernst, *Drei Leopardenkoepfe in Gold: Oesterreich in Dalmatien* (Vienna/Munich: Verlag Herold, 1973).
Bayer, Heinrich von Bayersburg, *Die K.u.K. Kriegsmarine auf Weiter Fahrt* (Vienna: Bergland Verlag, 1958).
Beehler, W. H., *The History of the Italo-Turkish War. September 29, 1911 to October 18, 1912* (Annapolis, MD: The Advertiser-Republican, 1913).
Bosworth, R. J. B., *Italy, the Least of the Great Powers: Italian Foreign Policy before the First World War* (London/New York: Cambridge University Press, 1979).
Braun, Theodor, 'Oesterreichische Kolonial-Bestrebungen', *Marine Rundschau* 11 (November 1928), pp. 509-11.
Brennecke, Hans J., *Panzerschiffe und Linienschiffe 1860–1910* (Herford: Koehlers Verlagsgesellschaft, 1976).
Brettner-Messler, Horst, 'Die Balkanpolitik Conrad von Hoetzendorf (Von seiner Wiederernennung zum Chef des Generalstabes bis zum Oktober Ultimatum, Dezember 1912 bis Oktober 1913)' (University of Vienna, unpublished Ph.D. dissertation, 1966).
Brettner-Messler, Horst, 'Die militaerischen Absprachen zwischen den Generalstaeben Oesterreich-Ungarns und Italiens von Dezember 1912 bis Juni 1914', *Mitteilungen des Oesterreichischen Staatsarchiv* 23 (1971), pp. 225-49.
Bridge, F., *From Sadowa to Sarajevo. The Foreign Policy of Austria-Hungary 1866–1914* (London: 1972).
Bridge, F., *Great Britain and Austria-Hungary 1906–1914. A Diplomatic History* (London: 1972).
Brusatti, Alois, ed., *Die Habsburger Monarchie 1848–1918 Vol. 1: Die Wirtschaftliche Entwicklung* (Vienna: Verlag der Oesterreichischen Akademie der Wissenschaften, 1973).
Chlumecki, Leopold Freiherr, *Oesterreich-Ungarn und Italien. Das Westbalkanische Problem und Italien. Kampf um die Vorherrschaft in der Adria*, 2nd edn (Leipzig/Vienna: Franz Deutzke, 1907).
Chmelar, Hans, *Hoehepunkte der Oesterreichischen Auswanderung. Die Auswanderung aus dem in Reichsrat vertretenen Koenigreichen und Laendern in den Jahren 1905–1914* (Vienna: Verlag der Oesterreichischen Akademie der Wissenschaft, 1974).
Csurda, Birgit, 'Die Diplomatischen Beziehungen zwischen Oesterreich-Ungarn und Italien von 1913 bis zum Ausbruch des Ersten Weltkrieges' (University of Vienna, unpublished Ph.D. dissertation, 1966).
Dainelli, Giotto, *La Dalmazia. Cenni Geografici e Statistici* (Novara: Istituto Geografico de Agostini, 1918).

Dell'Adami, Geza, *Zur Seepolitik Oesterreichs im Interesse seiner Volkswirtschaft* (Vienna: 1909).

Deutschmann, W., 'Die militaerischen Massnahmen in Oesterreich-Ungarn waehrend der Balkankrise 1912–13' (University of Vienna, unpublished Ph.D. dissertation, 1965).

Dietrich, R., *Die Tripoli Krise 1911-12 und die Erneuerung des Dreibundes 1912* (Wuerzburg: 1933).

Duca, G., 'Accordi e Convenzioni durante la Triplece Alleanza', *Rivista Marittima* 3 (March 1935), pp. 266–81.

Foerster, Wolfgang, 'Die deutsch-italienische Militaer-konvention', *Die Kriegschuldfrage* 5 (May 1927), pp. 395–416.

Gabriele, Mariano, *Le Convenzione Navali della Triplece* (Rome: Ufficio Storico della Marina Militare, 1969).

Gayda, Virgilio, *Italien und die englische Mittelmeerpolitik: Geschichte eines Hundertjaehrigen Kampfes* (Berlin: Junker und Duennhaupt, 1943).

Gayda, Virgilio, *L'Italia d'Oltre Confine (Le Provincie Italiane d'Austria)* (Turin: Fratelli Bocca Editori, 1914).

Gebhard, Louis A., 'The Development of the Austro-Hungarian Navy 1897–1914: a Study in the Operation of Dualism' (Rutgers University, New Brunswick, NJ, unpublished Ph.D. dissertation, 1971).

Gebhard, Louis A., 'Austro-Hungarian Dreadnought Squadron. The Naval Outlay of 1911', *Austrian History Yearbook, 1968–69* (Houston: Rice University Press, 1969), pp. 245–58.

Giesche, R. *Der Serbische Zugang zum Meer und die Europaeische Krise 1912* (Stuttgart: 1932).

Greger, René, *Austro-Hungarian Warships of World War I* (London: Ian Allan, 1976).

Grosz, Peter M., 'Austro-Hungarian Aircraft Armament: 1914–1918', *Cross & Cockade* 3 (Autumn 1974), pp. 227–83.

Halpern, Paul G., *The Mediterranean Naval Situation (1908–1914)* (Cambridge, MA: Harvard University Press, 1970).

Hanak, Harry, *Great Britain and Austria-Hungary During the First World War: A Study in the Formation of Public Opinion* (Oxford: Oxford University Press, 1962).

Handel-Mazzetti, Peter, *Die Oesterreichisch-Ungarische Kriegsmarine vor und im Weltkrieg* (Klagenfurt: Carl Roeschuar, 1925).

Handel-Mazzetti, Peter and Igaly, I., 'Oesterreich als Seemacht, Part 1: Entwicklung der Oesterreichisch-Ungarische Kriegs- und Handelsmarine mit besonderer Beruecksichtigung der Marinepolitik vor dem Kriege', *Marine Rundschau* 10 (October 1921), pp. 393–407; 'Part 2: Die politischen, nationalen und wirtschaftlichen Verhaeltnisse in den suedlichen Provinzen der Monarchie. Die Italienische und Suedslawische Frage bis zum Ausbruch des Weltkrieges', (January 1922), pp. 14–20.

Helbing, Guenther, 'Die deutsche Marinepolitik 1908-1912 im Spiegel der oesterreichischen-ungarischen Diplomatie', *Marine Rundschau* 6 (October 1961), pp. 32–70.

Helmreich, Ernst, *The Diplomacy of the Balkan Wars 1912–1913* (Cambridge, MA: Harvard University Press, 1938; reprinted, New York: Russell & Russell, 1969).

Historical Institute of the Yugoslav People's Army, *Prvi Balkanski Rat 1912–13 (Operacije Crnogorske Vojske)* (The First Balkan War 1912–13 (Operations of the Montenegrin Army)) (Belgrade: Istoriski Institut Jugoslavenski Narodne Armije, 1960).

Historical Section of the Foreign Office, *Peace Handbook, Vol. 4 The Balkan States* (London: HMSO, 1920; reprinted, Wilmington, DE: Scholarly Resources, 1973).

Hough, Richard, *A History of Modern Battleship: Dreadnought* (New York: Bonanza Books, 1979).

Institut fuer Oesterreichkunde, *Oesterreich am Vorabend des Ersten Weltkriegs* (Graz/ Vienna: Stiasny Verlag, 1964).

Jedina-Palombini, Leopold, Freiherr von, *Fuer Oesterreich-Ungarns Seegeltung* (Vienna: L. W. Seidel und Sohn, 1912).

Kabisch, Ernst, 'Die Militaer- und Marinekonvention der Triple Entente vor dem Ausbruch des Weltkrieges', *Kriegschuldfrage* 4 (April 1927).

Kennedy, Paul, ed., *The War Plans of the Great Powers 1990–1914* (London: George Allen & Unwin, 1979).

Khuepack, Alfred, 'Interessenten von der oesterreichischen Kriegsmarine', *Marine Rundschau* 19 (October 1940), pp. 609–19.

Kiszling, Rudolf, 'Die Entwicklung der oesterreichisch-ungarischen Wehrmacht seit der Annexionkrise 1908', *Berliner Monatshefte* 9 (September 1934), pp. 735–49.

Krenslehner, E., 'Die K.u.K. Kriegsmarine als wirtschaftlichen Faktor in den Jahren 1874–1914' (University of Vienna, unpublished Ph.D. dissertation, 1970).

Lowe, Cedrio J. and Marzari, F., *Italian Foreign Policy, 1980–1940* (Boston: Routledge & Kegan Paul, 1975).

Malgeri, Francesco, *La Guerra Libica (1911–1912)* (Rome: Edizione di Storia e Letteratura, 1970).

Manhart, George B., *Alliance and Entente 1871–1914* (New York: F. S. Crofts & Co., 1932).

Mansergh, Nicholas, *The Coming of the First World War. A Study in the European Balance 1878–1914* (London: Longman, Green, and Co., 1949).

Mantegazza, Vico, *L'Albania* (Rome: Bontempelli & Invernizzi, 1912).

Maranelli, Carlo and Salvemini, Gaetano, *La Questione dell' Adriatico* (Firenze: Libreria della Voce, 1918).

Marder, Arthur J., *The Anatomy of British Sea Power. A History of British Naval Policy in the Pre-dreadnought Era 1880–1905* (New York: A. A. Knopf, 1940).

Mayer, A., 'Die K.u.K. Kriegsmarine 1912-14 unter dem Kommando von Admiral Anton Haus' (University of Vienna, unpublished Ph.D. dissertation, 1962).

Michaelis, Herbert, *Die deutsche Politik waehrend der Balkanfrage, 1912–13* (Leipzig: E. Kastner, Waldenburg, 1929).

Michon, Georges, *The Franco-Russian Alliance 1891–1917* (New York: Howard Fertig, 1969).

Mirtl, Franz, *Unsere Flotte Sinkt* (Vienna/Leipzig: 1912).

Moerl, Anton, *Das Ende des Kontinentalismus in Oesterreich. Entwicklung und Bedeutung unserer Seegeltung* (Saaz: 1913).

Nereus. *Probleme der oesterreichischen Flottenpolitik* (Vienna: 1912).

Nowara, Heinz, *Die Entwicklung der Flugzeuge 1914–1918* (Munich: J. F. Lehmans Verlag, 1959).

Pacor, Mario, *Italia e Balcani dal Risorgimento alla Resistenza* (Milan: Feltrinelli, 1968).

Peteani, Luigi, *La Questione Libica nella Diplomazia Europea* (Florence: Casa Editrice del Dott. Carlo CYA, 1939).

Plaschka, Richard Georg, *et al.*, *Innere Front. Militaer-assistenz, Widerstand und Umsturz in der Donaumonarchie 1918*, 2 vols (Vienna: Verlag fuer Geschichte und Politik, 1979).

Pribram, Alfred Francis, *England and the International Policy of the Great European Powers 1871–1914* (Oxford: 1931).

Pribram, Alfred Francis, *Austria-Hungary and Great Britain, 1908–1914* (London: Oxford University Press, 1951).

Randa, Alexander, *Oesterreich in Uebersee* (Vienna/Munich: Verlag Herold, 1966).

Reichsluftfahrtministerium (German Air Transport Ministry), *Die Militaerluftfahrt bis zum Beginn des Weltkrieges 1914*, 2 vols (Berlin: E. S. Mittler & Sohn, 1941).

Reiter, Leo, 'Die Entwicklung der K.u.K. Flotte und die Delegation des Reichsrates' (University of Vienna, unpublished Ph.D. dissertation, 1949).

Rothmann, E., *Die Balkanfrage 1904-1908 und das Werden der Triple Entente* (Halle: 1932).

Saladino, Salvatore, *Italy from Unification to 1919: Growth and Decay of a Liberal Regime* (New York: Thomas Y. Crowell Co., 1970).

Salvatorelli, Luigi, *La Triplice Alleanza. Storia Diplomatica, 1877–1912* (Rome: Istituto per gli Studi di Politica Internazionale, 1939).

Sandona, Augusto, *L'Irredentismo nelle Lotte Politiche e nelle Contese Diplomatice Italo-Austriache*, 3 vols (Bologna: 1932–38).

Scheltena de Heere, R. F., 'Austro-Hungarian Battleships', *Warship International* 1 (Winter 1973), pp. 11–97.

Schloss, Max, *Die durch das Flottengesetz zu bestimmende Sollstaerke Kriegsflotte. Entwurf eines Motivenberichtes zum Flottengesetz* (Hamburg: 1909).

Schloss, Max, *Italien und Wir* (Vienna: 1915).

Schloss, Max, *Der Jammer Unsere Seemacht. Die Politischen, militaerischen und wirtschaftlichen Grundlagen des langfristigen Flottengesetzes* (Vienna: St Norbertus, 1914).

Schloss, Max, *Oesterreich-Ungarns Wacht zur See* (Hamburg: 1908).

Schloss, Max, *Die Wahrheit ueber die neuen Oesterreich-Ungarischen Schlachtschiffe. Ein Mahnruf in Letzter Stunde* (Hamburg: 1909).

Schloss, Max, *Wem sind die Oesterreich-Ungarischen Seeinteresse anvertraut* (Vienna: 1909).

Schmalenbeck, Paul, *Kurze Geschichte der K.u.K. Kriegsmarine* (Herford: Koehlers Verlagsgesellschaft, 1970).

Schmitt, Bernadotte E., *The Annexation of Bosnia 1908–1909* (New York: Howard Fertig, 1970).

Schaefer, Theobald, 'Das militaerische Zusammenwirken der Mittelmaechte in Herbst 1914', *Wehr und Wesen* (1926) pp. 213–34.

Serra, Enrico, *L'Intesa Mediterranea del 1902. Una Fase Risolutiva nei Rapporti Italo-Inglesi* (Milan: A. Giuffre, 1957).

Seton-Watson, R. W., *The Balkans, Italy and the Adriatic* (London: Nisbet & Co., 1915).

Seyfert, Gerhard, *Die militaerischen Beziehungen und Vereinbarungen zwischen den Deutschen und d. Oesterreichischen Generalstaeben vor und bei Beginn des Weltkrieges* (Leipzig: 1934).

Sieghart, Rudolf, *Die Letzten Jahrzehnte einer Grossmacht, Menschen, Voelker, Probleme des Habsburger Reiches* (Berlin: Ullstein, 1932).

Silvio, Pietro, *Italia, Francia, Inghilterra nel Mediterraneo* (Milan: Istituto per gli Studi di Politica Internazionale, 1939).

Skendi, Stavro, *The Albanian National Awakening 1878–1912* (Princeton: Princeton University Press, 1967).

Sokol, Anthony, *The Imperial and Royal Austro-Hungarian Navy* (Annapolis, MD: US Naval Institute Press, 1968).

Sokol, Anthony, 'Das oesterreichische-ungarische. Seeflugwesen', *Marine Rundschau* 5 (May 1976), pp. 292-313.

Sokol, Hans Hugo, *La Guerra Marittima dell' Austria-Ungheria 1914–1918*, 4 vols, trans. Raffaele de Courten (Rome: Istituto Poligrafico dello Stato Libreria, 1931–34).

Sokol, Hans Hugo, 'Einige nachtragliche Betrachtungen ueber Italiens Bedeutung fuer den Dreibund im Seekriege', *Marine Rundschau* 1 (January 1928), pp. 1–12.

Sosnosky, Theodor von, *Die Balkanpolitik Oesterreich-Ungarns seit 1866*, 2 vols (Stuttgart: Deutsche Verlags-Anstalt, 1914).

Steinitz, Eduard Ritter von, 'Die Reichsbefestigung Oesterreich-Ungarn zur Zeit Conrads von Hoetzendorf', *Militaerwissenschaftlichen Mitteilungen* 12 (December 1936), pp. 923–39.

Stickney, Edith Pierpoint, *Southern Albania or Northern Epirus in European International Affairs 1912–1921* (Stanford, CA: Stanford University Press, 1926).

Szilley, Bela von, *Oesterreichs Volkswirtschaftliche Interessen an der Seeschiffahrt* (Vienna: 1912).

Tapié, Victor L., *The Rise and Fall of the Habsburg Monarchy* (New York: Praeger Publisher, 1971).

Thadden, Edward, *Russia and the Balkan Alliance of 1911* (College Park: Penn State University Press, 1965).

Thursfield, James R., *Naval Warfare* (New York: G. P. Putnam Sons, 1913).

Tschuppik, Karl, *The Reign of the Emperor Francis Joseph I 1848–1916* (London: G. Bell & Sons, 1930).

Veiter, Theodore, *Die Italiener in der Oesterreichisch-Ungarischen Monarchie. Eine Volkspolitische und Nationalitaeten-Rechtliche Studie* (Vienna: Verlag fuer Geschichte und Politik, 1965).

Villari, Luigi, *The Expansion of Italy* (London: Faber & Faber, 1930).

Vojvodic', Mihajlo, *Skadarska Kriza 1913 Godine* (The Scutari Crisis of 1913) (Belgrade: Zavod za Izdavanje Udzbenika Socijalisticke Republike Srbije, 1970).

Volpe, Gioacchino, *L'Italia nella Triplice Alleanza 1881–1915* (Milan: Istituto per gli Studi di Politica Internazionale, 1939).

Wagner, Walter, *Geschichte des K.K. Kriegsministerium, Vol. 1: 1848–1866* and *Vol. 2: 1866–1888*, Studien zur Geschichte der Oesterreichisch-Ungarischen Monarchy Series, Vol. 10 (Vienna/Koeln/Graz: Hermann Boelhau, 1966 and 1971).

Wagner, Walter, *Die Obersten Behoerden der K.u.K. Kriegsmarine 1856–1918* (Vienna: Druck und Verlag Ferdinand Ber, 1961).

Waldersee, Georg Count, 'Ueber die Beziehungen des deutschen zum oesterreich-ungarischen Generalstabe vor dem Weltkriege', *Berliner Monatshefte* 2 (February 1930), pp. 103-42.

Wallace, William C. and Parker, Lillian, *Power, Public Opinion and Diplomacy. Essays in Honor of Eber Malcolm Carroll by his Former Students* (Durham, NC: Duke University Press, 1959).

Wallace, William Ray, *Greater Italy* (New York: Charles Scribner's Sons, 1917).

Wallisch, Friedrich, *Die Flagge Rot-Weiss-Rot. Maenner und Taten der Oesterreichen Marine in Vier Jahrhunderten* (Graz: Verlag Styria, 1956).

Wedel, Oswald H., *Austro-German Diplomatic Relations, 1908–1914* (Stanford, CA: Stanford University Press, 1932).

Williamson, Samuel R., Jr., *The Politics of Grand Strategy: Britain and France Prepare for War 1904–1914* (Cambridge, MA: Harvard University Press, 1969).

Zoellner, Erich, *Geschichte Oesterreichs*, 5th edn (Vienna: Verlag fuer Geschichte und Politik, 1974).

Zoellner, Erich, ed., *Diplomatie und Aussenpolitik Oesterreichs* (Vienna: Oesterreichischer Bundesverlag, 1977).

Annuals and periodicals

Almanach der K.u.K. Kriegsmarine (Pola: Gerold & Co.) 1900–14.
Berliner Monatshefte (formerly *Kriegschuldfrage*) (Berlin) 1925–38.
The Naval Annual, ed. Viscount Hythe Brassey and John Leyland (Portsmouth: J. Griffin Co.) 1901–14.
Die Flagge. Zeitschrift fuer Seewesen und Seeverkehr, Organ des Oesterreichischen Flottenvereins (Vienna) 1905–14.
Danzers Armee Zeitung (Vienna) 1904–9.
Internationale Revue ueber die Gesamten Armeen und Flotten (Dresden) 1904–13.
Jahresberichte der K.u.K. Kriegsmarine (Vienna: K.K. Hof-u. Staatsdruckerei) 1901–14.
The Journal of the Royal United Service Institution (London) 1906–12.
Marine Rundschau (Berlin) 1900–14.
Militaerische und Technische Mitteilungen (Vienna) 1922–28.
Militaerwissenschftliche Mitteilungen (Vienna) 1925–37.
Mitteilungen aus dem Gebiete des Seewesens (Pola: Gerold & Co.) 1895–1914.
Nauticus. Jahrbuch fuer deutsche Seeinteresse (Berlin: E. S. Mittler und Sohn) 1901–14.
Navy League Annual, ed. A. H. Burgoyne (London: J. Murray) 1908/9–1913/14.
Normalverordnungsblatt fuer die K.u.K. Kriegsmarine (Vienna: K.K. Hof- und Staatsdruckerei) 1901–14.
Rivista Marittima (Rome) 1900–14.
Statistik des Auswaertigen Handels der Oesterreich-Ungarischen Zollgebiete in Jahre 1904 (Vienna: K.K. Hof u. Staatsdruckerei) 1905 and 1914.
Statistik des Auswaertigen Handels der Vertraggebiete der Beiden Staaten der Oesterreichisch-Ungarischen Monarchie im Jahre 1913, Vol. 4: *Hauptergebnisse-Hafenverkehr* (Vienna: K.K. Hof-v. Staatsdruckerei, 1914).
Statistik der Seeschiffahrt und des Seehandels in dem Oesterreichischen Reich im Jahre 1904 und 1913 (Trieste: Tipografia Morterra, 1905).
Streufflers Oesterreichische Militaerische Zeitschrift (Vienna) 1904–14.
Ueberall. Zeitschrift fuer Armee und Marine (Vienna) 1910–14.

Index

211

Index